Closedown?

Closedown?

The BBC and Government Broadcasting
Policy 1979–92

Tom O'Malley

Pluto Press

LONDON · BOULDER, COLORADO

First published 1994 by Pluto Press
345 Archway Road, London N6 5AA, UK
and 5500 Central Avenue
Boulder, Colorado 80301, USA

British Library Cataloguing in Publication Data
A catalogue record for this book is available from the British Library

Library of Congress Cataloging in Publication Data
O'Malley, Tom, 1955–
   Closedown? : the BBC and government broadcasting policy
   1979–92 / by Tom O'Malley.
   236p. 22cm.
   Includes bibliographical references.
   ISBN 0-7453-0570-9 (hardback)
   1. British Broadcasting Corporation. 2. Radio broadcasting
   policy—Great Britain. 3. Television broadcasting policy—Great
   Britain. I. Title.
   HE8689.9.G7047   1994
   384.54'06'5442—dc20   94–18521
                                                                  CIP

ISBN 0 7453 0570 9 hardback

Designed and produced for Pluto Press by
Chase Production Services, Chipping Norton
Typeset from author's disk by
Stanford DTP Services, Milton Keynes
Printed in the EC by TJ Press, Padstow

Contents

Preface

This book is a preliminary, if detailed, survey and analysis of a recent phase in the history of the UK. The importance of the topic lies in the central role broadcasting has played in the UK's political and cultural life since the 1920s.

The book is based primarily on printed sources, most, but not all of which, are easily accessible. They are listed in the bibliography. Pressures of time and resources limited my investigations to these sources.

The fact that the events discussed in this book are part of contemporary experience makes it hard to develop and maintain a sense of perspective on their long-term origins and implications. I have tried to keep this problem in mind when writing.

I have also tried to present arguments in the debate clearly and fairly. When making judgements on the issues raised in the debates I have, I hope, provided adequate reasons and, or, evidence in support of my position.

This book could not have been written without the advice and support of a number of people, whom I would like to thank. The Campaign for Press and Broadcasting Freedom (CPBF) has provided the context within which many of the ideas in this book have, over the years, been argued and developed. There have been too many people involved in the CPBF to thank them all individually, however Kathy Darby, Mick Gosling, Mike Jempson, Tony Lennon, Jo Treharne and Granville Williams have all, in one way or another, helped me think through these issues.

A number of people commented on earlier drafts. They were Anne Beech (Pluto), Dr Richard Collins, Professor James Curran, Professor Nicholas Garnham, Peter Goodwin, Tony Lennon and Tim White. I am grateful for the time and effort they contributed and have benefited greatly from their comments and advice. Any errors of fact and interpretation which remain are my responsibility.

Finally, but most importantly, I would like to thank Ruth Shirtcliff and our children Patrick and Robert, without whose constant support this book could never have been seriously attempted, let alone written.

Tom O'Malley
March 1994

Introduction

Broadcasting is central to the political and cultural life of the United Kingdom. It occupies large amounts of the daily leisure time of ordinary people. Politicians, artists, trade unionists, teachers, academics and students, to name but a few, are all, in one way or another, interested in aspects of the broadcasting system. It goes without saying then that major changes to that system will impinge, for good or bad, on the leisure and working lives of millions of people. This book explores some of the major changes which took place in the 1980s and examines why and how these changes took place. It also tries to assess their significance for the political and cultural life of the UK.

A Success Story?

Broadcasting started in the UK in the 1920s when the British Broadcasting Corporation (BBC) was established. The BBC transmitted radio programmes and was funded by a licence fee levied on radio receivers. Its early experiments in television during the 1930s were suspended during the Second World War (1939–45). Television was restarted again in 1946. In 1954 the Television Act broke the BBC's monopoly and introduced a system of television funded by advertisements. This system was known as Independent Television (ITV) and was organised as a number of separate companies broadcasting to discrete regions of the country. The ITV companies were supervised on all matters of procedure, ownership and programming by an Independent Television Authority (ITA) which was modelled on the BBC's Board of Governors.

In 1964 the BBC opened a second TV channel, BBC2, and in 1967 began to set up a chain of local radio stations. In 1972 the Sound Broadcasting Act renamed the ITA the Independent Broadcasting Authority (IBA). The IBA was charged with regulating commercial television and establishing a system of commercially funded local radio stations, which became known as Independent Local Radio (ILR).

In 1979, at the start of the period covered in this book, the BBC was funded by a licence fee and operated two national TV services (BBC1 and BBC2), four national radio services (Radios 1, 2, 3 and 4), as well as regional services and 20 local radio stations. A grant from the Foreign Office funded the BBC's World Service radio. In 1979 the IBA supervised 19 ILR stations and 15 regional ITV companies, all of which were funded by advertising.[1]

The system was based on two fundamental principles. The first was that all broadcasting should be run as a 'public service'. This was not an easy concept to define or to put into practice. It required broadcasters to develop a range of services and programmes to meet the, albeit difficult to define, needs of the population as a whole. This was regarded as a key social purpose of broadcasting and, until the 1980s, was considered more important than the single-minded pursuit of ratings (BBC, ITV, ILR) and of profits (ITV, ILR).

Secondly, the system rested upon the fact that the BBC and the commercial system did not compete for the same source of revenue. This left room for both sides to develop programming which was not designed to maximise revenues but, in theory at least, to meet wider cultural and political goals. This contrasted sharply with the US, where commercial imperatives had dominated the system since the 1920s. On the continent of Europe individual states had a mix of systems with varying amounts of direct state funding or advertising, or a combination of both.

Measured in terms of the way the industry grew in size and output, and the volume of exports, the UK broadcasting system was a success. In 1938 there were about 5,000 people employed by the BBC, 11,000 in 1946, 14,350 in 1962 and 19,275 in 1967. The numbers employed continued to grow until the mid-1980s. ITV transmitted 47 hours of programmes a week in 1956. By 1976 this had become over 92 hours a week. BBC TV transmitted an average of 49 hours a week in 1955–6, which rose to 163 hours a week in 1975–6.[2] This increase in domestic output was matched by success in the international broadcasting sector. The UK had the advantage of being part of the world's dominant language group, English speakers, a fact which provided a huge potential international market for programmes. It has been estimated that, by 1985, the UK accounted for 68 per cent of the audio-visual exports of the European Community.[3]

Broadcasting also played an increasingly important part in the lives of ordinary people. In 1961 in the UK individuals watched an average of 13 hours and 30 minutes of television a week. By 1981 the figure was 18 hours and eight minutes. Television took up immense amounts of people's leisure time, providing a key source of information and entertainment.[4]

Broadcasting and Democracy

The importance of broadcasting extends well beyond the images conjured up by a bare repetition of statistics. Paddy Scannell has produced a powerful argument for 'broadcasting in its present form, as a public good that has unobtrusively contributed to the democratization of everday life, in public and private contexts, from its beginning through to today'.[5]

Broadcasting in the UK has provided access for the population to events, ideas and experiences ranging widely across cultural and political life, an access which has helped to shape democratic and cultural processes. The breadth and range of programming and ideas produced in the UK public service system stands in marked contrast to the commercially organised system in the US, and has provided, in the context of the UK's political life, a relatively balanced counterpoint to the increasing right-of-centre partisanship of the national newspaper press.

Change

We should be wary before burying ourselves under a heap of praise for the UK system. It had many major flaws, which are discussed in more detail in Chapter 1. The decade before 1979 saw a debate about the system's lack of accountability and the emergence of a number of campaigns for more openness, diversity and democratic control of broadcasting. A good part of this criticism came from the political left. In the 1980s the right took up the call for the reform of broadcasting, often using similar rhetoric.

During the 1970s Western economies entered a deep and prolonged recession. The years of relatively uninterrupted growth in the world economy which had followed the end of the Second World War came to an end. This influenced the economics both of national governments and of media organisations. Towards the end of the 1970s governments and industrialists became more aware of the need to restructure media industries to take account of the implications of developments in computer, satellite, video and fibre-optic technologies. This coincided with the emergence of right-of-centre governments in the US and the

UK. One feature of this shift to the right was the emergence of a new form of economic orthodoxy among policy-making elites in the US and Europe. This has been called neo-liberalism, or a new found faith in the capacity of free markets, stripped as far as possible of government interference, to bring economic growth. This challenged, and in some places replaced, the more interventionist strategies which governments in Europe and the US had pursued in the years since the great economic depression of the 1930s.

All these factors interacted with national conditions to produce a general move towards the national reregulation of broadcasting systems in the US and Europe, a process which invariably meant increasing the influence of commercial forces and marginalising or diminishing the role of public service broadcasting obligations in national broadcasting systems.

This was a complex and uneven process which worked differently in different states. This book examines how this process worked in the UK, in the context of policy towards the BBC. It recognises the importance of the global forces at work but seeks to add to our general understanding of these changes by looking in detail at how and why the changes took place in the UK. The changes in the UK were not unique, but the direction, nature and pace of change was shaped largely by conditions within the UK political system.

The State and the Market

Paddy Scannell is right to criticise those people who see broadcasting in the UK 'primarily as a form of social control'.[6] But broadcasting has always figured in the calculations of the people who run the state – politicians, civil servants and business people – as one instrument among many which can be used to maintain political and social stability, and to preserve the existing distribution of economic power in society. This was not the only function of broadcasting. Policy- and programme-makers believed that broadcasting had a wider set of social and cultural purposes, and sought to make sure that those purposes were pursued.

So, on the one hand the state has maintained formal and informal controls over the system. On the other, by imposing a positive programming remit and creating a financial environment in which that remit could be realised, the state has helped to create an innovative and rich system of broadcasting. But nonetheless it is important to remember that in the UK, as in all other countries, broadcasting has been actively used by the state to help to maintain political and social stability. I return to these themes in Chapter 8.

The changes which occurred in the UK system in the 1980s were, it will be argued, a modification of the established forms of control over broadcasting. The state relinquished some power over broadcasting to capitalists, intensified other forms of control and tried to maintain elements of the previous system. On matters of broadcasting policy the state in the 1980s was not monolithic. It was made up of a series of competing centres of power and influence, all seeking changes of a different order and import. The differences were not, however, fundamental; they did not lead to major splits within the state. No one in a position of influence advocated the democratisation of broadcasting and the removal of commercial control over the system. But, within the limited parameters of debate which will be outlined below, there were real differences of opinion which affected the outcome of policy.

In the middle of the nineteenth century the UK state relinquished a raft of formal controls over the newspaper press, opening the industry up to greater market control. Some argue that this was a major blow for press freedom, others that it was a conscious attempt to produce a politically safe press which, because it was controlled by capitalists and market forces, would provide continued support for the political and social system in the UK.[7] The result of the unfettered development of market forces in the UK press in the twentieth century has been to produce a press run by people whose economic interests are bound up with the maintenance of the existing distribution of wealth and power in the UK and who mobilise their considerable resources to crush any threat to that situation with a clear-minded sense of their own self-interest.

The changes to the broadcasting system in the UK set in train during the 1980s began to remove the legal and financial barriers which, relatively speaking, insulated broadcasting from the full impact of market forces. It might take a long time, but the outcome, unless checked, is likely to be a system which, in terms of its organisation and politics, mirrors the situation that obtained in the UK national press at the end of the 1980s. A broadcasting system which, because of the way it was regulated, had the financial and cultural space to pursue a relatively wide range of social, political and cultural goals in a relatively unpartisan manner, and which consequently helped to democratise our culture, was gradually dismantled in the 1980s – not fully but significantly. In one sense we witnessed a process in the 1980s which mirrors the shifts in control of the press that occurred in the 1850s and 1860s.

This book does not describe the complete abandonment of public service broadcasting to the forces of the market. But it does outline how the foundations of public service broadcasting were seriously undermined. The future is either one in which the values and practices of public service broadcasting, revived and democratised, are placed back at the centre of the system, or one in which the changes described in this book will finally erode that element of public service broadcasting which remains. If the latter happens, then public access to a wide range of information, entertainment and debate at low cost will be severely curtailed. The public will lose the benefits that come from a mass, public communications system, which is run for the public good and not just for the benefit of large commercial concerns.

It is in this spirit that the book is entitled *Closedown?*, with a question mark. I am convinced that the public service broadcasting system in the UK was mortally wounded in the 1980s, but I recognise that only time will test the accuracy of this diagnosis. I also recognise that, with information, motivation and, above all, self-organisation people can resist and reverse what at first seem like impersonal, insurmountable forces. This book aims to provide some of that information to members of the public, broadcasting workers, trade unionists, academics and students. Perhaps, if there is ever a second edition of this book, *Closedown?* can be taken off the title page. I hope I don't have to simply remove the question mark.

I take a particular view on the value of the changes which I describe. I have, however, tried to be detailed and fair in my exposition of the developments. The book opens (Chapter 1) with a review of the relations between governments and the BBC up to 1979 and some account of the key developments in the 1980s. This, I hope, will provide a context for what follows. The next two chapters examine the influence on the policy-making process of groups of people who, although not members of the government, were very close to the government and were either propagandists for the free market or capitalists interested in influencing policy in a particular direction.

Chapter 4 explores the high-profile political clashes between the government and the BBC after 1979 and tries to assess their impact on policy development. Chapter 5 describes and analyses the approach of Prime Minister Margaret Thatcher to the media and then analyses the policy pursued by her and the Home Office towards the BBC up to 1985 and aspects of the relationship between the Home Office, the Prime Minister and the BBC up to 1988. Chapter 6 examines the purpose, proceedings and findings of the Committee on Financing the BBC which reported in July 1986. Chapter 7 examines the development of broadcasting policy after 1986, focusing in particular on the development of policy towards the BBC. Chapter 8 outlines the impact of government policy on the BBC up to 1992. Chapter 9 draws some conclusions from the evidence surveyed in the context of debates about the relationship between the media and the state.

1 Some Background

It is important to remember that the sources of many of the tensions between the BBC and the government which exploded into bitter conflict during the 1980s, had existed and caused similar conflicts ever since the founding of the BBC in 1922. Overt political clashes between government and the BBC, newspaper attacks on the alleged bias of the Corporation, the problems faced by BBC management in dealing with controversial public issues on the one hand and hypersensitive governments on the other, and the politically sensitive issue of how to fund the BBC – these were all issues which had surfaced before the 1980s. Similarly the policy framework within which the BBC operated was, in spite of the Corporation's role as a public service broadcaster, always made by small groups of socially privileged and politically influential people. This 'closed' form of policy-making was still dominant in the 1980s.

Yet there were differences between policy under the Thatcher-led governments of 1979–90 and their predecessors. Policy-making on broadcasting, and in particular on the BBC, was, arguably, pursued with greater vigour and speed than had been the case under previous governments. Colin Seymour-Ure has described how:

> With cable and DBS (direct broadcasting by satellite) in the 1980s, the Thatcher government was more interventionist ... seeking to move ahead at a great pace compared with the deliberation that preceded the introduction of BBC2 and Channel 4. Later, the reconstruction of the entire broadcasting system in the 1990 Broadcasting Act was the most 'active' policy since the 1920s.[1]

This more active policy was driven by a vision of the future of broadcasting fundamentally different from that which had guided policy-making since the 1920s. When put into practice, it effected a radical change in the structure, financing and purpose of broadcasting in the UK.

A Brief Reminder

Broadcast politics has, from the beginning, given rise to unending acrimonious complaint from governments, political parties, lobby and pressure groups, academic researchers and members of the public ... Accusations of bias and distortion are as much a commonplace of television in the eighties as they were of radio in the thirties.[2]

Paddy Scannell and David Cardiff's remarks remind us how differences about the function, control and practice of broadcasting have been a recurring source of political conflict. Since 1945 the BBC had clashed with successive governments over issues such as the reporting of the Suez Crisis in 1956, of Ireland since 1968 and the day-to-day coverage of politics.

Prime Ministerial attacks on the BBC were a well established feature of UK politics by the time Mrs Thatcher took office in May 1979. Richard Crossman records how, in 1968, the Labour Prime Minister, Harold Wilson, had 'been listening to Radio One and noticed how some of the disc-jockeys bring in news items with an anti-Labour slant', and went on to make 'an extraordinary outburst about the wicked political bias of the BBC contrasted with the honesty of commercial TV under Charles Hill in the old days'. In 1969 Crossman recorded 'an attack by Harold on the BBC because young David Dimbleby had made a flippant commentary on the Nixon arrival. Harold had made a formal complaint ... He is obsessed with the BBC.'[3]

Similarly relationships between the BBC and the national press have always been complicated. Early attempts by BBC staff to cover controversial social and political issues such as unemployment, in the 1930s, provoked covert pressure from politicians which 'combined with well orchestrated campaigns in the right-wing national press, contributed to a retreat from controversy which reached crisis point for the BBC in 1938'.[4] The national press was to play a major role in focusing political attention on the politics, management and financing of the BBC in the 1980s, just as it had in the past.

The relationship between BBC managers and the government of the day was always an important factor in shaping the wider set of relationships between the government and the BBC. Hugh Greene, Director General from 1960 to 1969, played a vital role in preparing the BBC's response to the Pilkington Committee (1960–2) and in steering the Corporation through the difficult task of responding to the challenge of ITV. Lord Swann as Chairman of the Board of Governors from 1973 to 1980 ensured that the BBC put systematic preparation into the Corporation's response to the Annan Committee. Annan's findings were, with some minor exceptions, broadly in favour of the status quo.[5]

The relationship between top management at the BBC and the government of the day was always crucial. When it came under strain, as it did in the 1960s and 1970s, this could lead to severe conflicts. In the 1980s the relationship gradually broke down, almost completely, with major consequences for the Corporation. In the 1970s and for the first six years of the 1980s the relationship became increasingly tense. In part this tension reflected a critique of broadcasting which existed outside of government. During the late 1960s and the 1970s a wide range of criticisms of broadcasting were made by workers in the industry, academics, trade unionists and members of the Labour Party. The Free Communications Group, the '76 Group as well as the television union, the ACTT, campaigned for a more open, accountable system.

This agitation was felt within the Labour Party and was one reason why the Labour government established a committee on broadcasting under Lord Annan in 1974. Criticisms centred on the need for more independence from government, more public accountability and demands for the system to reflect more accurately the cultural and political diversity of the UK. These criticisms helped to shape the government's posture towards broadcasting at the end of the 1970s. In the medium term, notwithstanding their accuracy, the criticisms helped to foster a climate of hostility towards the BBC among those on the left of the political spectrum. This climate made it harder for some people to mobilise in support of the BBC and public service broadcasting when they came under attack from the right in the 1980s.

The Labour government's 1978 White Paper contained proposals to insert a new layer of Home Office appointed Service Management Boards into the BBC's management hierarchy. Broadcaster Robin Day felt that this was evidence of both 'an authoritarian streak in Callaghan and his Cabinet' and 'the anti-BBC feeling which had grown up among politicians of both main parties'. According to Ian Trethowan, Director General 1977–82, by the start of the 1980s distrust of the BBC was widespread among all political parties because of the Corporations's alleged contempt for the whole parliamentary process. Trethowan, a political journalist by trade, was careful to try to build bridges between the BBC and the government. During his tenure of the post he secured a three-year licence fee settlement and the renewal of the the BBC's Charter for 15 years from 1981 until 1996. Under his successor, Alasdair Milne, 1982–7, the conflicts between management and government were rehearsed again, only this time with greater intensity and in the context of a government prepared to take systematic action against the Corporation.[6]

Given the pre-1979 history of tensions between successive prime ministers, their governments, the national press and the BBC it is not surprising that the financing of the BBC was, at best, politically sensitive and, at worst, a potential source of serious political controversy. Proposals to fund broadcasting through sponsorship or advertising had been around since the 1920s. Successive governments had chosen, from the 1950s onwards, to keep funding the BBC by the licence fee but also to set up and maintain the advertising-funded Independent Television system (1954) and commercial radio (1971) as a concession to lobbyists from the advertising and equipment-manufacturing industries as well as to those who wanted more competition in broadcasting.[7]

Proposals to introduce advertisements on the BBC had been floated from time to time at Cabinet level. In November 1964, during negotiations between the BBC and the Labour government over the size of the licence fee increase, Postmaster General Tony Benn asked one of his officials to:

> think of alternative ways in which the money could be raised. These would include applying the TV levy to the BBC as a grant-in-aid, taking over the Light Programme and financing it by advertising, running a big Post-Office commercial light music programme, or taking away BBC2 and using the channel for educational television with advertising.

During the 1970s the slowdown in the growth of income from the purchase of new TV licences was coupled with a high level of inflation. This meant that the Corporation increasingly looked to regular large increases in the cost of the licence fee as a way of securing its financial position. As the 1970s gave way to the 1980s the size of the licence fee increase became a more sensitive issue. One solution, advertising as a source for financing the Corporation, was placed back on the political agenda in the more hostile political climate of the 1980s.[8]

Finally, a characteristic of policy-making around broadcasting in the 1980s was its relatively secretive or closed nature. Broadcasting policy has traditionally been shaped by small groups of people. These have included industry lobbyists, civil servants from key departments like the Home Office, and the Prime Minister of the day. Prime ministers could and did take key decisions without fully consulting the Cabinet, such as the decision to establish the Annan Inquiry made by Harold Wilson in 1970. In this respect the style of policy-making in the 1980s mirrored what had been done in the past. It remained a process in which only a small section of the politically active classes played a part, and within which an even smaller group of top industrialists, politicians and civil servants took key decisions. Although this book argues that the changes of the 1980s were of real long-term significance, another contention is that there was a strong element of continuity about the manner in which those decisions were taken.[9]

This section has skimmed the surface of aspects of the relationship between the BBC, politicians, the press and government before 1979. There are many more issues which could be raised but, for the purposes of this book, it is important to remember that the events of the 1980s, although in their own way unique, had precedents which went back to the origins of broadcasting in the UK. It is to the events of the 1980s that we now turn.

1979–83

During the period after the Conservative victory at the general election of 3 May 1979, the new government, under Mrs Thatcher, proceeded with a combination of public vigour in some areas, such as economic policy, and caution in others.[10] In broadcasting the main thrust was caution. Policy-making, except in the area of cable and satellite, remained essentially under the control of the Home Office and the Home Secretary, William Whitelaw.

Immediately after the general election the Home Office was occupied with drafting and implementing the 1981 Broadcasting Act which extended the three channel TV system – BBC1, BBC2 and ITV – by adding a fourth, Channel 4 TV. It was funded by advertising and started transmission in November 1982. Channel 4 was given a remit to cater for interests not serviced by the existing ITV companies. It was also intended to act as an outlet for programmes made by independent programme-makers, that is people who were not employed by the BBC or ITV companies. Its remit and use of independents was, in a sense, a response to many of the demands made by radical critics of broadcasting in the 1970s. But Channel 4 also provided a test bed for the development of a low-cost production sector which was later used by the government and others to justify policies which led to the cutting of staff and resources within the BBC and the ITV companies.

The main area of new policy in the field of broadcasting related to cable and satellite. In 1978 the Labour Prime Minister, Jim Callaghan, encouraged his Central Policy Review Staff, the Prime Minister's 'think tank', to examine issues relating to new technology. In addition, in September 1980, the Cabinet Office's Advisory Council for Applied Research, established in 1976, reported to the newly elected Thatcher government on information technology (IT). It recommended departmental coordination of computing and telecoms and that broadcasting should be brought into this brief. Shortly afterwards a special section of the Department of Industry devoted to IT was established with its own Minister for Information Technology. Early in 1981 Kenneth Baker was appointed to this post.

In July 1981 Mrs Thatcher announced the formation of an IT Unit in the Cabinet Office. She also established an Information Technology Advisory Panel (ITAP) which published a report on cable systems in March 1982. ITAP drew attention to the industrial benefits that the expansion of cable services would bring and argued that this should be privately funded. A number of interdepartmental committees were established involving the Home Office, the Cabinet Office, the Treasury and the Departments of Industry, Environment, Employment and Trade. The Home Office, under Whitelaw, set up a committee chaired by Lord Hunt, a former Cabinet Secretary, to report on the implications of cable expansion for broadcasting. Its brief was to, 'consider an expansion of cable services ... in a way consistent with the wider public interest, in particular the safeguarding of public service broadcasting'. Hunt reported in September 1982. The report recommended the expansion of commercially funded cable systems which would operate under a much looser regulatory regime than established broadcasting organisations.

The new system was not to be operated by existing TV companies nor would it be subject to the public service programming obligations under which the BBC and the commercial broadcasters operated. This marked the first significant break with the tradition of establishing new radio and TV services as public service broadcasters, a tradition which had shaped UK broadcasting policy since the 1920s.

In 1981 the Minister for Information Technology, Kenneth Baker, had encouraged the BBC to get involved in Direct Broadcasting by Satellite (DBS) as part of the government's industrial strategy, using market mechanisms, such as advertising, sponsorship and subscription, rather than public money in the form of additional licence fee income or grants.[11]

These initiatives had clear implications for the future shape of broadcasting policy and of the BBC. They reflected the fact that at this early stage Mrs Thatcher and others in government were committed to expanding the role of commerce in mass communications and were using the Department of Industry as the departmental base from which to achieve this goal. The Home Office, under Whitelaw, was clearly not regarded as an appropriate department to lead these new developments because of its closeness to the ethos and operation of existing broadcasting organisations. The lead came from the Prime Minister's Office and the Department of Industry.

While it is unclear whether these developments were, at the time, consciously designed to undermine the BBC, the BBC and the IBA recognised the implications. They presented evidence to Hunt and prepared a defence of existing funding arrangements in the form of a study of the daily cost of television to UK viewers.[12]

Whatever the government's long-term plans for the BBC at this time, it had already developed a critical attitude to the Corporation. In 1979 the government and the BBC clashed over the filming of an IRA roadblock at Carrickmore and the transmission of an interview with a member of the Irish National Liberation Army, the organisation which claimed it had assassinated Mrs Thatcher's close political colleague, Airey Neave. By 1981 Mrs Thatcher had embarked on a policy of appointing people to the BBC's Board of Governors who were known to be sympathetic to Conservative politics. This broke with a long tradition of bipartisan appointments to the Boards of the BBC and the IBA.

In 1982 Mrs Thatcher attacked the BBC for its coverage of the war in the Falkland Islands. By this time she had already made it clear to senior BBC executives that she felt the BBC should be more commercially minded and before the June 1983 general election there seems to have been some discussion at senior ministerial level about taking action against the BBC in the event of a Conservative victory at the election. The Conservative election manifesto contained no reference to any proposals for reshaping the BBC.

1983–7

Between 1984 and 1987 Mrs Thatcher took the lead in a sustained attack first on the finances and then on the management of the BBC. In early 1986, immediately after the loss of two of her senior ministers as a result of the controversy surrounding the Westland affair, her authority in the Cabinet was severely dented. The Westland affair raised questions about her involvement in breaching the Official Secrets Act and in attempts to discredit a Cabinet minister. There followed a period when her image-makers did their utmost to reestablish her popularity in the public mind in the run up to the 1987 general election. At the same time the policy of directly challenging the financial basis of the BBC gave way to one of openly campaigning, through the actions of her party Chairman, Norman Tebbit, for changes in BBC management.

After the 1983 election Leon Brittan was appointed Home Secretary. Shortly after this the BBC was attacked in three key reports. In May 1984 the right-wing pressure group, the Adam Smith Institute, published a report calling for the break up of the BBC and the expansion of market forces in broadcasting. In the autumn two advertising agencies, D'Arcy MacManus Massius and Saatchi and Saatchi, both published reports which argued that the BBC should take a small amount of advertising to limit increases in the licence fee.

Throughout 1984 the BBC was subjected to a barrage of criticism from the national press, in particular the quality papers owned by Mrs Thatcher's close political supporter, Rupert Murdoch. The press accused the BBC of being profligate, poorly managed and overweening in its ambitions.

In July 1984 Leon Brittan insisted on the BBC's inviting the firm of management consultants, Peat Marwick Mitchell (PMM), to conduct a value-for-money assessment of the Corporation to provide a benchmark for ministers when they were considering the BBC's bid for an increase in the licence fee. In December 1984 the BBC made public its bid for an increase in its colour licence fee from £46 to £65 and in its black and white licence from £15 to £18.

The bid unleashed a wave of criticism which was led by Mrs Thatcher and amplified by both the national press and Conservative MPs. The most sustained press criticism came from *The Times* which, on three successive days in January 1985, carried editorials entitled 'Whither the BBC?', which tore into the Corporation. A period of intense manoeu-vring then took place during which it was decided to grant the BBC a licence fee of £58 for two rather than three years and to appoint a committee of inquiry into BBC finances led by economist Alan Peacock.

In August 1985, while Peacock was sitting, Brittan publicly requested the BBC not to transmit a programme in the *Real Lives* TV series about the lives of two Northern Irish politicians. In the absence of Director General Alasdair Milne, who was on holiday, the BBC Governors agreed to ban the programme. The ban provoked the first ever national strike by BBC journalists. This episode illustrated the growing divide between the Governors and the management team led by Milne. This divide reached breaking point in January 1987 when the Governors dismissed Milne.

The Peacock Committee reported in July 1986, by which time Brittan had been replaced at the Home Office by Douglas Hurd. Peacock rejected the substitution of advertising for the licence fee but recommended a series of measures designed to replace the existing system, run on public service principles, with one driven by market forces. A Cabinet committee was established to look into Peacock's recommendations. In November 1986 Hurd announced that both BBC and ITV companies would eventually have to take 25 per cent of their output from independent programme-makers. In February 1987 he published a Green Paper on radio containing plans to subject the BBC to competition from hundreds of new, small-scale, lightly regulated radio stations. In January 1988 he announced that from the following April, for three years, the increase in the BBC's licence fee would be linked to annual increases in the retail price index (RPI). As inflation within the broadcasting industry ran at a higher rate than inflation in the rest of the economy, the decision imposed an annual cut in the BBC's real income.

In 1986 and 1987 a series of highly publicised clashes between the BBC and the government helped to create a climate in which the Governors, all appointees of Mrs Thatcher, felt able to dismiss Alasdair Milne as Director General and begin restructuring the BBC from management downwards.

In the autumn the BBC was attacked in Parliament for alleged bias in transmitting a drama on desertion by British soldiers in the First World War, *The Monocled Mutineer*, and for refusing to transmit a play on the Falklands because, it was alleged, the play provided too favourable a picture of the Prime Minister. In October, amid allegations of managerial incompetence and interference by the Conservative Party with key witnesses, the BBC withdrew its defence of a libel action which had been brought against it by two Conservative MPs and settled out of court. The situation was aggravated when, days later, a report commissioned by Conservative Cabinet minister and party Chairman Norman Tebbit, attacked the BBC for its anti-government bias in the coverage of the bombing of Libya by the United States Air Force. These events kept the BBC in the public eye throughout the autumn, shifting the focus of debate from the issue of BBC finances and placing it firmly on issues of managerial competence and political bias.

The decision by Alasdair Milne to ban the transmission of a programme about government spending on the Zircon Spy satellite, taken in December 1986, was followed in January and February 1987 by a concerted attack on the BBC by the government. The full weight of the courts and the police were used in an attempt to suppress transmission of the programme. At the height of this controversy, on 29 January, Milne was forced to resign by the recently appointed Chairman of the Board of Governors, Marmaduke Hussey.

Hussey, who had worked for Rupert Murdoch, had taken over in 1986. It was rumoured that he had been sent in to clean out the management at the BBC. By the end of 1987 Hussey had succeeded in dismissing Milne, replacing him with Michael Checkland and ridding top management of some of Milne's closest associates.

1987–92

By Mrs Thatcher's third administration the BBC was no longer at the centre of Conservative broadcasting policy. The focus shifted to restructuring the commercial broadcasting system by introducing more market-driven competition. This included issuing a White Paper on Broadcasting in November 1988 and a Broadcasting Bill in November 1989, which became the 1990 Broadcasting Act.

At the same time the DBS venture, Sky Television, launched by Murdoch in February 1989, helped to undermine the position of the IBA's chosen DBS provider, British Satellite Broadcasting (BSB). In November 1990 in contravention of the existing regulations, but with Mrs Thatcher's foreknowledge, Murdoch engineered a merger of Sky and BSB on terms widely seen as a takeover.

The government was deliberately introducing more commercial competition into the broadcasting industry which would, in time, eat into the BBC's audiences and make it increasingly difficult for the Corporation to justify its licence fee. The government encouraged the BBC to investigate the possibilities of subscription and, after March 1991, fixed the BBC's licence fee below the annual increase in the retail price index (RPI).

From 1987 onwards the management team at the BBC pursued a policy of gradually cutting jobs, closing down activities and introducing an internal market for resources known as Producer Choice. In 1991, with the encouragement of Hussey, the Board of Governors chose to appoint Checkland's deputy, John Birt, as the next Director General. As Checkland could have reasonably expected to have been offered another five-year term, this move was clearly a snub. From mid-1991 Birt and Hussey, supported by a management team imported from the private sector, began to establish a set of policies designed radically to reduce staff numbers and areas of activity. This was both in preparation for the review of the BBC's Charter, which was due for renewal in 1996, and inspired, as will be argued below, by a vision of the BBC similar to that developed by the Adam Smith Institute and the Peacock Committee.

In November 1990 Mrs Thatcher was sacked as Prime Minister by a revolt of Conservative MPs for a mixture of reasons. These included dislike of her autocratic style of leadership, rejection of her policy on Europe and a genuine fear that her economic policies and unbending support for the immensely unpopular form of local taxation, the poll tax, would lead to inevitable defeat at the next general election.

Her removal and replacement by John Major had little effect on policy towards the BBC. The managers that Hussey, Checkland and Birt had installed were committed to policies which had been laid out under Thatcher's premiership and which her successor showed no signs of wanting to alter significantly. Some doubt did exist over whether, in the event of a Labour victory at the 1992 general election, this management team would have to rethink their strategy or be replaced. There remained many within the BBC and outside who disapproved of developments under Hussey's chairmanship. In the event the Conservatives won the April 1992 election. By then the BBC had become very different to the organisation of May 1979. This book argues that the changes were profound and may prove to be long-lasting.

Why?

Why did all this happen? A number of explanations have been put forward. One view argues that the attack on the BBC was the consequence of a concerted campaign in 1983 and 1984 by a handful of advertising agencies, which then snowballed into a much more profound assault on public service broadcasting. Another suggests that it was the BBC's request in 1984 for an increase in licence fee which provoked the events leading to the establishment of the Peacock Committee. Yet another view argues that to 'trace the evolution of Mrs Thatcher's strategy' for broadcasting as a whole 'we have to go back to the Peacock Committee'. According to others, the Thatcher administration's broadcasting policy did not break significantly with past policy because it retained a strong public service element in the system. A similar view holds that the challenge from the right wing of the party acting through and with Mrs Thatcher to restructure broadcasting along thoroughly market lines was thwarted by the 'wets' or traditionalists who succeeded in maintaining the traditional framework of broadcasting by making a few necessary concessions to the market.[13]

What follows attempts to clarify the motives behind the timing and nature of the attack on the BBC. It provides a detailed survey of the events surrounding policy towards the BBC in the 1980s and analyses the nature and significance for broadcasting in the UK of Conservative policy.

2 Arguing for the Market: Pressures for Change

This chapter explores some of the factors which shaped the direction of broadcasting policy in general, and policy towards the BBC in particular, between 1979 and 1992. It looks at technological change, conservative or right-of-centre 'think tanks' and the advertising industry. What role did these factors play in the development of policy during this period?

Technological Mazes

the development of cable and satellite technologies has generated a momentum for more competition and more choice which no government, including the Eastern bloc, can stem or control. This has now been accepted by the British Government in its White Paper, *Broadcasting in the 90s*.

This was written in 1989 by Cento Veljanovski, an expert on the economics of cable and broadcasting who advised the Thatcher governments on policy and who strongly advocated introducing more market forces into the broadcasting system. In arguing that technology 'generated' a momentum for change 'which no government' could stem, Veljanovski was repeating a view which, from the early days of the Thatcher administrations, had developed into an orthodoxy.

The idea that technological change itself produced the kind of social consequences Veljanovski describes implies that, at best, technology has a clear impact on society, an impact which depends not on the actions of governments, industrialists or citizens, but which is simply the result of releasing the technology into society. At worst, Veljanovski's statement implies that inanimate objects, lengths of fibre optic cable or orbiting satellites, can act with a self-directed purpose to generate 'momentum'.[1]

Versions of this kind of argument were repeated in official publications and statements throughout the 1980s, in the Peacock Report and the White Paper on Broadcasting of 1988. Nigel Lawson, who was

Chancellor in two of Mrs Thatcher's administrations and sat on the key Cabinet Committee which helped to decide broadcasting policy, believed that the 'main forces for change were technological ... rather than any Government initiative'. Mrs Thatcher also recorded her view that, in the 1980s, the BBC/ITV 'duopoly was being undermined by technological developments'.

The government stressed the centrality of technical change to justify the nature of its intervention in broadcasting policy. Earl Ferrers, Minister of State at the Home Office, argued in December 1988:

> What the Government is seeking to do is to acknowledge that conditions have changed; that new technologies are here, and as a result that new possibilities have come about ... The Government's duty as we see it is to create a framework within which enterprise, opportunity and consumer demand will determine what is available.[2]

The second part of this statement is equally characteristic of the government's position on new technology and policy in these years. It implies that the only way to use new technologies is to create a framework in which 'enterprise, opportunity and consumer demand will determine what is available'. In other words only a market-driven framework provides the best conditions for the development of new technology.

These arguments were used frequently by advocates of change who were usually, but not exclusively, on the right of the political spectrum. Yet they obscured many important issues about the relationship between technological and social change. But it can also be argued that technical change is determined largely by the economic, social and political context of the society. It is equally plausible to argue that the market does not provide the best framework in which to develop technological change. Nonetheless the two arguments, stressing the centrality of technological change to policy development and linking technological change to a market-driven policy were at the heart of the case put forward by the government and its allies in the 1980s.[3]

This book holds that it was politicians, civil servants and industrialists determined to use the new technologies to generate profits and to maximise market control over mass communications who shaped policy on new technologies and broadcasting. There was nothing inherent in the nature of the technologies which determined the direction of policy. Had there been a government of a different political complexion, the shape of broadcasting policy would have been different and the new broadcasting technologies would have been introduced into a very different environment. One purpose of this book is to demonstrate that it was not the technologies that shaped policy changes but people acting in purposeful ways with specific goals in mind within complex political, economic and social frameworks.

Think Tanks and Pressure

It seems to me that just 10 or 12 years ago the place on the political horizon where there was something happening was the women's movement, now the people who are thinking interesting things are on the radical right. They have woken up partly because they now have the political power, and partly because the climate is changing.[4]

In the early 1980s, former journalists and Channel 4 TV executives like Liz Forgan were not alone in recognising the resurgence of right-wing thought in Conservative party circles. Many observers noted that the Conservative administrations after 1979 drew on a body of conservative economic and social thought developed and popularised in the 1970s and 1980s by organisations such as the Centre for Policy Studies (CPS), the Conservative Philosophy Group (CPG), the Institute of Economic Affairs (IEA) and the Adam Smith Institute (ASI).

These groups acted as centres for the discussion of conservative ideas, producing publications and promoting contacts between people of like minds. They were part of a network of contacts extending from academia through journalism and industry to the Cabinet. The people involved with these groups were not tied to a particular organisation nor did they always share the same perspective on problems. For instance there was a major contradiction between those who wanted both a free market and less state control over public and personal life and those who were strongly, or not so strongly, in favour of the free market but who believed that the state should play an active role in maintaining moral and ethical standards. It would be wrong to overestimate the newness of much of this thought, as it represented a revival of economic liberalism within the Conservative Party which had been eclipsed during the Tory party's accommodation with collectivist ideas on the state between the 1920s and the mid-1970s.[5]

These bodies owed their rise and subsequent influence to a number of factors:

In Britain the combination of relative economic decline, which has undermined many established political leaders and political and economic ideas, and the decline of the Labour Party provided the New Right with its opportunity ... [the groups gained] ... intellectual respectability, media support, approval of influential politicians, and electoral popularity.[6]

Individuals connected with the CPS, the CPG, the IEA and the ASI made interventions in the debate around broadcasting which played a major role in shaping the issues raised by the national press and the government.

The Centre for Policy Studies

The CPS was established in 1974 by Keith Joseph MP to act as an alternative unofficial think tank on the right of the Conservative Party. It published work by journalist and economic commentator Samuel Brittan, who later went on to serve on the Peacock Committee. David Young, who was to play a significant role in deciding broadcasting policy in the 1980s, was a close associate of Mrs Thatcher and of the CPS. Kenneth Baker was also associated with the organisation. A key figure in the CPS and a close associate of the Prime Minister was Alfred Sherman, who in 1986 was arguing that the BBC was too big for one person to control and that it had become 'a part of an oligopoly cushioned from public disapproval'. These views reflected the CPS's broad hostility to publicly regulated industries and Mrs Thatcher's own avowed aim to reduce the role of the state in controlling sections of industry.[7]

Conservative Philosophy Group

A more informal network existed in the CPG, a dinner club organised by two conservative academics from 1975 onwards which included many right-wing individuals and occasionally Mrs Thatcher. Sherman attended these meetings, as did the right-wing journalists Paul Johnson and T.E. Utley.[8]

The Institute of Economic Affairs

The IEA was a 'research and educational trust' established in 1957 'to study the role of markets and pricing in allocating resources and registering preferences'. It aimed to influence the climate of opinion among politicians and opinion formers in favour of the free market and of the lessening of constraints by government on consumer choice. The IEA played a role in changing the climate of opinion in influential circles in the 1960s and 1970s. It was helped by publicity from journalists who were later to play an active part in debates over broadcasting and the BBC in the 1980s, namely Peter Jay and William Rees-Mogg at *The Times* and Samuel Brittan at the *Financial Times*. Margaret Thatcher remained close to the IEA throughout her premiership and appointed a supporter of the Institute, Alan Peacock, to chair the Committee on the Financing of the BBC in 1985. She attended its 30th anniversary dinner in April 1987 and in 1988 paid tribute to the Institute's overall influence on her government's policies: 'What we have achieved could never have been done without the leadership of the Institute of Economic Affairs.' As late as June 1990, only five months before her removal from office, she was discussing future policy areas with IEA members.[9]

In the 1960s and 1970s the IEA published a number of analyses of broadcasting policy by economists, the main thrust of which 'was to advocate greater choice and competition, and subscription' in broadcasting. In 1962, at the time of the debate over broadcasting initiated by the Pilkington Committee, it published *TV: from Monopoly to Competition – and Back?* by W. Altman, D. Thomas and D. Sawers, arguing in favour of subscription. In 1965 it published Sidney Caine's case for subscription television, *Paying For TV*. Cento Veljanovski, a member of the IEA and an adviser to the Peacock Committee, says that the Caine book 'formed the cornerstone of Professor Alan Peacock's influential Report to the Government on broadcasting'. In 1983 the IEA published *Choice by Cable* by Velanjovski and W. Bishop, which Veljanovski later claimed was 'influential in an indirect way' on government cable and telecommunications policy.[10]

The pre-1980 publications clearly took a long time to become influential but by the 1980s the IEA was exerting a major influence on broadcasting policy through individuals such as Veljanovski, Peacock and Brittan. In *Choice by Cable* Bishop and Veljanovski argued that:

the main reasons advanced for excluding the market from broadcast TV are deeply flawed; and that a market in broadcast TV is feasible ... The hidden disadvantages of British broadcast TV in terms of foregone opportunities, unnecessarily high costs and monopoly profits are large because of a deliberate policy to ration television and place it in the hands of one public monopoly and a number of regional private ones.

They went on to conclude that:

The case for de-regulating broadcast TV should also be given serious consideration. The objective need not go as far as a full-blown market in frequencies, but there should be at least a thorough review of their present allocation ... Consideration should also be given to auctioning existing ITV franchises, to make available more frequencies for broadcast TV, and to allowing subscription TV. The purpose of a policy of de-regulating broadcast TV is not simply to privatise it but to ensure that the costs of current restrictions are justified and that pay-TV becomes more competitive.

These ideas were to frame much of the subsequent debate about the future of the BBC and ITV and formed the basis of the key proposals in the Peacock Report, the 1988 White Paper and the 1990 Broadcasting Act.[11] Samuel Brittan, the brother of the Leon Brittan MP who was appointed Home Secretary in June 1983, was closely associated with the IEA and had published under the IEA's imprint. Samuel Brittan, appointed to the Peacock Committee by his brother Leon, was a firm advocate of the futuristic ideas on broadcasting organisation advocated since the late 1960s by economic journalist Peter Jay, a populariser of ideas associated with the IEA. Jay's ideas heavily influenced the thinking behind the Peacock report. Alan Peacock was a trustee of the IEA. As we have seen, Veljanovski wrote on cable for the IEA, advised the Peacock Committee and by 1989 was the IEA's Research Editorial Director. According to one writer, Veljanovski was 'the economist who devised an auctioning system for the Peacock Committee on broadcasting'.

These strands running through the IEA's work, the celebration of the market, the critique of state provision in economic affairs and the support for consumer choice in broadcasting through the use of pay-TV or subscription methods clearly influenced the Peacock report and subsequent discussions about the BBC and ITV. The antistatist line of argument was expressed well by Veljanovski in 1989 when he attacked the BBC:

> The BBC must accept that its tenure as the dominant and protected broadcaster is running out. It must develop a strategy for the orderly withdrawal from the centre stage and accept that what the market does, a protected tax financed broadcaster has no business doing.[12]

By 1992 the BBC had indeed embarked on a withdrawal from the centre stage of broadcasting.

Adam Smith Institute

Fifteen months after the IEA published *Choice by Cable*, in May 1984, another conservative pressure group, the Adam Smith Institute, published a report entitled *The Omega File: Communications*, which attacked both the IBA and the BBC. The ASI was founded in 1977 in order to further 'the advancement of learning by research and public policy options, economic and political science, and the publication of such research'. The Institute has been described as 'fairly libertarian in personal and economic issues' and 'deeply critical of public-sector economics'.[13]

It published a string of documents throughout the late 1970s and the 1980s and by 1989 was claiming that it had influenced over 100 policy measures under the Thatcher governments. It maintained close links with Tory MPs including Christopher Chope, Michael Forsyth, Michael Fallon and Robert Jones. Fallon helped to write the Omega report, *Communications*. Jones was at the forefront of Parliamentary attacks on the BBC in 1984. In 1985 Jones and Chope called, in Parliament, for reform of the BBC. Giles Shaw, the Home Office Minister responsible for broadcasting from September 1984, spoke at the ASI conference on the future of the BBC in April 1985 and Mrs Thatcher lunched with the ASI in June 1990 in a search for fresh policy ideas for her government. In the world of broadcasting their ideas received support from some quarters. David Graham, an independent producer associated with Diverse Productions, an early supplier of programmes to Channel 4, rehearsed ASI themes on broadcasting during the 1980s. ASI ideas were also given much wider publicity by sections of the national press, particularly *The Times*, during 1984 and 1985. [14]

The Omega report echoed the free market, antistatist ideas on broad-casting held by writers associated with the IEA. It argued that the licence fee system, 'a lump sum imposed on those who own a television set', was flawed because 'there is no relationship between the viewer's satisfaction and the revenue that the BBC receives'. It added that in future the BBC should be financed by either advertising or direct-charging for services. This, it argued, was because the licence fee did not allow the exercise of 'consumer sovereignty'. By this it meant that there was no relationship between the price of television viewing – the fixed, lump sum licence fee – and the manner and quantity in which television was consumed.

It asserted that as the BBC was already engaged in commercially driven practices, such as chat shows where guests promoted books, records and films as well as in fierce competition with ITV for audiences, it would be wrong to suggest 'that any moves to encourage the BBC to become more market orientated would involve much change'. A move towards a more commercially driven system would allow broadcasters to serve the public in the way the national press did, and would increase the total number of quality programmes by increasing the supply of all kinds of programmes. It accepted that the average quality might decline but argued that this would be compensated for by the increase in choice that deregulation would bring. It compared this process to the one which occurred after the invention of printing when more and more books, of good and bad quality, were made available to a public previously denied access to expensive handwritten books.

Communications asserted that the argument put by defenders of the existing broadcasting system, that deregulation would lower the quality of programming, was 'clearly elitist'. Under the present system 'a small elite with access to the control of the existing duopoly, pass judgement on what is, and what is not a "good" programme, with the paying viewer having little or no say in what goes on'. As the definition of a quality programme was 'a highly subjective one', it followed that the 'only fair criterion for judging programme quality is by how many people like it, and not how much a few do'.

It then made recommendations for the future of the BBC.

1. The 'BBC should be improved by devolving many of its constituent parts into separate self-financing units ... The time has come to change the ... BBC ... to an association of independent and separately financed stations, operating under the guidance of the BBC board of governors.'

2. BBC1, BBC2 and Breakfast Time television should remain intact as one BBC TV unit, but the method of funding it would be changed. BBC1 and BBC2 should be funded by advertising, and BBC2 by a mix of advertising, sponsorship, subscription and subsidy from BBC1 and Breakfast Time.
3. BBC TV news should be a separate body, funded by a levy on the other BBC channels and subscriptions from other companies that wished to take its services.
4. Private capital should be attracted into BBC Radio's 1, 2, Scotland, Wales and Ulster, and all of these stations should take advertising.
5. Radios 3 and 4 would become separate units funded by sponsorship, subscription and advertising.
6. BBC local radio would be sold to the highest bidder and be removed from the authority of the Board of Governors.
7. The Foreign Office should continue to fund the BBC external services because they were of 'strategic and international significance'.
8. The BBC Board of Governors would play a similar role to the IBA where TV services were concerned, 'monitoring programme content, dealing with complaints, and ensuring due regard to standards'. They would be charged with making sure Radios 3 and 4 'retained their essential character' and with giving 'guidance' to BBC Radios Scotland, Wales and Ulster.[15]

The Omega report was published in May 1984 at the beginning of a period of intense political debate about the future of the BBC. Its ideas were used extensively by critics of the BBC during that debate. Key points from the report surfaced again and again: the attack on the licence fee, the attack on elitism among broadcasters, the celebration of consumer preference as a yardstick for quality, the assertion that the BBC was already 'commercial', the advocacy of breaking the BBC up into separate units, and the introduction of advertising, sponsorship and subscription. All these ideas were repeated by the press, MPs and Cabinet ministers, including the Prime Minister, and clearly influenced the deliberations of the Peacock Committee. They were also echoed in the strategy of BBC management after 1987.

Networks of Influence

The individuals associated with the CPS, CPG, IEA and the ASI were well connected with members of the incoming Conservative government of May 1979. The IEA and the ASI developed clear perspectives on how the future of broadcasting and the BBC should develop. These ideas were rooted in a version of economic thought which strongly supported the extension of market relations into areas previously regulated and financed by the state. These general ideas were applied to broadcasting and were well received by sections of the Conservative Party who were themselves already committed to the promotion of free-market politics.

In broadcasting policy, as in other areas of policy-making, small numbers of people, of similar outlook, connected through networks of group membership, personal and political association talked to each other about how to deal with broadcasting institutions. Radhika Desai has pointed out that conservative think tanks often:

> operated in a common environment, a distinct sub-universe which was not only geographically close to, but also had close links with, the political, journalistic and financial worlds of London, being located within the two or three square miles that contain Westminster, Whitehall, the City and Fleet Street.... They consciously aimed to effect a transformation in the views of the strategic policy-making elite.

On matters relating to broadcasting there is no evidence that the IEA and the ASI ever represented or reflected the view of significant numbers of people in the country, or that, they won people over to their arguments. Influential and, in Forgan's words, 'interesting' as their ideas might be, their influence depended upon close contact with politicians and ready access to the pages of the national press, not on widespread support.[16]

The Advertising Industry

> When the Prime Minister let it be known last week that she was personally in favour of allowing the BBC to carry advertising this was the ultimate endorsement of a remarkably successful lobby campaign by a handful of people in the advertising business. [December 1984][17]

Another force for change which shared many of the ideas associated with the IEA and ASI, but from its own particular perspective, was the advertising industry. The comments quoted above overestimate the influence of this lobby on the specific issue of the licence fee, but they do highlight the importance of the industry in the debate.

Using their personal connections with politicians and the support of significant parts of the national press, sections of the industry had, by 1990, succeeded in gaining legislation which expanded the number of commercially funded broadcasting outlets in the UK, and which contributed to a major restructuring of the BBC.

Persistent Lobby

From the earliest days of British broadcasting advertising agencies and many of their clients had lobbied for more commercially funded broadcasting. For advertising agencies the prospect of more advertising or sponsor-supported channels held out the possibility of more business on more favourable terms. For those advertisers who supported them it held out the prospect, at times, of being able to reach more potential customers at cheaper rates. So when advertising agencies intervened in order to influence the future of broadcasting policy in the 1980s they were following a well-established tradition.

Although advertising as a means of financing the BBC was ruled out by successive inquiries and governments, it was frequently resurrected as an issue. Advertising agencies supported the English-language radio 'pirate' stations which broadcast to the UK from Europe in the 1930s. Agencies played a key role in the successful lobby for the introduction of commercial television in the UK in the early 1950s. They also lobbied for the introduction of commercial radio in the 1950s and 1960s and gave support to the commercial offshore pirate radio stations which began transmitting to the UK in 1964 and helped to win Conservative Party support for the introduction in 1972 of commercial local radio, known as Independent Local Radio. The agencies played a role in the debate about the second ITV channel in the 1970s and, by the 1980s, UK advertisers were involved in international pressure groups working to influence the media policy of the European Community.[18]

As we have seen, the Wilson governments of 1964–70 discussed advertising as a source of finance for the BBC. When the funding of Channel 4 was being discussed before the passage of the 1981 Broadcasting Act the Conservative's Backbench Media Committee received a paper from the advertising firm, D'Arcy McManus Masius, advocating adverts on the BBC. By the 1983 general election the issue was clearly on the agenda of the advertising industry.

In 1984 the advertising industry added its weight to a growing number of influential voices questioning the future of public service broadcasting and of the BBC. Mrs Thatcher had queried the basis of BBC funding in her first term of office and, by early 1983, the IEA was questioning the future funding of television. Then, in May 1984, the ASI's Omega report was published. It is unclear whether the intervention of the advertising industry was spontaneous or the result of coordination with politicians and others anxious to use the opportunity of the licence fee renewal to cut the BBC down to size. But the context and timing of the intervention, the arguments used, and the strong personal links between the people from the industry leading the attack and members of the government, suggest that the attack was consciously designed to be part of a multifronted assault on the BBC.[19]

Two large agencies led the attack, D'Arcy MacManus Masius and Saatchi and Saatchi. They were joined by the Institute of Practitioners in Advertising (IPA) and the Incorporated Society of British Advertisers (ISBA). These bodies had to persuade other sections of the industry that the plan to put advertisements on the BBC had some value. In December 1984, after two reports on the BBC and advertising had been published by D'Arcy MacManus Massius and Saatchi and Saatchi, the trade journal *Admap* argued in a leader that it was:

by no means clear that the advertising industry itself had yet fully thought through the implications of a change of this nature ... the problem requires more profound examination than it has so far had.

Nor could the lobbyists count on support, automatic or otherwise, from all the organisations in which advertisers played a role. The *Advertising Association*, which drew on membership from all parts of the media industry and not just advertising agencies and advertisers, was unable in 1985 to reach the 'internal consensus' necessary to make a submission to the Peacock Committee. Nevertheless in July 1985 a survey of 63 agencies revealed that only 13 were opposed to placing advertisements on the BBC.[20]

D'Arcy MacManus Masius (DMM)

The campaign focused initially on two reports published in the autumn of 1984 when the BBC was preparing its bid for the 1985–8 licence fee settlement. D'Arcy MacManus Masius's report, *Funding the BBC from Advertising*, was published in September 1984. It stated that the report was produced because the government 'proposes to re-examine the funding of the BBC'. The views of advertising interests should be taken into account, it asserted, as well as those of viewers and broadcasters. The report argued that if the licence fee was pegged at £46 and the BBC were to take 15 seconds of advertising per hour in 1985 and 30 seconds per hour in 1986, this would generate approximately £60 million for the BBC, enough to meet its additional revenue requirements.

Advertising on the BBC would provide enough money to produce good programmes, mean no increase in the licence fee and do no serious harm to ITV's profits. By organising its advertising sales on a regional basis, thereby shadowing the ITV regions, the BBC could provide 'real advertisement competition to ITV'. The licence fee D'Arcy asserted 'is regarded as socially unfair, falling on rich and poor alike and is resented by those who mainly watch ITV ... costs £50 million to collect and evasion costs something like another £65 million'. The BBC it argued, refused to take advertising for two reasons:

> First, it is part of the British Establishment that looks down on tradesmen, salesmen, commerce in general and advertising in particular. It is the perpetuation of this attitude that has helped reduce Britain's share of world and home markets.

The second reason was that the Corporation feared a ratings war which, as in the US, would drive down programme standards. D'Arcy pointed out that the BBC and ITV already took part in ratings wars and that these were 'not at all a bad thing' as it 'certainly concentrates minds on giving viewers what they want'. Control by the BBC and IBA, DMM added, could prevent a lowering of standards and many newer advertisers would react against programming going down market as they 'want to reach a more affluent market'. In fact 'the emotive bogeyman of a ratings war is advanced by those who want to retain the status quo'.

Advertising should be introduced into the BBC at a rate limited to covering the progressive loss to the Corporation through the licence fee remaining the same. This would exert downward pressure on costs within the industry, for 'the BBC is clearly spread in far too many directions and profligate with resources'. D'Arcy criticised staffing levels at the BBC and its incursion into local radio and breakfast TV as a diversion from its main role 'designed to keep up with the IBA'.

The report then implied that the Home Secretary's decision in July 1984 to initiate an independent audit of the BBC would lead to a 'whitewash'. Finally D'Arcy argued that an increase in the amount of advertising on television would lead to an increase in retail activity in the economy as a whole.[21]

These arguments, about providing money for the BBC through advertising, pegging the licence fee, promoting competition in the sale of advertising, criticising the unfair nature of the fee, attacking the BBC's management's attitude to trade, celebrating consumer choice, rejecting ideas that adverts would lead to lower quality, promoting efficiency within broadcasting and stimulating economic growth, echoed ideas in the IEA and ASI publications.

Rodney Harris, DMM's media director, made it clear that the report had been published with the intention of influencing the licence fee negotiations and made sure that copies of it were sent to MPs and ministers. Harris worked with John Perris of Saatchi and Saatchi through the IPA to promote their views. D'Arcy also commissioned polls which received a fair amount of publicity, purporting to show public support for these ideas. For example an NOP poll commissioned by the agency showed that of 1,879 people interviewed in late 1984, 77 per cent wanted one commercial each hour on the BBC and the licence fee pegged. Polls such as this seem to have been designed to create the impression that there was a wave of public support for the agencies' views. But this was not borne out when the polls were subjected to close scrutiny during the subsequent debate.[22]

Saatchi and Saatchi

The second report, *Funding the BBC – the Case for Allowing Advertising* by Saatchi and Saatchi, was published on 1 October 1984. It argued that 'allowing advertising to increasingly fund the BBC will give the Corporation the resources to develop its services more fully without the need for the public to bear the burden'. The views expressed in this report were almost exactly the same as those in the D'Arcy MacManus Masius report:

1. Advertising should be permitted on all television and radio networks.
2. The licence fee was inequitable. Those who avoided paying were subsidised by those who paid and the number of evaders would

increase with increases in the fee which hit those least able to pay the hardest. Collecting the fee was expensive and burdensome.

3. Commercial broadcasters brought in more revenue than the BBC and the gap was likely to grow while the BBC's commitments and costs rose. The BBC was also 'increasingly and unsuccessfully having to fight for viewers'.
4. 'Advertisers needed more, preferably competitively sold television air-time to offset steeply rising television costs.' Indeed, if advertising were allowed on the BBC 'many "ex-television" brands could be "resurrected" and many product categories which do not advertise might be persuaded to do so'.
5. Viewers liked advertising.
6. Standards would not drop. The tradition of high standards in non-commercial and commercial TV in the UK would help to prevent such a drop. Anyway, other countries where ' "state controlled" television has taken advertising have not suffered from lowest common denominator programming'.
7. If the BBC took advertisements, it might 'pose problems to the financial viability' of some Independent Local Radio stations.[23]

Both reports attacked the licence fee and argued that if the BBC took advertisements it would benefit advertisers and viewers. Both argued that quality would not drop. The Saatchi report focused more strongly on the economic issues than did D'Arcy's. Differences of emphasis aside, both agencies shared the same goal and worked together to achieve it.

Lobbies and Networks

The Saatchi report was sent to the Home Office. Saatchi also commissioned opinion polls. One of these showed that 48 per cent of those interviewed favoured advertising on the BBC. Both reports were given wide coverage and editorial support in sections of the national press. The publicity provoked responses from the Chair of the BBC Board of Governors and the Director General, something which Rodney Harris saw as proof of the impact of the documents:

> The fact that extensive press coverage has forced public statements from both Alasdair Milne and Stuart Young on the matter is an indication of the seriousness ... The BBC normally keeps its head down when the flak is flying.[24]

Saatchi's connection with the Prime Minister and other Cabinet ministers was excellent. Saatchi had run the Conservative Party's election publicity in 1979 and 1983. Tim Bell, the ex-Chairman of Saatchi and Saatchi, was 'one of the Prime Minister's most trusted consultants' at this time. Although he denied any involvement in the Saatchi report he was very critical of the BBC. For instance, in the trade publication *Media Week* in 1985 he stated, 'I want the BBC to fail because I don't want that system to work. It only works now because it has a monopoly.' Michael Dobbs, another Saatchi employee, enjoyed close access to the Prime Minister. While still employed by Saatchi, he and Bell attended a 'major discussion on tactics' with the Prime Minister, Norman Tebbit, Cecil Parkinson, Ian Gow and other advisers in June 1983 at Chequers. He was later Norman Tebbit's 'special adviser and a key member of the Saatchi campaign team' in the run up to the 1987 general election at a time when Tebbit was leading a well-planned public attack on the BBC.

Saatchi and Saatchi and the people associated with it maintained close links with the inner circles of the Conservative Cabinet throughout the 1980s and could no doubt be confident that their views on the BBC or other media-related activities would receive a sympathetic hearing. Again, as in the case of the IEA and ASI, these advertising agencies enjoyed access to power through the political networks in which they were involved, networks which provided the opportunity for the transmission of ideas and policy options.[25]

As well as operating within these networks the two agencies worked alongside two trade organisations, the Incorporated Society of British Advertisers (ISBA) and the Institute of Practitioners in Advertising (IPA). These organisations sought to win support for the idea that the BBC should take advertising. They also kept up the pressure for more commercially funded broadcasting outlets after the Peacock Committee rejected the idea of advertising on the BBC.

The ISBA described itself as:

> the representative of all areas of industry and commerce, for whom advertising, sponsorship and all aspects of publicity are important. We describe our members as 'the advertisers' to make a clear distinction between our point of view and those of advertising agencies and of the media owners.

Ken Miles, the ISBA's Director, wrote to MPs of all parties urging them to support a Bill promoted by the Labour MP Joe Ashton, debated in

January 1985. Ashton tried, unsuccessfully, to force the BBC to take advertising. The ISBA's submission to Peacock read in places like a summary of the main points in the Saatchi and DMM documents. The ISBA recommended that BBC1 should take two minutes of advertising each hour or that BBC2 should take six minutes per hour initially:

> The ISBA believes that a controlled and phased introduction of advertising to the BBC would produce all round benefits. The BBC's income growth would be more secure; viewers would not need to suffer continual licence fee increases; many disadvantaged viewers could be exempted from licence fees; industry would have more opportunities for television advertising and competitive activity, and would benefit from stable costs. Extravagance in aspects of television would be contained.[26]

The IPA, which represented most of the UK's advertising agencies, received a report from John Perris in November 1984 advocating advertising on the BBC. In December the IPA decided to press for a Committee of Inquiry on the future funding of the BBC which would draw up recommendations for the planned introduction of advertising. In April 1985 it organised a debate at which Michael Grade, then a BBC executive, opposed the idea of advertising on the BBC while Perris argued that it was 'inevitable'. Once Peacock had reported, the IPA prepared a document aimed at the Prime Minister, the Home Office and the Department of Trade and Industry, reasserting the case for the phased introduction of advertising on the BBC.[27]

There is no doubt that the two agencies at the centre of this debate were well placed to use their high-level political contacts to lobby for, publicise and promote the case for advertising on the BBC. By the summer of 1985 their arguments had received widespread publicity in the national press and the endorsement of the Prime Minister. They had been circulated to Tory and Labour MPs and had been discussed and publicised by the IPA and the ISBA. The IPA's call in December 1984 for a committee of inquiry into the BBC had, in part, been implemented with the establishment of the Peacock Committee.

Shaping the Debate

This chapter has shown that the direction of broadcasting policy in the 1980s was the subject of systematic attention by right-wing 'think tanks' and advertising interests. All of these groups had close contacts with senior politicians within the Conservative government. The arguments they promoted found expression in a series of broadcasting policy initiatives taken by the three Thatcher administrations. Some of these initiatives had the effect of reshaping the framework within which broadcasting operated. Not all of the ideas were taken up. Those that were, as with Mrs Thatcher's support for placing advertisements on the BBC, were not all implemented. But some, like promoting more competition, auctioning franchises and creating favourable conditions for pay-TV were.

These groups were not, formally, part of the state but their views were respected by those who exercised power within the state – the politicians and civil servants. In effect these lobbyists, most notably the IEA, were advocating modifications in the formal relationship between state, broadcasters and the economy. The general thrust of this view was that broadcasting should be more tightly controlled by market forces and that the state should be used to facilitate this. It was a view which had powerful supporters among many senior politicians during the 1980s.

3   The Press and the BBC in the 1980s: a Survey

The advertising lobby was at that time merely trying it on again as they had done many times in the past. But the campaign to try to get ads on the BBC caught fire, to the surprise of all concerned, and struck sparks all the way from the Tory backbenchers to Downing Street because the BBC, ignoring the spirit of the times, asked for more money to continue expanding without any accompanying savings.[1]

This explanation of what triggered the campaign against the BBC assumes that the initial attack was routine, but that the scale of the 'fire' was unpredicted and essentially accidental. It implies that if the BBC had payed more attention to 'the spirit of the times' the attack would not have taken place. The argument is vague. What is meant by 'the spirit of the times'? It also dispenses with explanation, preferring to invoke accident – 'to the surprise of all concerned'. It fails to place the developments of the early 1980s in the context of the debates and manoeuvres of the time. More significantly it fails, as do most of the published accounts of what happened, to focus on and examine the role of the national newspapers in stimulating and sustaining the attack. In reality, by 1984 there was a host of actors pushing against the door of broadcasting policy, by and large, in the same direction. One key actor was the national press.

This chapter argues that, just as the majority of the national press gave open support to the broad range of Mrs Thatcher's policies throughout the 1980s, so significant sections supported her policy of restructuring British broadcasting, starting with the BBC. They promoted a range of opinions and policies which directly paralleled those held by Mrs Thatcher, her allies in the Cabinet, the advertisers, and right-wing pressure groups. The section which was most vociferous in supporting the attack on the BBC was the Murdoch-owned press. This organisation was close to Mrs Thatcher and was strategically placed to benefit from changes in broadcasting policy which would open the UK system to more commercial pressures.[2]

Throughout the 1980s most of the national press gave consistent support to Mrs Thatcher and the Conservative Party. There were exceptions. Some, like *The Times* under the editorship of Harold Evans, were occasionally distant from the Prime Minister and the ruling party. Others were more or less critical of the government, like the *Guardian*, the *Observer*, the *Daily Mirror* and the *Sunday Mirror*. In 1986 the *Independent* was launched and adopted a broadly supportive but frequently critical stance towards the government, especially on social policy.

Loyal Supporters

The rest of the national press, the *Financial Times*, the *Daily Telegraph*, the *Daily Express*, the *Sunday Express*, the *Mail*, the *Mail on Sunday*, *Today* (from 1987), *The Times* and *Sunday Times*, the *Sun*, and the *News of the World*, supported the policies of the government with varying degrees of intensity. In 1987 73 per cent of national daily circulation and 81 per cent of national Sunday circulation was controlled by papers which actively supported the Conservative government. The Tories could count on important periodicals like the *Economist* and the *Spectator*. Although, on individual issues, all national papers could and did criticise aspects of policy, most commentators would endorse the judgement of a former Tory MP and director of the Conservative Party Political Centre, Lord Alport, who in 1985 pointed out that the national press had, 'for the most part gone to extraordinary lengths to support the government's policies and flatter the Prime Minister'. In 1989 Viscount Rothermere, proprietor of the *Mail* and the *Mail on Sunday*, summed up his attitude in a way which reasonably reflected the position occupied by most national newspapers in this period:

> These newspapers have always been conservative. Mrs Thatcher is the leading exponent of true Conservative policies. David English and myself are enthusiastic supporters, though that is not to say we don't take an independent line.[3]

Mrs Thatcher received active, enthusiastic support from these proprietors and editors before the 1979 general election and many of them were subsequently rewarded in one way or another. The day after Mrs Thatcher's election victory, on 4 May 1979, 'a celebration lunch was hosted' by the proprietor of the *Daily Express*, Lord Mathews, and his deputy Jocelyn Stevens. Rupert Murdoch was among the guests.

Murdoch was also on the top table at the select tenth anniversary dinner held by Mrs Thatcher in 1989. Knighthoods were given to the editors of the *Sun* (1980), the *Express* (1980) and the *Mail* (1982), and an OBE was given to the editor of the *Daily Star* in 1990. Lords Mathews and Stevens, who both ran the *Express* during the 1980s, owed their peerages to Mrs Thatcher. She also maintained close contact with Fleet Street editors and journalists directly through her Press Secretary, Bernard Ingham, and through her private Secretary, Charles Powell.[4]

Not a Good Press

It is within this context that attacks on the BBC in the national press should be viewed. Milne dates the assault from January 1984 when journalist Max Hastings launched an attack in the pages of the London *Evening Standard* (hereafter the *Standard*), a paper owned by Viscount Rothermere. Milne suggests that the BBC's coverage of the Falklands War provoked the attacks as well as its involvement in DBS, which made it a potential rival for some national newspapers whose proprietors were considering involvement in this area. But, as already discussed, there were also by this time other groups lobbying for change in broadcasting who provided ample material for use by the press.[5]

All the national papers covered the issue of the BBC, the licence fee and related issues, but they did so with varying degrees of emphasis. Some, such as the *Daily Telegraph*, the *Sunday Telegraph* and the *Financial Times* ran stories which reflected the critical agenda of other papers and of the government, but did not lead a sustained attack on the BBC. They ran material sympathetic to the values embodied in the BBC and to its difficult position under the Conservative government. These papers showed that there was a debate about the BBC and took their own line on that debate.[6]

Some papers, like the *Sunday People*, the *Daily Mirror* and the *Sunday Mirror*, ran pieces critical of the BBC but stopped short of an all-out attack on the Corporation. The *Observer* and the *Guardian*, on the other hand, reported the criticisms but gave prominent coverage to the other side of the debate. Their editorial line was, by and large, hostile towards government policies on broadcasting and remained so throughout the period under consideration.

The small-circulation weeklies of the right, the *Economist* and the *Spectator*, took up the arguments against the BBC and the duopoly with some vigour. The *Spectator* published critical articles by Paul Johnson who, in January 1985, took on the BBC, the Labour Party and the trade unions within commercial television all in one article. The *Economist*, three months later just after the Peacock Committee was established, attacked the duopoly of the BBC and ITV as costly and restrictive.[7]

Tony Elliot, owner of *Time Out*, a London-based leisure magazine, put his weight behind a campaign to abolish the monopoly of the BBC and ITV on publication of their programming details. The campaign was supported by *Sunday Times* editor Andrew Neil. It also succeeded in winning the support of the Parliamentary Home Affairs Select Committee in 1988, and of the government. The 1990 Broadcasting Act gave the campaigners what they wanted.[8]

Other publications took a clearly hostile approach. Max Hastings' article in the *Standard* in January 1984 was called 'Who will halt the runaway Beeb?' Although it appeared four months before the publication of the Adam Smith Institute report, it rehearsed many of the arguments which were used by the ASI as well as by the advertising lobby and the Murdoch press. According to Hastings the BBC lacked proper leadership, was bankrupt of ideas and, with its incursion into Breakfast Television and plans for DBS, had exhibited a tendency to take on more than it could handle:

> For a start, the Corporation could be compelled to divest itself of many of its irrelevant fringe activities such as local radio ... it should seek to initiate and sponsor far more outside programme making by independent producers ... and ... should set itself an absolute target of cutting its own staff by, say, a third over the next decade.

The *Standard* continued to provide a platform for criticism of the BBC. It joined in the chorus accusing the BBC of being too left wing, an allegation which, by the mid-1980s, had become a recurrent theme in parliamentary and newspaper attacks on the Corporation. On 11 November 1986 it carried a headline which dominated the front page: 'Yes, The BBC is Biased'. The story reported the findings of what the *Standard* described as the 'independent media research group, the Media Monitoring Unit' which alleged that BBC current affairs programmes were biased. Within a matter of days it emerged that the Media Monitoring Unit was closely linked to known right-wing activists who were connected with the Conservative Party.[9]

A similar consistency of critical tone characterised articles in the *Mail*. In January 1984 the BBC *Panorama* programme 'Maggie's Militant Tendency' provoked fury at Tory Central Office because of its allegations about the extent of right-wing influence within the party. Milne had a series of meetings with Conservative Party Chairman John Selwyn Gummer and the government's Chief Whip, John Wakeham, to discuss the dispute. No agreement was reached at the meeting and, as a result, Milne records in his memoirs, 'Central Office fed the *Daily Mail* with a whole list of charges against us suggesting the programme was a tissue of lies'. In December 1984 the *Mail* attacked the BBC's bid for an increase in its licence fee and in March 1985 supported the decision to establish the Peacock inquiry. It argued in favour of introducing advertising into the Corporation and in August 1985 attacked BBC management demanding that Milne should go. It denounced *The Monocled Mutineer* as the latest example of left-wing bias at the BBC. Once the spotlight was off the BBC, after the 1987 general election, the paper wholeheartedly supported the government's 1989 Broadcasting Bill. It took on the Labour Party, the BBC and the ITV companies all in the same editorial:

> To listen to Labour you would think that this government was forever trying to force through reforms against the popular grain ... [the Bill] ... breaks the cosy BBC–ITV duopoly of television. There is to be more choice.[10]

The *Mail*'s rival in the middle market of the national press was the *Daily Express*. During the mid-1980s it repeated many of the same themes as the *Mail*. In October 1984 the *Express* carried a fierce attack on the BBC by Geoffrey Levy. Levy argued that the licence fee was unfair because ITV viewers had to pay it whether or not they watched BBC, that the Corporation had too many staff and that it would be more efficient if it had to earn a living. It cited the views of ASI Director Eamon Butler, attacked BBC management and echoed the views of D'Arcy MacManus Masius on the gentlemanly culture of the BBC, but from a slightly more populist perspective: 'There is a vanity about the BBC which is not unlike the polished performance of a confidence trickster who must look and behave like a first-class gent to succeed. For generations the BBC has done just that.'

Like the *Mail*, the *Express* attacked the BBC with arguments drawn from a repertoire of criticism which had become well established by October 1984. They were timed to coincide with the run up to the BBC's bid for a new licence fee settlement. The *Express* attacked the bid in December 1984, supported the establishment of the Peacock Committee in March 1985, called for Milne to go in August 1985 and, in its editorial in October 1986, summed up its general position on the

Corporation: 'The BBC is professionally and financially out of control ... No wonder there is mounting pressure at Westminster for the smug head of Director General Alasdair Milne.'[11]

Rupert Murdoch's Newspapers and the Attack on the BBC

No one should underestimate the importance of the national press in helping to set, reflect, sustain and develop the agendas of public policy debates in the UK in the 1970s and 1980s.[12] In the 1980s a large section of the national press was owned by Rupert Murdoch's companies, known as the News International Group. During this period Murdoch's extensive media interests in the UK were used to support the Prime Minister, and his companies received direct material benefits as a consequence of policy decisions taken by Margaret Thatcher's government. Rupert Murdoch allowed, some argue even encouraged, his papers, especially *The Times*, to attack the BBC when it was also under attack from the Prime Minister using arguments drawn from and paralleling those developed by the ASI and the advertising lobby. This helped to promote ideas in favour of allowing commercially funded media such as those operated by Murdoch's companies to establish more of a foothold in UK broadcasting.

'Mr Prime Minister'

In spite of occasional disagreements, Murdoch 'made no secret of his devotion to Margaret Thatcher and her policies'. His UK papers supported her premiership, with few reservations, throughout the 1980s. One former editor of *The Times* is reported to have commented that: 'Rupert and Mrs Thatcher consult regularly on every important matter of policy, especially as they relate to his economic and political interests. Around here he's often jokingly referred to as Mr Prime Minister.' Thatcher was known as 'a close friend and admirer' of Murdoch and at a private lunch, celebrating her tenth anniversary in office: 'There were no fewer than 60 guests seated at 10 tables. At the top table the men, with Mrs Thatcher, consisted of Lords Whitelaw, Carrington, Thornycroft, Forte and one commoner, Mr Rupert Murdoch.'[13]

This closeness yielded mutual benefits. Murdoch's papers the *Sun* and the *News of the World* had campaigned vigorously for Mrs Thatcher in the 1979 general election. In early 1981 Murdoch was trying to buy *The Times* and the *Sunday Times*. Under the terms of the 1973 Fair Trading Act, he faced a delay if the Secretary of State for Trade deemed that the bid should be referred to the Monopolies and Mergers Commission. Thatcher intervened and insisted that there should be no inquiry by the Commission. The move was justified by Secretary of State for Trade John Biffen on the grounds that a referral would be inappropriate as both papers were losing money.

Within ten months of Murdoch's purchase of *The Times*, Mrs Thatcher had developed doubts about the 'reliability' of the paper's editor, Harold Evans. As Evans has put it in his memoirs: 'My offence in the eyes of the Prime Minister and the Chairman of the party was unreliability: there was a doubt, aggravated by Murdoch, whether *The Times* under Evans would back Mrs Thatcher and the Tories wholeheartedly.' According to Evans, Murdoch took a series of steps which forced him to resign as editor in March 1983.[14]

In 1985 the government decided to legalise Small Mast Antennae TV receivers – a move which allowed homes to have small dishes designed to receive satellite signals. One commentator argued at the time that Murdoch would be 'the prime beneficiary' of this decision. It opened the market for the sale of domestic satellite receivers which would allow programmes transmitted by satellite to reach homes which were not cabled. Murdoch had begun investing in satellite TV projects in 1983 and did indeed exploit this opening by launching the DBS Sky TV service in 1989.

In July 1987 the government allowed Murdoch to take over the middle market tabloid *Today* without a reference to the Monopolies and Mergers Commission. In 1988 he was consulted by government advisers on broadcasting policy. In 1990 he informed Mrs Thatcher of the planned merger between Sky and BSB a matter of days before it happened. The merger flouted the terms of BSB's operating licence and the authority of the IBA. Downing Street did not pass on its privileged information to either the IBA or the Home Office. These are just some of the more dramatic ways in which Murdoch's relationship with Mrs Thatcher benefited both parties.[15]

This pattern of mutual support was repeated in the context of his papers' coverage of the BBC. There is no doubt that his newspapers were used to attack certain aspects of the UK broadcasting system. The attack on the BBC was sustained and, according to Milne, damaging. Journalist Paul Foot argued at the time that Murdoch 'personally ordered a sustained attack on the BBC and all its people'. Alastair Hetherington, a member of the Peacock Committee, accused *The Times* of running 'a vendetta against the BBC in its leaders, news stories and features'. In September 1985 Murdoch attacked the licence fee as 'wasteful, very unfair to the public and unnecessary'. He said that the BBC should be allowed to take advertising, but only if it were privatised. If it were not privatised he would be against the Corporation's taking advertisements as this would be 'very unfair'. Murdoch later denied that he had supported the idea that the BBC should take advertising, but there is absolutely no doubt that his flagship paper, *The Times*, gave extensive and sympathetic coverage to views advocating this course of action.

It was not just the BBC which was subjected to attacks from Murdoch's stable in the 1980s. ITV companies received similar treatment, particularly after 1987. He also used his papers to promote his interests in satellite TV. A report by the European Institute for the Media on the coverage of Sky Television and its rival BSB during 1989 revealed that Murdoch's papers covered the affairs of Sky TV at much greater length and in more detail than the affairs of the rival BSB.[16]

The Attack

The *Sun* did not devote as much attention to the issues of the BBC and the future of broadcasting as *The Times* and the *Sunday Times*. However, it sustained a critical perspective on the BBC and later in the decade did much to promote Murdoch's UK satellite interests. The *Sun* attacked the BBC over its coverage of the Falklands War in 1982 and over its licence fee bid in December 1984. It called for Milne to go in August 1985 and warmly supported the government's White Paper on broadcasting in 1988, exclaiming: 'Roll on the Government's plans to promote competition and freedom in TV.'[17]

Today was launched in 1986 by Eddie Shah. It was purchased by Murdoch in mid-1987 and from then on gave consistent support to the News International perspective on how UK broadcasting policy should develop. It even went as far as criticising the 1988 White Paper on Broadcasting for being too soft on the ITV companies: 'Mr Hurd's reforms will leave the BBC and the ITV companies holding a privileged place at the centre of the TV stage.'[18]

The two most prestigious publications in the Murdoch stable, the *Sunday Times* and *The Times*, held a consistent line on broadcasting from 1984 until the end of the period. They promoted the liberalisation of broadcasting regulation in order to open up the UK market to greater commercial exploitation. The various techniques used by the papers included open criticism of the BBC and ITV, publishing and commissioning opinion polls which suggested public disquiet with the duopoly and support for advertising, and stimulating controversy around the BBC. The papers also promoted specific changes in broadcasting regulation and management, often based on those advocated by the ASI, the IEA and the advertising industry. They also gave a favourable interpretation of the direction, if not always the detail, of government broadcasting policy.

The Sunday Times

Rupert Murdoch appointed Andrew Neil as editor of the *Sunday Times* in 1983. In 1988 Neil asserted that the *Sunday Times* had 'never questioned the BBC licence fee' but that, in his view, UK broadcasting was 'the most cartelised industry in this country'. He was also at pains to assert his independence from his proprietor on this topic claiming that he had 'never had a discussion with Rupert Murdoch over what *The Sunday Times* writes about broadcasting'.[19]

The claim that the *Sunday Times* had never questioned the BBC's licence fee may be true if the comment is strictly confined to a consideration of the paper's position as expressed in its leaders. But the news pages of the paper suggest a different interpretation. From early 1984 the *Sunday Times* ran a series of stories, occasionally based on polls commissioned by the paper, which highlighted problems with the licence fee and with the BBC. In presentation and in timing – these stories were run during the period preceding the discussions around the renewal of the licence fee – they could reasonably be interpreted as hostile copy designed to raise questions in the minds of readers about the desirability of continuing with the status quo.

On 4 March 1984, for example, the paper ran a story with the headline 'Public tells BBC: we want better value for money'. It was based on the findings of an opinion poll which had been commissioned by the *Sunday Times*. The story was written to emphasise those aspects of the results which were negative to the BBC:

Only one person in seven thinks the BBC licence fee represents 'very good value for money'. As many as 42 per cent of people are dissatisfied with the TV service they are receiving from the BBC. An exclusive MORI/Sunday Times poll reveals these facts this week as

BBC executives prepare for the battle to persuade a hostile government to raise the price of the colour licence, currently £46, to at least £60.

By not revealing the methods used in questioning the public, by opening the report with two negative 'findings' about the BBC, and by representing these as 'facts', the story was clearly constructed to echo criticism of the licence fee and the BBC.[20]

In June 1984 the paper brought the issue of the BBC's funding sharply into focus when it ran an article based on comments made by Home Office Minister Douglas Hurd, who was responsible for broadcasting, under the headline, 'Who should pay for the BBC?' In October 1984 an article 'Making the money go around' implied that it was the BBC's request for an increase in the licence fee which had triggered the government's hostile response to the Corporation rather than the considerations discussed in this book.[21]

In addition to its willingness to focus on critiques of BBC funding the paper promoted the extension of market forces into the broadcasting system. In September 1984 its 'Memo to Maggie' column advocated the deregulation of commercial radio. This was to involve the creation of a new tier of lightly regulated radio stations and the removal of some of the public service obligations under which commercial stations operated. These views, which reflected those expressed in the Omega report and echoed demands from sections of the commercial radio industry, found legislative expression in the 1990 Broadcasting Act.[22]

In May 1985, when the composition of the Peacock Committee was announced, the paper carried an article which suggested that the Committee would be more independent in its handling of the issues than other commentators believed at the time: 'The five men and one woman who have been appointed to serve on [Peacock's] committee appear, for the most part, to be obstinately open-minded.'

Later in the year the *Sunday Times* sparked the controversy over a BBC film 'At the Edge of the Union' in the *Real Lives* series. The controversy brought the Home Secretary into open conflict with the BBC Governors, the Governors into conflict with senior BBC management, and journalists into conflict with both the government and the BBC Governors. The key issues at stake were the BBC's coverage of Ireland and the Corporation's independence from the government, or as it seemed to many at the time, lack of it. The *Real Lives* affair, by fostering a perception already widespread among senior figures in the government that the BBC was poorly managed, arguably helped to contribute to the wholesale restructuring of BBC management. This began with the sacking of Alasdair Milne from his post as Director General in early 1987.

The paper played a similar role in relation to the Thames TV programme, 'Death on the Rock', in 1988. This programme, in its detailed refutation of aspects of the government's account of the death of three IRA members in Gibraltar in 1988, provoked the government into criticism of the standards of TV journalism and the role of the IBA at a time when the whole future of public service commercial broadcasting was being reviewed. The *Sunday Times* took a vigorous position which, in systematically criticising the programme-makers, implicitly helped to foster doubts about the state of investigative journalism on television and about the role of the IBA.[23]

Later in 1988 the *Sunday Times* welcomed the government's White Paper on broadcasting, which contained plans to restructure commercial television along market lines and to promote more competition by facilitating the spread of cable and satellite television. The new commercially driven environment announced by the White Paper had serious implications for the BBC. Shortly afterwards Jonathan Miller, editor of the paper's media section since mid-1987, was 'seconded for six months to Sky Television as special assistant to Andrew Neil the executive Chairman'. By this time Murdoch was clearly focused on promoting his interests in commercial broadcasting by creating an opening for his Sky TV satellite service. It seems that Murdoch considered the track record of Neil and Miller on media issues sufficiently in harmony with his perspectives to give them sensitive, senior posts in this strategically important venture. The paper then adopted an approach to the coverage of issues associated with ITV and the IBA similar to its coverage of the BBC.[24]

So it is evident that the *Sunday Times* pursued a pro-active policy in favour of the deregulation of public service broadcasting from at least 1983. It advocated an approach to broadcasting policy which, even if we accept Neil's testimony that he never discussed the paper's coverage of these matters with Murdoch, were conveniently in harmony with those of his employer and the Prime Minister.

The Times

A similar line was adopted by the other flagship title in Murdoch's UK stable. *The Times* systematically attacked the BBC and openly tried to influence government policy on the future of the Corporation.

In September 1984 the former Labour MP turned fierce advocate of Conservatism, Woodrow Wyatt, attacked the BBC. That same month the paper reported the D'Arcy MacManus Masius report on BBC finances under the headline 'Advertising on BBC "could peg licence"'. There followed a series of stories whose headlines highlighted negative aspects of the Corporation's affairs. On 30 November a report about the BBC's Annual Report for 1983–4 was headlined, 'Quality of BBC TV programmes threatened by soaring costs'. On 11 December 1984 it carried a piece headed 'The BBC still not sending out a clear picture', which asked: 'Is the sale of some of the Beeb's assets such a heinous suggestion? Every other nationalised industry has been forced to do it, is the BBC so special?'

On 4 January 1985 an article headlined '£60 licence would kill BBC plans' took an argument developed by the BBC, that it needed an adequate fee settlement to implement its plans, and used it to remind its readers of the suggestion that the Corporation should take advertising: 'A BBC analysis of its budgets, which have been released for the first time, shows there is little room for cosmetic cuts without bringing in advertising as some backbenchers have hoped.'[25]

All of these articles appeared while the advertising agencies were lobbying for advertisements on the BBC, during the period immediately before and just after the BBC made its bid for a higher licence fee and when the attention of the Home Secretary, the Prime Minister and MPs was on the renewal process. The articles were clearly meant to play a part in this debate.

On 15 January 1985 the House of Commons debated Joe Ashton's bill which was designed to introduce advertising into the BBC. This initiative coincided with the consideration by the Home Secretary and the Prime Minister of the Peat Marwick Mitchell audit and of the government's response to the BBC's request for a £65 Colour TV licence fee. *The Times* published three leaders on 14, 15 and 16 January attacking the BBC and public service broadcasting, all under the slightly comic and archaic headline, 'Whither the BBC?'

The 14 January leader, timed to coincide with the debate over the Ashton Bill, opened by agreeing with those critics of the BBC who accused it 'with varying degrees of fairness, of inefficiency, unaccountability, self-aggrandizement' and of 'feather bedding its employees'. Pressures were at work, it argued, which would 'burst' the ITV/BBC broadcasting duopoly apart. The pressure of competition for audiences with ITV had, it argued, led to the two systems looking 'remarkably similar'. In addition the BBC's costs had expanded with its activities in local radio and breakfast TV and these costs would grow further with its involvement in cable and satellite. By extending 'consumer choice', cable and satellite would make it 'still harder for the BBC to achieve its chosen level of domination in the market'. Finally, the leader asserted 'the political climate has changed' and it was now necessary to justify both a duopoly and the licence fee which was a 'poll tax ... that is fast rising, and looks set to rise still faster'. As a result of these pressures 'various questions should now be asked – and answered – by politicians and broadcasters'.

Adopting its traditional, self-appointed role as guide and mentor to the political nation, *The Times* set about addressing these questions in its leader of 15 January. There it argued that advertisers 'can clearly play some part ... in generating the revenue to pay for many programmes'. Where publicly generated money funded programmes there should be 'more open discussion' about the use to which this money was put. Public money, it suggested, should 'provide finance last (and preferably not at all) to those programmes which the advertising market would be most likely to generate by itself'. It went on to argue that the 'Government might consider critically the question of whether British television really is better than that of the Americans and the rest of the world'. There was no reason 'to be certain that finance by advertising will overthrow' the creative impulse underpinning BBC TV; broadcasters created their own 'propaganda' by setting their own standards of quality and awarding themselves prizes according to those standards. The government, it said, should establish whether the consumer really wanted to pay for the current system. It concluded by calling for 'a more open – less monolithic – system of broadcasting in which customers can chose what qualities they want from their television screens and radio sets' and suggested that 'others outside the BBC' should have a role in programme-making.

Next day's leader argued that the 'Government should concede no increase in the BBC licence fee' but that the 'future of British broadcasting' required a 'rapid and radical enquiry first'. It continued, 'Advertising must eventually pay for some of the "quality television" now financed by the BBC licence' and advocated that sections of the BBC should be auctioned off and financed by advertising. The licence fee should be pegged and used to fund a system of public service broadcasting with news and current affairs at its centre. It ended: 'In the next few weeks the Government has the opportunity to begin the process of redefining public service broadcasting in a way that will ensure its survival for the 1990s and beyond. It should seize it with a will.'

The central themes of these editorials repeated and supplemented those developed by the IEA, the Adam Smith Institute and the two advertising agencies discussed in Chapter 2. These were that consumers should be given more choice, that the BBC was too costly and over-extended, that it should take advertising, that parts should be hived off, and that the government should not accept the broadcasters' own definition of quality.

The leaders were a timely intervention in the debate. First, they gave status to what had until then been a relatively arcane aspect of politics, namely the funding of broadcasting. Second, they advocated a political device, the 'rapid and radical enquiry' for dealing with the issue, a device which was known to be favoured by the Prime Minister. The idea was already being mooted in public and became the solution adopted by the government in March 1985.[26]

Alasdair Milne responded vigorously to these attacks, accusing the paper of reflecting the commercial interests of its proprietor in its coverage of the BBC. Charles Douglas Home, the paper's editor, protested and *The Times*'s independent directors were called in to investigate the allegations. They found in favour of the paper.[27]

Thereafter the paper continued its criticism. In response to the BBC's claim that the Peat Marwick Mitchell report had broadly given the Corporation a clean bill of health, *The Times* replied that the Home Office felt the report had no bearing on the licence fee discussions. The original brief to which Peat Marwick Mitchell worked excluded consideration of key issues such as manning and the more efficient use of technology. On 29 March 1985, two days after the Home Secretary announced the establishment of the Peacock Committee, *The Times* reminded readers that it had called for an inquiry and encouraged readers to support it. On the day of the first full meeting of the Peacock Committee *The Times* leader proffered comment and advice. The BBC's definition of quality was attacked and it was criticised for making 'petulant threats'.[28]

Any effect?

The policy of restructuring UK broadcasting was supported at the highest level of government from the early 1980s. In promoting the restructuring of broadcasting, sections of the national press were doing for broadcasting policy what they had been doing for other policies favoured by the Conservative administrations.

As shown here, there was a general prejudice against the BBC and ITV in key national publications which were traditional supporters of the Conservatives. The bias on broadcasting was more systematically sustained in the middle-market publications (*Mail*, *Express*, *Today* (after 1987)) and the Murdoch-controlled papers. The tabloids did not cover these issues with the same detail and continuity as the qualities. Among the qualities the most unambiguous criticism of broadcasters came from the Murdoch press and the small circulation right-of-centre periodicals (*Economist*, *Spectator*).

There are three main considerations to bear in mind. The national press was neither uniformly nor unremittingly hostile to the BBC and ITV. The *Guardian*, the *Observer*, the *Telegraph*, and later the *Independent* were either openly hostile, critical or doubtful about the drive to restructure broadcasting. The lead was taken by the Murdoch press. These divisions within the press reflected the fact that there were divisions among politicians and opinion-makers on this topic.

Second, the policy debates in the national press were concentrated in the quality papers. The mass of viewers and listeners who would be affected by any policy changes read tabloids and were not exposed to even the limited debate which took place in the qualities.

This reflected a divide between the popular and quality press which, according to some people, makes it unreasonable to argue that the qualities and the tabloids can both be described as newspapers. Qualities contain news and opinion for a small section of the population, the tabloids offer entertainment and some overt political content of varying level and depth for the masses. The national press therefore fed one section of the population with a lot of information on the issues and deprived the rest, the great mass of readers, of information and debate on a topic which was central to their own leisure time. There is no doubt that this issue deserves further, detailed examination.[29]

Third, press coverage had an influence. Cabinet ministers took the press coverage of major issues very seriously, as did people within the BBC when broadcasting was being discussed. Former Cabinet Minister James Prior has recorded how important the right-wing press was in setting the tone of Cabinet debates. Margaret Thatcher has recorded how on 9 January 1986 she opened a Cabinet discussion of the Westland affair by: 'rehearsing the decisions which had been made by the Government. I then ran over the damaging press comment which there had been in the New Year. I said that if the situation continued, the Government would have no credibility left.'

The Times clearly believed its views on broadcasting had an effect on decision-makers, claiming in 1988 that the policies it had been supporting since 1983 had 'subsequently taken root' and were present in the government's 1988 White Paper on broadcasting.[30]

Within the BBC the attacks in the press were taken very seriously. Milne noted in early 1985 that the BBC 'had taken a drubbing and some of the mud stuck'. He stated in public that if *The Times*'s recommendations were acted on, they 'would have the practical effect of enabling its owner, Mr Rupert Murdoch, to acquire some of the most valuable broadcasting action in the United Kingdom'.

In May of the same year, in an interview in the *Stage and Television Today*, Milne commented on national press coverage and in particular on the *The Times*'s effect on relations between governors and managers at the BBC:

> the national press, and *The Times* in particular, were malevolent to a degree. There were one or two exceptions – the *Daily Telegraph* for example, who don't like the BBC and make that opinion very clear, were meticulously careful in reporting all that happened ... Everyday – and it was everyday – there was some distortion, some half-truth, or something turned to the disadvantage of the BBC. Obviously I know who owns *The Times*, but the way the campaign against us was run – with five leaders and the daily drip-on-the-stone technique – was a surprise to me. You have to accept that when someone throws enough mud, some will stick. Even some of the BBC governors believed some of the things that appeared in *The Times* and I had to disabuse them.

In 1985, just after the *Real Lives* affair, an internal report on the relationship between BBC management and the Governors was commissioned. It found that: 'The Governors feel themselves often to be inadequately informed and insufficiently forewarned. Too often the first knowledge they have of some development affecting the public position of the BBC is when they read about it in the press.'

At the height of the press attacks on the BBC, according to one source, 'Producers and executives felt they were living in a bunker having the stuffing knocked out of them.' Later, in January 1987 senior BBC executive Michael Grade attacked the national press for 'regular, persistent and malign criticism of the BBC'. Press coverage mattered. Milne's sensitivity to the affect of the attacks on internal relationships within the Corporation testifies to the significance of the press coverage. It was a significance recognised by all the major protagonists within the battle over public service broadcasting.[31]

4 The Public Battles over Broadcasting

Throughout the 1980s Conservative MPs attacked the BBC. During the same period the Corporation clashed repeatedly and openly with the government on a range of issues. This chapter outlines and explores these two aspects of the political history.

The reasons for the attacks and clashes sometimes reflected long-standing Conservative criticisms of the BBC. Others were more orchestrated, designed to put the Corporation on the defensive or to achieve changes in its management. All were conducted within a context shaped by the fact that the Prime Minister and some of her senior colleagues were known to be critical of the BBC and wanted change.

Parliamentary Criticism

The clashes between the BBC and the government had a parliamentary dimension, in the form of regular attacks on the Corporation by Cabinet ministers and backbench Tory MPs in the House of Commons. These focused initially, in 1979, on the BBC's coverage of Ireland. In 1982 the BBC's coverage of the Falklands War was deemed by some tabloids, notably the *Sun*, as well as by the Prime Minister and many Tory MPs, to be insufficiently patriotic. As Bernard Ingham, the Prime Minister's Press Secretary, put it: 'It was ... rather trying when notably the BBC gave an impression of neutrality as between Britain and Argentine. This caused some outrage among MPs and the Prime Minister herself was not best pleased.'

Senior BBC managers were summoned before a noisy meeting of the Conservative Backbench Media Committee and subjected to a fierce barrage of criticism. In this context the committee, according to Ingham, served a useful function:

I found the criticism of the BBC by MPs was a valuable safety valve. It put the issue before the public and thereby helped the Government to avoid becoming more deeply embroiled in such essentially ephemeral matters when it had bigger issues on its plate.[1]

In late 1984 the BBC was about to apply for an increase in the licence fee. After a summer and autumn of newspaper attacks on the Corporation which had given widespread publicity to the arguments of the advertisers and the ASI, a group of Tory MPs tabled a motion opposing any moves to increase the licence fee to £60. As one commentator put it: 'Friends of the BBC in the Commons were few and far between, particularly on the Tory benches, and the latest reports of excess spending by the Corporation were not improving attitudes.'[2]

In December 1984 Labour MP Joe Ashton indicated that he intended to introduce a Ten-Minute-Rule Bill designed to put advertisements on the BBC. This was not Labour Party policy. He justified his move by describing the licence fee as a regressive poll tax. He argued that the Labour Party's own paper, *Labour Weekly*, took adverts, and that ITV programmes were good in spite of being funded by advertising. He noted that the BBC already contained material which could be regarded as advertising. His arguments echoed those of the advertising industry. In fact the Incorporated Society of British Advertisers lobbied MPs to support the Bill. According to one commentator the Bill had the merit of providing 'an opportunity for a first reading vote by which Government ministers can see the strength of feeling on both sides', at a time when the government was considering the BBC's application for a licence fee increase. The Bill was defeated but provided an opportunity for the ideas circulating in the press and elsewhere to be more widely aired and given the credibility that Parliamentary debates can confer on such ideas.[3]

Shortly afterwards, on 27 March 1985, Leon Brittan, the Home Secretary, announced that the BBC's licence fee would be £58 not £65 and that the government was establishing the Peacock Committee. Few of the 25 Tory MPs who spoke in the debate that followed had anything favourable to say about the BBC. Within two hours of the announcement 50 Tory MPs had signed a motion of protest against the increase. Criticisms included the BBC's lack of patriotism and its lack of good economic housekeeping. There were attacks on the principle of the licence fee and calls for new forms of funding including the introduction of advertisements. These criticisms reflected a view among some Tory MPs that the BBC had been let off too lightly.[4]

The attacks on the BBC's politics by Tory MPs continued throughout the 1980s. Tony Marlow accused the BBC of giving an 'obsessive and therefore possibly misleading view' of events in South Africa in 1986.

A few days later, on 3 July, John Stokes MP echoed the sentiments he had expressed in the debate on the licence fee in March 1985. He attacked the BBC for 'its utter lack of patriotism and left-wing bias' alleging that its producers were 'entirely out of hand' and 'trying to brainwash much of the population'.[5]

Stokes's comments were made in the House, after Home Secretary Douglas Hurd had announced the government's initial response to the Peacock Committee's report. In this debate, speakers ranged widely across the issues, expressing concern about continuation of the licence fee, the implications of the report for commercial broadcasting and the morality of broadcasting. The emphasis on market forces within the Peacock report was, however, welcomed by the government and Tory backbenchers. Michael Forsyth MP later welcomed Peacock for 'its clear recognition of the role which market choice must play in the future of broadcasting'.[6]

By the end of 1986 it was clear to some observers that parliamentary support among Tory MPs for the immediate introduction of advertisements on the BBC had waned: 'Ministers have not sensed any great pressure from within their party for making the BBC take advertising.' Nonetheless sentiment against the licence fee lingered on. In January 1987 when Hurd announced that the government was linking future increases in the BBC licence fee to the retail price index, one Tory MP claimed that the public were 'fed up with paying an enormous fee for old films and ... biased current affairs programmes'.

The shift occurred for a variety of reasons. The number of Conservative MPs involved in attacking the licence fee was a minority of the parliamentary party. They were articulate and won support at moments of heightened interest in the issue. But it seems that they did not represent the majority of Tory MPs. Once the licence fee issue had been dealt with by Peacock, the immediate focus of government policy shifted and consequently the motive and opportunity for attacks on the licence fee diminished. The government, following the lead taken by Tory Party Chairman Norman Tebbit, focused more sharply on criticising the quality of the BBC's management and its alleged political bias. In addition legislation on the future of broadcasting finance was now unlikely to be introduced before the general election. Peacock's recommendations (see Chapter 6) meant that any changes would probably centre primarily on commercial broadcasting. By early 1987 the BBC's problems had partly been solved in the eyes of the government and many backbench MPs by the introduction of a new management regime under Marmaduke Hussey, Michael Checkland and John Birt.[7]

Two further aspects of parliamentary interest in the BBC provide a useful insight into the methods used by parliamentarians and the government to air and win support for particular policies. They relate to the activities of the Tory Backbench Media Committee and Conservative Party Chairman Norman Tebbit.

The Backbench Media Committee

The Tory Backbench Media Committee was one of many backbench committees. Its spokesman for much of the period 1983–5 was former broadcaster Tim Brinton. At this time its membership was open to all Tory backbenchers, but the key participants were its officers and one or two activists. It did not take minutes nor, according to one source, did it 'take a view' on issues. The opinions expressed by its officers were their own.

The officers of the committee seem to have acted as a point of contact between backbench Tory MPs and the Home Office, the department mainly responsible for broadcasting. Officers of the Committee canvassed the views of Tory backbenchers on broadcasting matters.[8]

This situation was ambiguous. The Committee was independent of but also clearly linked to the government. It ostensibly canvassed backbench views but at times seemed to pursue a policy line which reflected the thinking of certain sections within the government. It was described as a committee which automatically gave its officers some public status. But it did not operate like a normal committee in a political organisation. It is this ambiguity which makes it difficult to assess properly the motives and actions of individuals associated with it except in so far as cultivated ambiguity is a tried and tested feature of parliamentary politics.

In December 1984 Tim Brinton, as Chairman of the Committee, urged the Home Secretary not to agree to the BBC's £65 bid. He said the BBC should be encouraged to cut its spending. This view clearly had the support of many Conservative MPs as the March 1985 licence fee debate showed. In his capacity as Committee Chairman, Brinton's views were canvassed and published in influential trade publications such as *Broadcast* and national papers such as *The Times*. Usually his views were reported without questioning the credentials of the Committee, examining its function or explaining the role or status of the Chairman.

The opinions of the Committee were often cited as if the views of all its members were in agreement, even though it is not clear how many views were being represented and by whom. For instance in January 1985 *The Times* reported the following:

The Conservative Party's media committee, which is opposed to an increase in the present £46-a-year licence fee, has suggested that breakfast television should be scrapped and local radio and Radio 1 be sold off to reduce the corporation's costs.

These views clearly echoed those developed by the ASI and the advertisers.

In December 1984 Giles Shaw, the Home Office minister responsible for broadcasting, refused to rule out advertising as an option for funding the BBC. Mrs Thatcher had, by then, openly declared her support for it. In January 1985 one commentator suggested that the Committee was acting as a mouthpiece for some of her views: 'The Tory media committee, clearly operating with the personal approval of Mrs Thatcher, have declared not only that the BBC's expansion plans are unnecessary, but that there should be massive cutbacks.' These views echoed what had emerged as a consensus on broadcasting policy among ministers, namely that the BBC should curtail its plans for expansion and put its house in order.

Brinton questioned the licence fee but did not come out in favour of advertising, a position very similar to the one underpinning Home Office thinking which was the official government line: 'The question is should a compulsory tax be levied which in effect provides music hall and pop music. It is rather like taking income tax from the Treasury and subsidising Mars bars.' By early March 1985 he appears to have been testing the water on behalf of the government for the option of an inquiry: 'I would be happy if the Government said that the BBC could have between £55 and £60 for two years during which time we would set up some sort of inquiry.'

An inquiry meant that the BBC would not be forced to take advertisements immediately but it left open the possibility of advertising finance replacing the licence fee in the medium term.

Brinton's views clearly did not reflect those of Tory MPs who wanted advertisements introduced immediately. He seems to have acted as a mouthpiece for a range of criticisms of the BBC both inside and outside the government. He gave an apparently independent backbench gloss to views which, on closer examination, seem to have had significant support in government.

The Committee was part of a wider process under way at that time. Opinion on the BBC was being shaped outside of Parliament, as we have seen. But among Tory MPs in Parliament it was divided. The pronouncements made by the Committee Chairman give an insight into those divisions. The Committee did not come out wholly in support of advertising on the BBC and from late December 1984 Brinton's statements were closer to those being made by Home Office ministers – see Chapter 5 – than to those of Thatcher. It could be argued that the Committee was acting, at this stage, as a weapon in the Home Office's battle to win parliamentary and wider support for a more moderate pace of reform than that advocated by the Prime Minister and those Tory MPs who wanted swift action. According to Alan Peacock, who chaired the Committee on Financing the BBC in 1985–6, members of the Backbench Committee: 'tried very hard to draw me on what our conclusions were likely to be and how they would view them, but there was a notably lack of unanimity of view on broadcasting finance amongst its experienced members'.

The fact that the Backbench Committee never formally backed advertising on the BBC, the defeat of the Ashton Bill and the absence of any real revolt among Tory MPs over the announcement of 27 March 1985, suggests that the majority of Tory MPs in early 1985 did not favour it. Most Tory MPs lacked the time and expertise to take a detailed interest in the issue of broadcasting finance. Those who did seem to have been trying to gauge and influence backbench opinion on key policy issues as part of a process which was being driven by the government and lobbyists outside the House of Commons.[9]

Party and Parliament

If the factors shaping the formulation and expression of backbench opinion on the issue of advertising were complex, so too was the interaction between Conservative MPs, their supporters in the Party nationally, the government, the press and the BBC. This is shown by the attack on the BBC led from Conservative Central Office by Norman Tebbit, MP, Cabinet Minister and Chairman of the Conservative Party from 1985–7. This was a concerted effort to provoke criticism of the BBC in the Conservative Party, among MPs and in the press. In this Tebbit succeeded.

In 1986 the Conservative Party's internal publication, *Newsline*, which went to members around the country, ran a campaign encouraging its readers to monitor bias on radio and TV. In the summer it was announced that a one person unit had been set up in Central Office to monitor TV bias. Speaking at the 1986 Radio Festival in Glasgow, Scottish Secretary Malcolm Rifkind said there was a built-in anti-government bias in the media and he supported the work of Tebbit's monitoring unit. In October and November Tebbit clashed publicly with the BBC over a libel case involving Tory MPs and the publication of a Conservative Central Office report alleging bias in coverage of the April 1986 bombings of Libya by the US government. In late October 1986 over 100 Tory MPs signed a motion calling for a restoration of standards at the BBC. In January 1987, when Milne was sacked, his 'departure was greeted with unconcealed glee by many Tory MPs'.

Tebbit's attack on the BBC then was a concerted effort, using the resources and media platform provided by the Conservative Party machine and his position as a senior Cabinet minister. The attacks appeared to be coming from many quarters but, in reality, they were either being initiated, or exploited by Conservative Central Office. The aim was to alter the nature of BBC management.[10]

Parliamentary criticism of the BBC by the Tories combined spontaneous dislike of the Corporation, with the influence of externally generated critiques and manipulation by ministers and party managers. As a result of all this the BBC, between 1984 and 1986, was the subject of constant attacks in Parliament. These helped to generate a political climate in Parliament, the press and the BBC which made it possible to effect major changes in the management of the Corporation during 1987.

Clashes

The parliamentary criticisms outlined above were frequently linked with clashes between the BBC and the government, clashes which reflected the rapid deterioration in relations between the two parties in the years 1979 to 1987.

The causes of this conflict went beyond any differences which might have been expected between a government committed to minimising the role of the public sector and an institution which was a prominent part of that public sector. They were rooted in a heightened sense among many senior figures in government that the BBC and the public service broadcasting ethos was anti-Tory or, in a more general sense, anti-authority. The former view was held by many Conservatives and predated the 1979 election. It was certainly held within the inner circles of the Thatcher administrations. Bernard Ingham described attitudes towards public service broadcasters in government circles during this period:

> the main irritant in relations between Governments and television – and not merely BBC television – has for long been current affairs programmes, whether for example, Granada's 'World in Action', Thames's 'This Week' or the BBC's 'Panorama' programmes. With their record one might assume that they have a more tender mercy for the sinner than the sinned against; for the criminal rather than the victim; and for the terrorist rather than the dead and bereaved. They seldom appear to be on the side of the forces of law and order.[11]

These factors, combined with the views of the Prime Minister, the attitude of senior BBC managers and pressures for change in the status of public service broadcasting, caused relations between the government and the BBC to become increasingly fractious. Problems which might have been solved quickly or with relatively little fuss became major sources of conflict. Others were clearly provoked by the government, especially during Norman Tebbit's tenure as Party Chairman. Each of the events discussed below is rooted in this complex web of factors all of which were combining in this period to force radical change on the BBC.

A Difference of Opinion

BBC coverage of Ireland was a major source of conflict. In 1979, despite an attempt by the Northern Ireland Secretary to stop it, a programme was transmitted containing an interview with a member of the Irish National Liberation Army, the organisation which had claimed responsibility for killing Mrs Thatcher's close colleague, Airey Neave MP. The Corporation was criticised by Mrs Thatcher in the Commons, by the national press and by MPs. That same year Mrs Thatcher, sections of the national press and MPs savaged the BBC for filming a road block set up by the IRA in a small town called Carrickmore. Mrs Thatcher was reportedly highly critical of the Corporation's decision, under pressure from BBC journalists, to reinstate the producer responsible for the incident.[12]

The Falklands

The next major clash came in 1982 over the BBC's coverage of the Falklands War. Internal BBC minutes leaked in April 1982 revealed that BBC management, including the Director General, were acutely aware of the problems it confronted in covering the conflict evenhandedly. In May two BBC programmes, *Newsnight* and *Panorama*, transmitted at a tense period in the conflict, were deemed insufficiently patriotic by Mrs Thatcher, many Tory MPs and sections of the national press, notably the *Sun*. One Conservative MP asserted that the *Newsnight* programme was 'almost treasonable'. On 11 May Mrs Thatcher attacked the BBC in the Commons for failing to support 'our boys'.

There seems little doubt in the minds of participants and commentators that this highly publicised clash soured the BBC's relations with government for the next five years. Norman Tebbit, in his autobiography published in 1989, has written:

Amongst the casualties of the Falklands War was the relationship between the Government and the BBC. Whilst the BBC correspondents with our forces in the South Atlantic upheld the highest standards of courage and journalism of their wartime predecessors, the unctuous 'impartiality' of the BBC's editorialising was a source of grief and anger ... the wounds inflicted by the BBC have still not healed.

Milne believed that the row over the Falklands: 'sowed the seeds of enmity in the minds of some newspapers and politicians which would come to fruition at a later date'.[13]

These rows reflected a profound difference of outlook between senior government figures on the one hand and managers and production staff at the BBC on the other. The former seemed to believe that, on matters of terrorism and war, broadcasters should support government policy unquestioningly. Broadcasters felt that these were matters in which the normal rules of impartiality might be modified, as indeed they were, but that they should not be abandoned.

Tensions

There were other less dramatic incidents which reflected and exacerbated the tension between the government and the BBC. In 1983 Mrs

Thatcher's Press Secretary threatened the BBC with 'incalculable consequences' unless the Corporation agreed to share film of Mrs Thatcher's pre-election visit to the Falkland Islands with Independent Television News and other outlets. The object of the exercise was to secure maximum publicity. In the end the BBC capitulated and under direct pressure from the government shared with its rivals what should have been exclusive coverage.

Norman Tebbit has written of what he perceived as a deep political distance between the government and the staff at the BBC on the election night 6 June 1983:

> From the count I drove to the BBC to take part in their election night coverage. The atmosphere in the studio was terrible – almost everyone on the staff seemed to be in mourning with no attempt to conceal their regret that their side had lost.

Tensions surfaced during the Westland crisis of 1985–6 when Michael Heseltine MP came into open conflict with Mrs Thatcher over the future of a small helicopter manufacturing company, a conflict that led to Heseltine's resignation from the Cabinet in January 1986. At one point Downing Street put pressure on the BBC to cut an item on the affair on the Radio 4 programme, *Weekend World*, in December 1985, at a particularly sensitive point in the dispute. 'The BBC refused. Even as Heseltine prepared to speak, another call came through from Number 10, presumably from Ingham. Heseltine declined to take it.' The interview was broadcast. As with the previous incidents, sections of the government clearly felt the BBC ought to be more accommodating when confronted by government requests for co-operation.[14]

Tebbit's perception that BBC staff were anti-Tory gained further support from the transmission on 30 January 1984 of the *Panorama* programme 'Maggie's Militant Tendency'. The programme explored allegations of extreme right-wing influence within the Conservative Party. Within two weeks five Conservative MPs had issued writs for libel against the BBC. Tory Party Chairman John Selwyn Gummer MP was reported to believe that 'very serious action' would have to be taken over the programme. Gummer and the Chief Whip, John Wakeham, had a series of meetings with Milne to discuss the programme, but no agreement was reached. According to Milne, Central Office then fed the *Daily Mail* with a list of charges against the BBC. The incident dragged on until late 1986 when the BBC withdrew its defence of the libel action and settled out of court. This was used by sections of the national press to argue for Milne's removal.[15]

Real Lives

In 1985 the BBC clashed with the government over the transmission of a programme, 'The Edge of the Union' in the *Real Lives* TV series. The programme was about two politicians on either side of the political divide in Northern Ireland. It was cleared by BBC management using its usual special vetting procedures for programmes on Ireland. Shortly before transmission the London office of the *Sunday Times* managed to get a quote from Mrs Thatcher condemning programmes which gave publicity to terrorists.

Home Secretary Leon Brittan then wrote to the Chairman of the Board of Governors. He wanted the BBC to stop transmission of the programme. In the absence of Milne, who was on holiday, the Governors agreed to the request. This decision overrode the one taken by BBC managers and provoked the first ever nationwide strike by BBC journalists on 6 August 1985. The Governors and the Home Secretary were widely condemned for censoring the Corporation's programmes.

The significance of the affair was immense. It 'marked a new low point in relations between the Prime Minister and the BBC and led to the gravest internal crisis in the Corporation's history'. It crystallised the conflict setting certain members of the Board of Governors against Milne and his senior management team. It projected a public image of a BBC, at best, divided at the highest levels and, at worst, prepared to accept uncritically the unjustified demands of the government. It showed more clearly than ever the differences between the government and the Governors on the one hand and BBC managers and journalists on the other over the proper role of public service broadcasters in covering sensitive issues. It was bad publicity for the BBC at a time when its future was being investigated by the Peacock Committee.

The affair brought the underlying conflicts between the Thatcher government and the BBC into sharp focus. Leon Brittan's handling of the issue was ill-judged – he could possibly have got what he wanted by the time-honoured method of working behind the scenes – but it was Milne who eventually suffered most. It made him vulnerable to attacks from those who believed his tenure as Director General was an obstacle to reforming the BBC.[16]

In the summer of 1986 the journal of the right-wing pressure group, the Freedom Association, published an allegation by playwright Ian Curteis that a play he had written on the Falklands War had been dropped because he refused to portray Mrs Thatcher in an unsympathetic light. Milne had initially agreed to the production but had changed his mind in July 1986. The reason given by the BBC was that 'it would not be possible to mount such a play with so many political overtones in a period that is likely to precede by only a few weeks or months a general election'. The decision was attacked in Parliament and by sections of the national press where the contrast was drawn between this decision and the decision to transmit an allegedly anti-patriotic series, *The Monocoled Mutineer*.[17]

The Last Days of Milne: Libya, Libel and Zircon

The clashes reached a new intensity in the summer of 1986. They all involved Tebbit or Thatcher or both in attacking BBC management. This created a political climate dominated by calls from the government, Tory MPs and sections of the national press for the removal of Milne and a shakeout at the top of the BBC.

Norman Tebbit organised a major, public assault on the BBC in the form of the publication in October by Conservative Central Office of a report alleging anti-American and anti-government bias in BBC coverage of the US bombing of Libya. The attack on Libya, using some bombers based at UK air bases, was highly controversial. Many of Mrs Thatcher's supporters were doubtful about the wisdom of allowing UK territory to be used as a base for launching the attack. There was concern at Cabinet level about the TV coverage of the affair. Tebbit wrote: 'many reasonably minded people were uneasy, especially as they watched the misleading and unbalanced BBC coverage'. According to David Young, until the bombings had shown their effectiveness by limiting the President of Libya's 'more public support of terrorism ... there was quite a field day for all harbingers of doom and gloom amongst us, particularly at the BBC'.[18]

Tebbit also wrote that in his view complaints made to the BBC about political bias were often met with 'arrogance and willingness simply to brazen things out', so he decided that 'to be effective we would have to choose an example where the "we'll redress it next time" response would be clearly invalid'. Although it is difficult to prove, it was believed at the time – a belief subsequently supported by evidence allegedly acquired from a source at Central Office – that Tebbit's attacks had been 'carefully considered at Conservative Central Office with the objective of intimidating the BBC and softening up programme-makers prior to the general election'. In the summer of 1986 the Conservative Party's internal newspaper, *Newsline*, promoted the idea that TV coverage was the key to the election and could, according to a letter from Tebbit's secretary at the House of Commons, 'win or lose the next election for us because it brings into everyone's home the biased and distorted views of the Left'. Conservative supporters were encouraged to jam the switchboards of the TV companies with their complaints.[19]

It also seems that by the summer of 1986 senior Cabinet members were aware that the Peacock report would not recommend advertising on the BBC and that there was no time for any major legislative reform of broadcasting to be attempted before the general election. The strategy which emerged was to exert maximum pressure on the Corporation to reform itself from within. This was made explicit in material accompanying the publication of the Central Office report which was based on monitoring ITN and BBC coverage of the bombing of Libya. It alleged that the BBC 'made the principle feature if its news the "worldwide condemnation" of America – a subjective and emotive description – but never substantiated it throughout the broadcast'. It also asserted that:

> There can be little doubt that ITN succeeded far better than the BBC in introducing the news in a balanced and impartial fashion. They were scrupulous in not attempting to lead the viewer either to a pro-American or pro-Libyan opinion.

The BBC was aware that the report was on the way and one senior manager tried to get Tebbit to come and discuss the issue in advance of publication. But Tebbit delayed his acceptance of the invitation until after the report was published on 30 October. In the letter sent to the BBC with the dossier he pinpointed his concern about BBC management, demanding 'a thorough reappraisal of the managerial and editorial standards currently in operation for TV news coverage'.

On 5 November the BBC published its rebuttal. In response to this, Tebbit again focused his attack on the journalists and management: 'Our criticisms are of the editorial and managerial standards used in compiling the whole of the reports.'[20]

The Conservative Central Office report received massive publicity in the national press with a run of front page stories and leading articles.

The Independent, a paper with a record of, at best, equivocal support for the Thatcher government, nonetheless carried a leader which accepted the report's two key points. First:

> There is little doubt, with hindsight and thanks to Central Office research, that ITN gave a more balanced, less alarmist account of the attack, the reasons for it and the likely implications than did the BBC.

Second it echoed, by implication, the idea that the less balanced coverage was due to mistakes at managerial level: 'The BBC needs all the support it can get from its journalists and from the public. It should not offer hostages to fortune and ill will.'

This theme was taken up much more openly in the leader of the Conservative Party's traditional supporter in the quality market, *The Daily Telegraph*:

> We have frequently argued in these columns that there should be a re-evaluation of the structure and management of the BBC. It has become such a vast and unwieldy organisation as to defy effective management by even the best-intentioned of senior executives.[21]

The signals coming from Central Office which were being picked up and amplified by the press were that the Corporation was at best poorly managed and at worst out of control. The opportunity to put this right was provided by the premature death of the Chairman of the BBC's Board of Governors, Stuart Young, in 1986. Tebbit's office was reported to have believed that the appointment in October of Young's successor, Marmaduke Hussey, provided an opportunity to sort out the BBC. Tebbit's assault on the Corporation provided the context in which a dramatic rearrangement of top management by Hussey was made politically possible.

Hussey removed Milne within a matter of months. Tebbit's attack on BBC managers had succeeded and so too, he believed, had his onslaught on editorial standards:

> Despite the furious reaction of the BBC and its usual total rejection of my conclusions I have little doubt that they struck home and that members of the editorial staff began to look more critically at their own work.[22]

The changes introduced into BBC news and current affairs after the appointment of John Birt in 1987 are discussed in Chapter 8 and tend to confirm Tebbit's observation.

Pressure on BBC management was also exerted by Central Office as a result of the settlement out of court by the BBC of the outstanding libel action brought by Tory MPs over the *Panorama* programme, 'Maggie's Militant Tendency'. In October 1986 the cases brought by Neil Hamilton MP and Gerald Howarth MP reached the High Court and began to attract publicity. Milne says that by the first week in October he was trying for an out-of-court settlement because of problems with witnesses and because 'counsel said we had less than fifty per cent chance of winning'. The case went to court before a settlement had been reached and Milne came under pressure to settle from acting Chairman Joel Barnett in the run up to and during the next meeting of the Board of Governors. Tebbit suggests that the impetus for a settlement came not from Milne but from Barnett who 'shortly after his appointment as Deputy Chairman ... asked to see the BBC's legal advice on the case. Soon after that the BBC settled, paying substantial damages to both MPs.'

The settlement was a humiliation inflicted on senior managers by the Governors and it was followed by a Commons motion signed by 100 Tory MPs calling for Milne's resignation. Allegations then surfaced in Parliament that Central Office had sought to interfere with the case by putting pressure on witnesses to withdraw from giving evidence. The outcome was a costly climbdown by BBC managers. It provided more evidence in the eyes of many Tory MPs that BBC managers had shown political prejudice in backing the defence action and managerial incompetence in not settling much earlier. Hussey and Barnett subsequently made it known to Milne that they thought he and his senior managers had 'made a proper hash of the whole thing'.[23]

While the row over the BBC's coverage of the Libyan bombings and the libel affair were both still fresh, a new attack was launched on broadcasters by a pressure group, the Media Monitoring Unit. On 19 November it published a report which claimed to identify 150 examples of left-wing bias in TV reporting including examples from BBC's *Panorama*. The Unit's Director was Simon Clark who had been recruited to the post by former Tory candidate Justin Lewis. Lewis was director of Policy Research Associates, an offspring of the right-wing pressure group, the Coalition for Peace Through Security, which had links with right-wing politician Lord Chalfont, a close associate of Mrs Thatcher's. Chalfont wrote the foreword to the Unit's report, the timing of which gave more credibility to calls from the right for an overhaul of BBC management.[24]

The final major clash occurred immediately before Milne's dismissal. The BBC planned a programme on the Zircon spy satellite in the *Secret Society* series, the main thrust of which was that the government had misled Parliament about the cost of the project. Nigel Lawson says the 'government managed to lean on the BBC to ban the programme'. The Board of Governors, in particular Dame Daphne Park, a former employee of the security services, agreed to the ban. The matter did not stop there. According to Lawson, when Duncan Campbell, the journalist who had researched the programme:

> published a *New Statesman* article instead, Margaret instructed Michael Havers, the Attorney General, to issue an injunction against him and every newspaper in the country ... the police raided the offices both of the BBC in Glasgow and of the *New Statesman* in an attempt to discover the source of his information.

This stimulated a major row about media censorship. The very fact that the BBC had commissioned the programme was felt by the government to be 'proof positive that under Milne the Corporation was out of control'. Coming so soon after the Libyan affair, the libel case and the attack on current affairs coverage, the Zircon affair provided more damaging evidence in support of the case for change at the top in the BBC. In retrospect the attacks from Tebbit and Thatcher appear calculated to create a climate in which it would be possible for the new Chairman of the Board of Governors to remove Milne and his associates.[25]

A Running Sore

Public clashes with the BBC continued after the removal of Milne in January 1987 and beyond the 1987 general election. The underlying theme of these attacks remained the alleged left-wing political bias which the Conservative Party still detected within the Corporation. In April 1987 Tebbit asked why recently published '"unexpected and very good" trade figures had not been mentioned on the BBC's early evening news bulletin when ITN devoted nearly two minutes to them'. This was interpreted by the Liberal Chief Whip in the Commons as 'a direct attempt ... to lean on the BBC in the run-up to the election campaign'. On election day David Young attended a party at the Corporation, where he noted that when it became clear the Tories were winning, many of 'the BBC people were very glum'. The feeling that the BBC contained people who were directly opposed to the government clearly continued at the highest levels of government after the dismissal of Milne. It increased pressure on the new managers to sort out the politics of its news and current affairs staff.

Bernard Ingham felt that most 'damage to Government BBC relations was done between 6.30 and 9am' on the BBC Radio 4 *Today* programme. In 1987 it ran a mini-saga competition. The winning entry, announced in January 1988, was in Ingham's view on the theme of Mrs Thatcher's legalising hard drugs in the interests of promoting individual choice: 'Only a sick mind could sanction such a broadcast. No one needed to be a Tory to be revolted by it. Yet the "Today" programme broadcast it.' Sentiments such as those of Tebbit, Young and Ingham clearly helped to sustain the attacks on the BBC before and after January 1987.[26]

In May 1988 Foreign Secretary Geoffrey Howe attempted to stop transmission of a BBC 'Spotlight' programme on Irish issues. The same month Tory MPs attacked the BBC for showing *Tumbledown*, a play about the experiences of a former soldier in the Falklands War. In June the Corporation came under sustained attack from MPs and sections of the national press for its decision to transmit a concert celebrating the 70th birthday of imprisoned South African leader Nelson Mandela. By the end of 1988 Woodrow Wyatt, a right-wing journalist close to Mrs Thatcher, was attacking the BBC over a *Panorama* programme which he felt was not impartial. During 1989 and 1990 attacks on the BBC and specific programmes for their lack of impartiality were mounted by the Media Monitoring Unit, the Conservative Party Chairman Kenneth Baker, Woodrow Wyatt and Tebbit. These provided a context in which it was possible to justify the introduction of controversial clauses on impartiality into the 1990 Broadcasting Act. The clauses, promoted by Woodrow Wyatt, enjoyed Thatcher's support and were interpreted by broadcasters as an attack on independent investigative journalism.[27]

Conclusion

Throughout the 1980s the BBC was publicly attacked by MPs and clashed repeatedly with the government. The main themes of these attacks concerned the BBC's finances, the quality of its management and its alleged left-wing political bias. The attacks reflected a real distaste for certain aspects of BBC policy among some MPs and ministers. But they were not much different from the kind of attacks broadcasters had been subjected to earlier. Some simply reflected pressures outside Parliament and the thrust of government policy.

Some attacks in Parliament and clashes with the government were the result of unpredictable circumstances such as the Falkland's conflict. Others formed part of the ongoing pressure being exerted on the BBC by pressure groups, the advertising industry, sections of the national press, Cabinet ministers and their supporters in Parliament. On the issues of finance and management the intensity of the attacks and of open clashes with the government increased when the government was actively seeking political support for change. Finance dominated the run up to the 1985 licence fee settlement and management dominated the run up to the removal of Milne. The links between some MPs and the ASI, the support of the ISBA for Ashton's Bill, the statements of Backbench Media Committee, the interventions over Libya, the *Panorama* libel case and the Zircon affair suggest that many of the attacks and clashes occurred because the government, and supporters of change outside of Parliament, were using the House of Commons to win support for and publicise their preferred solutions for the BBC.

The evidence goes some way towards illustrating how Parliament was used by different forces to manipulate political opinion around broadcasting. The major forces at work were parts of the state system and politicians acting in concert with their supporters outside of the system. Given the divisions of opinion in Parliament and government (see Chapter 5), there was no guarantee that the dominant pro-reform grouping in the government could win support for drastic measures against the BBC. Hence the ferocity of the attacks. Some of the attacks aimed at winning support for reform outside Parliament among the wider politically influential classes such as those who read the qualities and who, like the leader writer of the *Independent*, could be persuaded of the rectitude of the government's position, if it shouted long and loud enough.

5 Policy-making at the Centre: Prejudice and Power

This chapter discusses aspects of the decision-making process on broadcasting between 1979 and 1988. It focuses on the role of the Prime Minister, the Cabinet and the Home Office. In so doing it describes the actions of a very small group of people with immense power who took decisions about the future of the BBC and broadcasting within the context of the pressures, motives and events outlined in previous chapters.

Changes in policy would have occurred regardless of the party in government in the 1980s. The nature and pace of policy was affected by the specific political context in which it was developed during these years. This context was characterised by a division between those parts of the government that wanted fast, relatively radical changes and those seeking a more measured, evolutionary development. The Home Office and some Cabinet ministers promoted change in broadcasting at a slower pace than that sought by the Prime Minister, her advisers and some key members of her government. The process was not always clear cut, and the Prime Minister and her supporters on this issue did not get all they wanted. But by the end of the 1980s they had succeeded in making some radical changes to the broadcasting system. How did this happen? This chapter addresses that question by focusing mainly, but not exclusively, on the period up to 1986.

Mrs Thatcher and the Media

'Since the mid-1950s when people have been asked where they got most of their news about politics from, 80 per cent have answered "from television".' Bernard Crick's comment illustrates how, as the number of TV sets in homes rose in the 1950s and 1960s, more people looked to TV as a source of information on politics. This prompted all major political parties to take the medium increasingly seriously.

Michael Cockerell, describing the relationship between successive prime ministers and television, has shown how the Conservative Party under Mrs Thatcher sought to use television to promote their leader, government and party in the best possible light. Television became central to the projection of the government throughout the electoral cycle. As a result a lot of time, money and manpower were devoted to the task of manipulating TV coverage of the government and the Prime Minister. Mrs Thatcher was acutely aware of the political importance of TV and radio throughout her period as leader of the Conservative Party from 1975 to 1979 and as Prime Minister 1979–90.[1]

In spite of this awareness, those close to her have suggested that her interest in the newspapers and television was in some ways narrowly utilitarian, nor was she as obsessed with press coverage as some of her predecessors. But she was keen on BBC Radio 4's news programmes. William Whitelaw points out that:

Prime Ministers … have different approaches to the press. Some, like Wilson, never stopped reading the newspapers and were obsessed with what was written about them. Atlee never read any papers at all. Margaret Thatcher is much closer to Atlee than she is to Wilson.

According to Ingham: 'Mrs Thatcher's natural habitat … was not the media. She regarded journalism as the haunt of the brittle, the cynical and the unreliable.' Although she had friends who were journalists, 'she was never … a Prime Minister who would court them or generally enjoy their company'. She was 'simply not interested in the press, radio and television unless she came to feel that the Government's message was not getting over'.

Ingham prepared a precis of the press for her by 9.30 every morning. She occasionally read the front page of the *Standard*, the news digest in the *Wall Street Journal* and raced through some of the Saturday and Sunday papers. 'Most of her knowledge of what was going on in the world was imbibed from the BBC's "Today" programme (except when she cut herself off from its mischief), the Press Association's club tape outside her Private Office … and her staff.'

'Firm Views and Prejudices'

Although not as obsessed with reading the press as some of her predecessors, Thatcher took care to use her staff and some of her own time to keep abreast of news stories. Her interest in the *Today* programme was shared by other senior politicians and, perhaps, helped to fuel the attacks on the programme which appeared throughout the 1980s.[2]

In addition to this professional interest in the media portrayal of her government she held a range of views which reflected a belief in the power of television to influence the behaviour of individuals and governments. In her memoirs, Mrs Thatcher recalls how at one point during her premiership she had argued that: 'television was special because it was watched in the family's sitting room. Standards on television had an effect on society as a whole and were therefore a matter of proper public interest for the Government.'

In a speech to the Parliamentary Press Gallery in July 1981, during a period of urban uprisings throughout England, she echoed views put forward in the press about television encouraging copy-cat rioting and helping to 'spread the violence from one city to another by its immediate transmission of the methods and weapons used by the rioters'. In 1982 she expressed concern to Milne about the portrayal of violence on television and, the following year, told members of BBC management that, in her view, TV had helped the US to lose the war in Vietnam.

Her support for spreading the influence of market forces in broadcasting was tempered by her view that the media was so powerful that it still needed regulating in the interests of social and moral stability. Nigel Lawson has written that she 'was deeply concerned at actual and potential political bias on television especially in news programmes, and with the prospect of moral degradation'. This meant, he argued, that 'she suffered from the delusion that tends to afflict all politicians, even professedly free-market ones, that they can regulate anything if they really wish to'. As she told a group of broadcasters: 'I am a regulator ... it is the government's duty to restrict too much violence and pornography. We must get the framework right.'[3]

Her utilitarian approach to reading the press was matched by a simple view of the power of the media and a strong desire to control aspects of its output. She has since, in her memoirs, expressed the view that broadcasters were simply a special interest group hiding behind the increasingly dated theory of public service broadcasting:

> Broadcasting was one of a number of areas – the professions such as teaching, medicine and the law were others – in which special pleading by powerful interest groups was diguised as high-minded commitment to some greater good.

As for public service broadcasting, it was 'extremely difficult to define' and, in so far as it could be defined, was a 'somewhat nebulous and increasingly outdated theory'.

To these attitudes were added a political distrust of some of the people who managed the BBC. Before the 1979 election during a visit to the BBC, she attacked it for its coverage of Ireland, showing scant awareness, according to one source, of the problems associated with reporting such a complex issue. She wanted to know whether Alasdair Milne, who took over from Ian Trethowan in 1982, was politically acceptable to the Tories: 'Trethowan ... paid a farewell visit to Downing Street and Mrs Thatcher had only one question to ask about his chosen successor, Alasdair Milne: "Is he one of us?"'

This distrust reflected a prejudice, which she shared with other members of the Cabinet, that the world of broadcasting was populated by left-wingers. In 1986 a journalist very close to the Prime Minister noted how, in government circles, 'the BBC itself is ... feared, since it seems to breed a kind of trendy leftism ... '. Nigel Lawson shared this prejudice: 'It is a fact of life that bright young people on the left tend to seek and get jobs in broadcasting and journalism just as those on the right tend to choose the City.' In a speech to Conservative Central Council in March 1988, Thatcher echoed this view when she 'blamed the rising crime rate on – among others – "the professional progressives among broadcasters"'.[4]

She saw Channel 4 as an extension of market forces within broadcasting, having urged the Channel's first Chief Executive, Jeremy Issacs, to 'stand up for free enterprise' at a reception to celebrate the Channel's launch in 1982. However she apparently felt that the financing of Channel 4, which was based on ITV companies selling advertising on its behalf, was insufficiently market driven. In 1983 some ITV executives believed 'that Mrs Thatcher would like to see Channel 4 handle its own advertising rather than having the shortfall between programme costs and advertising revenues met by the ITV companies'. Nonetheless, she later viewed the Channel as an important initiative opening up the broadcasting system to new commercial operators: 'I wanted to see the widest competition among and opportunities for the independent producers – who were themselves virtually a creation of our earlier decision to set up Channel 4 in 1982.'

As well as wanting to see Channel 4 operate on a more market-driven basis, Ingham testifies to her desire to assist TV AM and Murdoch's Sky Television by giving them interviews, 'both of which Mrs Thatcher wanted to help and encourage as further competition for the BBC and as examples of entrepreneurial developments during her time in office'.

Nigel Lawson was not impressed by the coherence of her thought on broadcasting. He has written that, 'Broadcasting was a subject on which Margaret held a great many firm views and prejudices which she would air at some length.' He pointed out that her position on the licence fee, which she detested, was at variance with her support for the poll tax, the method of local government finance she introduced in the late 1980s:

> While eloquent on the 'everyone pays' argument for the Poll Tax, she welcomed increases in personal tax allowances which took people out of the income tax net altogether. And of all the imposts on the statute-book, the one she detested most was the television licence fee, the closest approximation to a poll tax in the entire system, with precisely the same regressive characteristics.

Thatcher's views on broadcasting were neither coherent nor particularly well informed, but they decisively influenced the development of broadcasting policy in the 1980s.[5]

Mrs Thatcher and the Exercise of Power

On all policy issues Mrs Thatcher acted in theory as the first among a Cabinet of political equals. Thus all major policy interventions which she favoured had, in principle, to be assessed in the light of their likely impact on Cabinet colleagues and her backbench MPs. In practice she wielded a great deal of autonomous power which was based on her control as Prime Minister over ministerial appointments:

> The Prime Minister's influence on economic policy comes from the same sources as his or her influence in other fields of policy. They are the 'hire and fire' power, the Prime Minister's position at the centre of the Whitehall machine, and the self-fulfilling belief of media and academe that the British system has become presidential.

This enabled Thatcher to have her 'own policy agenda' which was often 'separate from that of the Cabinet or Conservative party'. This, in turn, meant she used a range of techniques to achieve the maximum amount of success for her own agenda with the minimum amount of opposition from the Cabinet.

These techniques included placing more decision-making in Cabinet committees, using informal groups of Cabinet ministers to decide policy, exploiting her control over the agenda of Cabinet meetings, reducing the number of Cabinet meetings and papers to limit the scope for collective Cabinet opposition, bouncing the Cabinet into policy positions through her public pronouncements and leaking material to the media critical of Cabinet ministers. In developing broadcasting policy she used many of these techniques to try to set both the agenda and pace of reform. She encountered opposition from within the Cabinet and the Home Office. This, together with developments external to broadcasting policy, played a part in slowing the pace and modifying the nature of the change.[6]

Reshaping the Cabinet

Margaret Thatcher inherited a Cabinet containing many colleagues who were there because of their position within the Conservative Party, not because she agreed with them. As the years went by she reshaped its composition to include more of her supporters. But in spite of this she had to retain a very few people who represented different strands of thinking in the Party – people such as Douglas Hurd and Peter Walker. Tebbit records how, towards the end of 1980, she made it clear to him that 'she wanted to begin the reconstruction of the Government to bring forward more of those who believed in the policies on which we had been elected rather than those who still hankered after those on which Ted Heath had been defeated'. As late as the summer of 1981 her Cabinet was still, according to Lawson, 'a visible descendant of the Shadow Cabinet ... inherited from Ted Heath' and it was not until September of that year that she 'at last secured a Cabinet with a Thatcherite majority'. Thatcher confirms Lawson's view of the autumn 1981 reshuffle: 'The whole nature of the Cabinet changed as a result of these changes. After the new Cabinet's first meeting I remarked ... what a difference it made to have most of the people in it on my side.'

Although the Cabinet increasingly became, in the words of one former minister, a 'rubber stamp' for many of her policies, it could never be taken for granted that this would always be the case. During periods when Mrs Thatcher's star was in decline the Cabinet's rose, such as in 1986 when: 'After the damaging Westland affair and the loss of two senior Cabinet ministers ... Mrs Thatcher apparently took greater care to consult the Cabinet more fully.'

The Westland affair was followed by the dramatic decline in her popularity which was caused, in part, by her decision to allow planes from the USAF to take off from UK airfields on their mission to bomb Libya. Westland and Libya immediately preceded the receipt, by Cabinet, of the Peacock report. The relative weakness of Thatcher in the Cabinet at this point, combined with her low ratings in the public opinion polls, may have contributed to the Cabinet's allowing the Home Office to make the running on the government's initial response to Peacock, a response which was gradualist in tone. Cabinet opposition remained a problem for her throughout her premiership and it proved to be the public denunciation of her style of government by her longest-serving senior minister, Geoffrey Howe, which precipitated the chain of events in the autumn of 1990 that led to her being jettisoned.[7]

Committees, Informal Groups and Advisers

Mrs Thatcher made frequent use of small committees and informal groups to arrive at decisions. Lawson records that:

> key decisions were taken in smaller groups – either the formal Cabinet Committees, of which the most important ... were like the Cabinet itself, chaired by the Prime Minister; or at still smaller informal meetings of Ministers which she would usually hold in her study.

She had used this method while in opposition from 1975 to 1979 and continued it in government. Tebbit had been part of one such group while a backbencher in the 1970s. Looking back with his experience as a Cabinet member he could 'see how irritating to senior members of the Shadow Cabinet these informal groups ... must have been'. The advantage of these informal groups was that unlike Cabinet, or formal Cabinet Committees, they could be the sole creatures of the Prime Minister and could be formed, used, reformed and dissolved at will.[8]

These informal groups gave the individuals involved a potentially powerful role in influencing policy. Individuals who at one time or another advised Thatcher on media issues informally or who were known to be close to her and held parallel views on broadcasting included Tim Bell, Professor Brian Griffiths, David Young, Jeffrey Sterling, Paul Johnson and Woodrow Wyatt.

Tim Bell had been her Saatchi and Saatchi contact in the 1970s and the early 1980s. He remained very close to Mrs Thatcher and top Tory ministers, including Young, throughout the 1980s. Although he was linked to Saatchi, Bell maintained that he was not involved in writing the 1984 Saatchi report on BBC finance. Just after Peacock was established he was openly hostile to the BBC. In an interview in 1985 he said, 'I want the BBC to fail because I don't want the system to work. It only works now because it is a monopoly.' Milne, it is said, met Bell in 1985 and, in what he called a 'pre-emptive strike', 'Bell was apparently "turned" to fight the cause of the BBC.' He was later appointed as an image consultant for the Corporation. But Mrs Thatcher was close to a man intimately linked to Saatchi and Saatchi, a company which, as we have shown, was at the centre of the campaign against the BBC and who, until at least 1985, was personally hostile to the Corporation.[9]

Brian Griffiths was the head of Mrs Thatcher's policy unit at Number 10 from 1985. He took an active part in formulating broadcasting policy after the 1987 election. He helped to organise, with Jeffrey Sterling, a series of executive breakfasts on broadcasting policy, one of which Rupert Murdoch attended. He supported measures to introduce more market forces into government policy. According to one source he both opposed the licence fee and was 'obsessed' with breaking up the BBC.[10]

David Young, Secretary of State at the Department of Trade and Industry after 1987, served the Thatcher administrations as an unpaid special adviser at the Department of Industry and as head of the Manpower Services Commission. He was a keen supporter of small businesses and of the then fashionable idea that encouraging the entrepreneur was a key to reviving the UK economy. Thatcher believed that he 'shared Keith Joseph's and my view about how the economy worked and how jobs were created – not by government but by enterprise'. He remained close to Thatcher throughout the mid to late 1980s. Under Young, and with Thatcher's encouragement, the DTI adopted a vigorously proactive role in developing broadcasting policy. Its remit in this area and its relationship to the Home Office are discussed in Chapter 7. This initiative gave departmental force to proposals for change not held in high favour at the Home Office.[11]

Jeffrey Sterling had been an associate of Young's since the 1960s. In the 1980s he acted as special adviser to successive Industry ministers, including Keith Joseph and Norman Tebbit. After the 1987 election he worked with Young and Griffiths on developing DTI views on broadcasting policy. He took part in the series of executive breakfasts involving business people, politicians and broadcasters designed to help to develop broadcasting policy.[12]

Journalist Paul Johnson was a former Labour Party supporter who became a keen supporter of Mrs Thatcher. In 1984 he was appointed for a five-year term to the Cable Authority, the body established to promote the spread of cable on free market lines. During the debate on the renewal of the licence fee he vehemently attacked both the BBC and broadcasting unions, suggesting that Mrs Thatcher wanted the BBC to accept advertisements of it own volition without having them forced on it. He clearly believed that the attack on broadcasting was not a marginal political issue but central to the success of Thatcher's aim of promoting an entrepreneurial culture in the UK. Writing in 1989 he argued that:

> One of the reasons Mrs Thatcher has not yet cured the British disease – witness the trade figures and the return to stop–go economics – is that she waited ten years before tackling the television duopoly instead of doing it right at the beginning. It is absurd, for instance, that the BBC licence fee, the very lifeblood of the anti-enterprise culture, should still be in existence, suitably adjusted for inflation, a whole decade after Mrs Thatcher took power.[13]

Another journalist closely associated with Thatcher was Woodrow Wyatt, the former Labour MP and columnist on Murdoch's *News of the World*. According to one writer he was someone who could 'telephone Downing Street, ask for the Prime Minister and get her'. Wyatt held similar views to Mrs Thatcher about the left-wing politics of broadcasters. He was especially instrumental and, it has been argued, colluded with Mrs Thatcher in devising and promoting an amendment on impartiality to the 1989 Broadcasting Bill which successfully imposed new sets of responsibilities on broadcasters. This measure was perceived by broadcasters at the time as an attempt to gag investigative journalism.[14]

So Thatcher had close advisers, who shared a similar perspective on broadcasting, to whom she could turn for advice on policy before it went to Cabinet. They, in turn, were linked to the world of right-wing journalism, the Murdoch press and the advertising industry, all key forces lobbying for change at the BBC.

1979–83: Channel 4, the Licence Fee and Cable

The BBC was not the focus of an assault by the first Thatcher government of 1979–83, although by the spring of 1983 the issue was being discussed by her Central Policy Review staff. But Mrs Thatcher did show an early interest in the question of the BBC's future: '"What are we going to do about the BBC?" she had asked during her first formal visit to the Home Office as Prime Minister.' In 1980 she 'went to lunch at Broadcasting House and asked Aubrey Singer, managing director of radio, why he did not take advertising on Radio 1, the pop channel'.[15]

In its first term the government was faced with a series of acute problems not related to broadcasting which militated against major shifts in broadcasting policy. Developments which did take place in relation to broadcasting, but not cable, were supervised by the Home Office under Home Secretary William Whitelaw and did not break with the evolutionary approach to broadcasting reform which had dominated policy since the 1950s.

Setting up Channel 4 was the major innovation in this period. This measure had broad, cross party support. Combining the introduction of more competition in programme-making and more choice for the viewer with the existing duopoly framework, exemplified the Home Office's gradualist approach to change. Whitelaw's Home Office also supervised a three-year renewal of the licence fee, a process which did not, in this instance, provoke a full-scale debate on the future of the BBC. The settlement negotiations were over by 1981 and there is no evidence that at this point the idea of an all-out assault on the Corporation had taken root in the Prime Minister's mind.

The thrust of entrepreneurial policy in broadcasting came from work centred around the introduction of cable TV. This policy was driven from the Prime Minister's office and the Department of Industry. As outlined in Chapter 1 cable policy was meant to be dominated by market forces. It marked the first major break under Thatcher with the tradition of evolving broadcasting policy within a public service framework and, in the eyes of one commentator writing in April 1983, signified a victory over Whitelaw:

> The much-delayed, yet comprehensively leaked White paper on cable television is due to appear on Thursday. It will show that the free market sentiments which, for the most part, informed the Hunt Report have overridden Home Office caution and the Home Secretary's own instinctive feeling for paternalist regulation. Though

there will be a cable television authority, the principles guiding its actions will be far from those of the BBC Charter.[16]

These developments signalled to broadcasters, politicians and lobbyists that the future direction of broadcasting policy was likely to be dramatically influenced by the ideas that were shaping cable policy.

Thatcher, the Licence Fee and the Home Office 1983–5

Broadcasters quickly recognised that the debate around cable carried implications for the future regulation and finance of broadcasting. The BBC and the IBA commissioned a report by Aske Research Ltd on the cost of television to the consumer which was presented in July 1982 and published in 1983. The report put the case in support of the financial and regulatory regime which underpinned the BBC and ITV. It argued that new services like cable and satellite would best be delivered by 'suitably adapting the UK's traditional forms of programme controls'. It also recognised one of the long-standing and important economic reasons why advertising agencies wanted more opportunities to place advertisements on television. It noted that advertisers 'sometimes argue for the breaking of the ITV monopoly, for instance by the BBC also carrying commercials', their purpose being to 'reduce the advertising cost per 1,000 viewers'.[17]

In February 1983 the IEA published a report on cable TV which argued that the 'case for de-regulating broadcast TV should ... be given serious consideration' in order to 'ensure that the costs of the current restrictions are justified and that pay-TV becomes more competitive'. This kind of thinking had clearly gained a foothold amongst the Prime Minister's circle. According to one commentator writing in April:

Already the case for the dismemberment or even the abolition of the BBC is gaining ground among the Prime Minister's advisers. And the Central Policy Review Staff (think tank) has been asked to consider the future of broadcasting policy. For once the analysis will go further than a sterile debate about the size of the licence fee ... It seems that if Mrs Thatcher has a second term there will be a radical reappraisal of public service broadcasting. The present structure conceived in an era of optimistic collectivism – is creaking, expensive and out of touch with its taxpayer viewers.

If this was the intention among her advisers it was not one which found its way in any shape or form into the 1983 Conservative Party election manifesto.[18]

As we have seen, the press attacks on the BBC started in earnest in early 1984. In May the Adam Smith Institute published its Omega report on *Communications* at a time when the advertising agencies were on the verge of producing their reports and the BBC was in the process of preparing its bid for an increase in the licence fee.

At the end of May 1984 Douglas Hurd, then the Home Office minster responsible for broadcasting, briefed the press that the government intended to consider alternative means of financing the BBC. The ideas floated to journalists by ministers included putting advertisements on the BBC, and privatising the Corporation. For example in June: 'Leading Ministers are privately advocating that BBC Radio should be opened up to commercial advertising to limit increases in the licence fee.' Again, in September, there were reports of 'doubts in the highest reaches of government about the long term viability of the BBC ... some government ministers are said to favour "privatising" the Corporation, perhaps by breaking it up'.[19]

These reports signalled that the government intended to subject the BBC to an intense public debate. During the autumn of 1984 Mrs Thatcher made public her desire to see rapid change at the BBC. This was an example of how she could put pressure on her colleagues by public statements which were not the official views of the government. The official view was expressed by the Home Office, under Leon Brittan, which indicated that change would occur but at a more measured pace than the one being advocated by the Prime Minister.

There can be no doubt that Mrs Thatcher favoured the rapid introduction of advertising on the BBC and opposed a large increase in the licence fee. In October 1984 she lunched with Milne and told him that a £100 licence fee was a political impossibility. Milne had no doubts about her views on advertising. Stuart Young, the Chairman of the Board of Governors was, at around this time, well aware that 'certain Government ministers favour privatisation of the BBC and/or the break up of the corporation'.[20]

During the winter of 1985–6 Thatcher became the most prominent public supporter of the views about BBC finance canvassed by the advertising agencies. On 12 December 1984 the BBC announced its bid for a 41 per cent increase in the colour TV licence fee from £46 to £65. The same day Mrs Thatcher's Press Secretary briefed national newspaper journalists on her views: the BBC was 'over-committed, over staffed and inefficient, it should no longer be protected from the fresh winds of market forces. Advertising was the answer.' Her views were taken up in the national press and framed coverage of the BBC's bid.

Next day at Prime Minister's Question Time in the House of Commons, speaking for the government her words were more measured. She echoed the position outlined by Home Office Minister Hurd in June which at this time, in spite of her own pronouncements, was the agreed government position. Referring to the Home Secretary she said: 'I doubt whether, this time, he will consider the introduction of advertising although, in the longer term, we might have to consider other methods of raising the requisite revenue for the BBC.'[21]

In 1983 Brittan had committed himself to a three-year settlement. But the signals coming from Downing Street indicated that the Prime Minister favoured tougher action. It became known, through press briefings, that Thatcher favoured a one-year settlement to allow the BBC to decide itself whether to cut its services or take advertising. This, she was alleged to believe, would stimulate a wide-ranging debate. The leaks indicated that she favoured measures to dismantle the BBC, which included privatisation of Radios 1 and 2 and the introduction of a limited amount of advertising. In December 1984 and in January 1985 rumours circulated that the government was in favour of an inquiry to sort out the issue. By January 1985 Paul Johnson was indicating that Thatcher wanted the BBC to agree to take advertising voluntarily.

In the closing months of 1984 and at the start of 1985, Thatcher adopted an aggressive stance on the future of the BBC which received widespread publicity. When speaking on behalf of the government, however, she adopted a more cautious line more in harmony with the views expressed by her Home Office ministers.[22] Home Office Minister Giles Shaw trod a cautious line. He stressed the official position that 'we have made it clear that the Government does not want any radical departure from the licence fee system for the BBC … at this stage'.[23]

Although there seems to have been agreement by this stage between Downing Street and the Home Office that the size of the BBC bid could not be met, it appears there was disagreement over the length and terms of the settlement. The pressure for a settlement plus an inquiry seems to have been regarded critically by Home Office officials. The final package announced on the 27 March 1985 had been put together by Brittan, Chancellor Nigel Lawson and Thatcher, and the decision to hold the Peacock inquiry seems to have been taken quite 'late in the day'. Alan Peacock was offered the job only a few days before the announcement and it was May before the members of the Committee were announced.[24]

From the outset, the decision to set up the Committee had the hallmark of a compromise between the Prime Minister's Office and the Home Office. Instead of the BBC receiving a new licence fee with the minimum of fuss it got £7 less than it had requested and a major inquiry into its finances. The issue of advertising on the BBC, never ruled out by Hurd, Shaw or Brittan, but never publicly supported by them, had been placed firmly on the agenda. It formed a central part of the terms of reference of the inquiry and, in one sense, marked a clear victory for those who had been lobbying for advertising on the BBC. But the inquiry had its disadvantages from the point of view of those wanting rapid change at the BBC. It extended the period in which a decision could be taken, making it less likely that legislation could be drawn up and enacted before the next general election due on or before June 1988. This not only provided an opportunity for the Home Office and the BBC to mount a defence of the licence fee, it also meant that the report could fall victim to changes in personnel and the balance of power in Cabinet.

Peacock reported in July 1986 and ruled out the possibility of advertisements on the BBC in the short term, but provided an alternative plan designed to restructure UK broadcasting along market lines, an option which Thatcher enthusiastically embraced. Thereafter Mrs Thatcher concentrated on two main approaches to broadcasting. She chaired a Cabinet Committee on broadcasting where, along with other measures, she continued to press for advertisements on the BBC, and a watered-down commitment to this was introduced into the 1988 White Paper.[25]

The other approach had been implicit in her earlier attempts to pressurise the BBC into reforming itself from inside. This was a policy she had already been pursuing by appointing Governors with known Tory sympathies to vacancies on the Board and in sanctioning Tebbit's public assault on BBC managers. When Stuart Young died prematurely in 1986, she seized the chance to achieve rapid internal reform. The man chosen to succeed Young was Marmaduke Hussey. He was appointed to alter the management and culture of the BBC as quickly as possible:

the word from Norman Tebbit's office was that Hussey was appointed 'to make it bloody clear things have to change; he is to get in there and sort it out – in days and not months'. Tebbit immediately began to fill the Chairman's agenda.[26]

By the end of her second term (1983–7) Mrs Thatcher had brought the issue of broadcasting and the BBC to the centre of the political stage. She had echoed and amplified the views expressed by advertisers, pressure groups and newspapers, which harmonised with her own perspectives. She did this by forcing the Home Office, the department most allied to the existing broadcasting system, to adopt a more aggressive stance on broadcasting reform than it had under Whitelaw. This was clearly not to the liking of Home Office officials. In spite of failing to get advertisements on the BBC, she established a radical framework for change in the industry in the form of the agenda set out by the Peacock Committee.

The Home Office and Broadcasting Policy after 1979

If Mrs Thatcher's role could be summed up as one of seeking to force the pace of change in this period, the role of the Home Office after 1979 was to exert a moderating influence on the pace and direction of change.

Home Secretaries after Whitelaw owed their senior ministerial positions almost exclusively to the patronage of Thatcher. All of them after the 1983 election faced a Prime Minister, backed by the lobby described in Chapters 2 and 3 and powerful ministers like Tebbit and Young, who were determined to force the pace of change. It was inevitable then that, whatever their misgivings and despite pressure and advice from their officials, they had to move down the road of restructuring broadcasting at a pace dictated largely by the Prime Minister.

This section traces aspects of the relationship between the Home Office and its ministers to broadcasting policy from 1979 to 1988. It provides evidence to support the view that policy was affected by the interaction between the views of the Prime Minister and her supporters and the perspectives on broadcasting change which came from the Home Office. The Home Office clearly sought, through the advice given by officials and the actions and statements of its main ministers, to modify the force of Prime Ministerial policy.

This was because Home Office civil servants supported the existing system and because successive ministers and Home Secretaries were concerned to promote their own careers by fighting the corner, successfully, for their departmental interests. Moreover, at key periods during these years two of the three Home Secretaries who held the post long enough to have a major impact on policy, Whitelaw and Hurd, were on the traditionalist wing of the Conservative Party where broadcasting was concerned. The third, Brittan, wanted change, but at a pace which did not result in sinking the BBC overnight by the imposition of advertising. Nevertheless, Thatcher's authority overrode Home Office preferences and succeeded in forcing rapid change on the BBC and broadcasting as a whole.

The Home Office and Broadcasting Policy under Whitelaw

The Home Office had, since the 1970s, been the main seat of policy-making on television and radio. William Whitelaw was Home Secretary during Mrs Thatcher's first term from 1979 to 1983 and acted as a moderating influence on the Prime Minister on matters relating to broadcasting policy. According to Lawson he 'best represented the old Tory tradition'. He was a senior figure within the Party and had, according to Norman Tebbit, a 'genius for conducting difficult political manoeuvres under a smokescreen of apparent confusion'. Thatcher considered him 'indispensable to me in Cabinet', but recognised that 'Willie and I knew that we did not share the same instincts on Home Office matters.' Whitelaw was personally committed to the BBC as were officials within his department. Mrs Thatcher commented on this fact: 'Unfortunately, in the Home Office the broadcasters often found a ready advocate.' One commentator argued that the BBC would have been attacked much earlier had it not been for Whitelaw who 'was an ally of the BBC, yet his total loyalty to the Prime Minister enabled him to curb her more radical instincts'.[27]

Whitelaw was prepared to put pressure on the broadcasters when necessary. In 1979 he phoned the Chairman of the Board of Governors, George Howard, on Thatcher's behalf over the dispute surrounding the filming of an IRA roadblock at Carrickmore. He was part of Mrs Thatcher's inner circle of ministers during the Falklands War and put pressure on the IBA, unsuccessfully as it turned out, to prevent the transmission of an interview on ITV with General Galtieri, leader of the Argentinian military junta.[28]

His attitude to change in broadcasting policy reflected the gradualism traditionally associated with Home Office policy-making. He steered through the creation of Channel 4 television, but in a way which built on and developed existing structures while allowing some room for innovation. In 1981 he presided over the renewal of the BBC's Charter and a licence fee settlement, processes which provoked nothing like the controversy that the 1985 settlement did. According to Milne, Whitelaw had 'most certainly not' been in favour of advertising on the BBC. He was also prepared to allow a gradual expansion of commercial radio, but within the framework established in the 1970s, of a heavily regulated independent local radio sector. One advocate of less control over radio, broadcasting analyst William Phillips, described Whitelaw as 'that loyal pal of parish-pump radio'. Under pressure from the IBA and the commercial radio industry he eventually agreed, in 1983, to establish a national commercial radio network.[29]

At times he distanced himself from other policies advocated by the government. In 1981 when Kenneth Baker, the Minister for IT, was encouraging the BBC to get involved in the costly Direct Broadcasting by Satellite project, Whitelaw was urging caution on George Howard. Baker noted how in 1982 Whitelaw was 'apprehensive' about cable and satellite, 'principally because of its effect upon the BBC and ITV'. In addition Whitelaw was clearly concerned about the nature of relations between the government and the BBC. Baker records how, at a Cabinet meeting in November 1982:

Willie was worried that Cable TV would outbid the BBC and ITV for major sporting events ... Willie remained strongly against pay-per-view, arguing 'We have an appalling relationship with the BBC, the worst of any government in recent times' (to which the Prime Minister nodded) 'and I have to take the brunt of that relationship. It is all very unpleasant and they have made it clear to me that pay-per-view is not acceptable.'

Thatcher confirms Baker's view of Whitelaw's commitment to the BBC:

I would have liked to find an alternative to the BBC licence fee. One possibility was advertising. Peacock rejected the idea. Willie Whitelaw too was fiercely opposed to it and indeed threatened to resign from the Government if it were introduced.

In 1986 he allegedly played a role, through his chairmanship of the Cabinet's Home Affairs Committee, in moderating the government's response to the recommendations made in the Peacock Committee. In 1988, when he sat in the House of Lords, he voiced his concerns about the direction of government policy by criticising the White Paper on broadcasting. He was critical of proposals to auction ITV franchises, to change the funding basis of Channel 4 and of the likely effect of changes in the ITV system on the BBC. He asserted that he did not 'think the BBC could stand against a trend if other television companies go more down-market'.[30]

Whitelaw had the authority to ensure that changes in broadcasting policy proceeded at a pace in tune with the gradualist traditions of the Home Office. There would have been change, but it is doubtful whether the pace of change would have accelerated as it did from 1983 if he had remained Home Secretary.

Brittan and the BBC

In June 1983 Leon Brittan became Home Secretary. Brittan had been at the Home Office under Whitelaw until 1981. His move to the Treasury in that year was, according to Lawson, due to Whitelaw, who was 'the main sponsor of his promotion'. His return to the Home Office as Home Secretary in 1983 clearly owed something to Whitelaw's support for his career. He supported the view that the BBC should control its expenditure more carefully and was in favour of a more market-orientated approach to broadcasting policy. He was not, however, keen on the rapid introduction of advertising into the BBC.[31] In a speech delivered in 1983 to the Royal Television Society he: 'urged broad-casters to demonstrate clearly and publicly that they are husbanding their resources with care. He declared his support for longer term licence fee settlements.' At this point he was in favour of a three-year licence fee settlement.[32]

By June 1984 Brittan and his junior minister, Hurd, were echoing the themes raised in the press and the Omega report. Hurd announced the government's willingness to investigate other methods of funding the BBC and Brittan criticised the IBA's role as supervisor of independent local radio and showed support for the spread of small scale 'community radio'.[33]

As the political pressure built up in the summer of 1984 Brittan asked the BBC to conduct an independent audit of its financial and management performance. The audit was ostensibly meant to provide information which would inform the autumn negotiations on the licence fee. In addition Brittan seems to have been anxious both to generate evidence, for public consumption, of the BBC's value for money and to be seen to be responding to the mounting public criticisms of the BBC by putting pressure on the Corporation to justify its spending.[34]

In the winter of 1984/5 Brittan published an article in the IBA's quarterly magazine, *Airwaves*, in which he expressed the evolutionary perspective on broadcasting policy favoured by the Home Office. It was a perspective which had little room for abrupt changes of direction:

> Reports of the death of public service broadcasting are greatly exaggerated. What is undeniable, however, is that like our predecessors 30 years ago we are moving forwards into a new age where some of the old assumptions no longer hold good. For them the task was to make a smooth transition from monopoly to duopoly, for us it is the passage from duopoly to multiplicity.[35]

The Home Office under Brittan engaged in a cautious balancing act. On the one hand it recognised the importance of the debate about public service broadcasting but on the other it made no commitment to introduce advertising. In December Giles Shaw, who had replaced Hurd as Home Office minister responsible for broadcasting in September 1984, told MPs in a debate initiated by critics of the BBC: 'Advertising deserves the most careful debate and decision ... That is why we have made it clear that the Government does not want any radical departure from the licence fee system for BBC finance at this stage.'

This speech was made after it had been reported that Home Office civil servants were 'under orders to come up with alternative methods of funding the corporation'.[36]

By early January the view that ministers had decided the BBC would only get £58 not £65 was circulating in the press. The audit of the BBC, conducted by Peat Marwick Mitchell, was being considered by the Home Office that month and had been promoted by the BBC as broadly supportive of the Corporation. In spite of the positive aspects of the audit for the BBC, Brittan was keen to stress its negative side at a private meeting with Milne. At the same time he confirmed the view then circulating in the national press that 'the BBC has more hope with him than any other minister'. Milne reports that Brittan:

> told us with, I thought, some pleasure that he found the PMM report critical of the BBC. In the same breath, he also assured us there was no question of the BBC being invited to consider taking advertising at this stage.[37]

Milne took the view that Brittan was 'less immediately persuaded' of the need for the BBC to take advertising than the Prime Minister, but clearly believed that Brittan felt under pressure to do something. This led to the acceptance by the Home Office of an inquiry into the BBC. The idea of setting up an inquiry was not something that had been uppermost in the minds of Brittan's officials:

> All the indications are that the decision to set up Peacock was taken late in the day and that senior officials believed that the launching of cable TV, the endless meetings over DBS and the inquiry into the ITV levy was enough broadcast policy to be getting on with.

The pressure to do something more than just settle the licence fee was clearly coming from Downing Street as well as from the national press at this point. When Brittan informed Milne and Young on 26 March 1985 of the decision he reminded Milne 'of the pressures on him to agree to no increase at all'.[38]

When he announced the decision in the House of Commons, Brittan was at pains to stress the complexity of the issue, a position which reflected a more cautious approach than that advocated by the Prime Minister and the lobbyists for change. The inquiry was:

> A way of bringing independent expertise to bear on a problem which has implications not just for the BBC but for the independent television sector and broadcasting generally, for the newspapers and for a wide variety of other interests.

In his statement he was equally concerned to stress that in his view the BBC needed to provide greater value for money:

> I believe, however, that the BBC could and must achieve greater productivity than it has done in the past or has so far planned for the future. The BBC already has a useful programme of activity review and has stressed its commitment to achieving value for money. But, in the light of the report from Peat Marwick Mitchell ... I believe there is scope for the BBC to achieve greater efficiency through improved management procedures and strengthened management attitudes.

He was equally determined to answer the charge that 'the figure announced today will be seen as a victory for the BBC'. He noted: 'When yesterday I told the BBC what I would announce today the demeanour of those emerging from my room was not that of victors.'[39]

Like junior minister Shaw, Brittan acknowledged the demand for advertising but indicated that it would have to be more carefully considered before any action could be taken.

Other factors suggest that Home Office officials and ministers, while accepting the need for an inquiry, were disinclined to throw the BBC to the wolves, lock, stock and barrel. For instance, the civil servant in charge of the broadcasting unit at the Home Office from 1984–8 and who oversaw work on the Peacock report was Quentin Thomas. One journalist who maintained contacts with Thomas in these years placed him firmly within the evolutionary camp: 'he is no technology obsessed deregulator: he shares Douglas Hurd's instincts for the cultural value of broadcasting, and its place in society'. Home Office officials were anxious to consult the BBC on sensitive aspects of the March 1985 announcement. According to Milne, interviewed in 1985, the brief to which Peacock worked was 'a brief which we insisted on'. Likewise the BBC was consulted on the composition of the Committee.

In the week that Peacock met for the first time, Giles Shaw once again stressed that the government was not formerly committed to advertising on the BBC, and singled out *The Times*, the most strident advocate of advertising on the BBC, for particular attention: 'But ... on advertising – whatever *The Times* may say – we have an open mind.' This reference to *The Times* was inserted into the prepared text of the speech and interpreted by a journalist present as indicating: 'A certain ministerial impatience with being told what to think.'

Even when the report was ready for publication early in the summer of 1986 the Home Office responded cautiously. It closed ranks to dampen expectations that the radical proposals in the report would be accepted uncritically. Hurd, who was by then Home Secretary, was less than enthusiastic about it in public. Samuel Brittan, a key member of the Committee, has argued that the Home Office did its best to undermine the report before its publication.[40]

Home Office reluctance to move fast on the deregulation of commercial broadcasting was also reflected in its handling of the community radio experiment. In 1985, under what appears to have been pressure from Tebbit's Department of Industry (see Chapter 7), Brittan announced a plan which took an initial step towards deregulating radio by announcing plans to set up an experiment in lightly regulated community radio. This was criticised heavily by representatives of the established commercial radio stations: 'Setting a virtually unregulated local radio system alongside the two existing tightly regulated ones ...

would have been a nonsense.' The Association of Independent Radio Contractors lobbied fiercely against it. The Home Office moved slowly and plans for the experiment were eventually dropped in 1986 and replaced by a commitment to producing a Green Paper on the future of all radio. In retrospect agreement on the experiment seems to have resulted from pressure being exerted on a reluctant Home Office which then simply dragged its feet.[41]

As Home Secretary Brittan may have been treading a thin line between the demands of Downing Street and his own, and his department's perspective. But his commitment to lasting change in broadcasting was not in question. He welcomed the Peacock report for containing 'radical and imaginative proposals for the future of broadcasting generally'.[42] Had he remained Home Secretary the tone of Home Office statements on broadcasting reregulation may have taken on a more enthusiastic edge, rather than the cautious tone adopted by his successor, Douglas Hurd.

Hurd's Home Office remained keen to keep any developments to a manageable minimum although it clearly supported change. Officials were prepared to accept Peacock's recommendation that the BBC and ITV should take a quota of independent productions, but resisted attempts to impose this too quickly: 'The Home Office broadcast section is understood to be satisfied that the BBC and IBA are moving as quickly as possible in ensuring that the new minimum is met.'

When Mrs Thatcher insisted that a new watchdog on sex and violence on TV should be set up – what became the Broadcasting Standards Council (BSC) – she met with opposition and, to some extent, successful resistance from Hurd's Home Office. Although the BSC's first Chairman was a known Thatcherite, William Rees-Mogg, its first executive director, Colin Shaw, was a man with a long career as a senior executive in the BBC and ITV. He had experience of dealings with the Home Office over many years. His deputy director, David Houghton, was a Home Office civil servant on secondment to the BSC. Not content with placing safe hands at the helm of the new ship, the Home Office got a commitment that the BSC would conduct research into media effects and not just pronounce in an ill-informed way on matters of sex and violence. The BSC beast, then, had a head – Mogg. But Home Office resistance ensured that it was given few sharp teeth and a conventional pair of handlers to keep it as close to the traditions of British broadcasting as could be achieved in the circumstances.[43]

Mrs Thatcher's response to this resistance centred around the DTI and is described in Chapter 7. She also kept up pressure on her ministers at the Home Office throughout the 1980s. She has described how she 'took a close interest in senior appointments in the civil service from the first because they could affect the morale and efficiency of whole departments'. She used her power of appointment to top posts in the civil service to modify the political culture within the Home Office. This was par for the course. As one commentator put it in 1988:

All of the present permanent secretaries were appointed under her premiership. The committee of permanent secretaries, chaired by Sir Robin Butler, which appoints deputy and permanent secretaries, now regularly has its candidates queried, knowledgeably by the Prime Minister. The recent retirement of Sir Brian Cubbin from the Home Office (he was appointed in 1979) and his replacement by Sir Clive Whitemore (who served as the PM's private secretary from 1979–82) is seen as the last change from the old guard to the new.

Clive Whitemore, who had been described as a 'prime ministerial favourite', became Permanent Secretary in March 1988. He was seen as someone who, on broadcasting policy at least, was prepared to countenance a break with the more traditional regime of his predecessor, Brian Cubbin. He presided over the Home Office's involvement in the production of the 1988 White Paper which, according to *The Times*, rang 'the changes from the Cubbin regime, when the old verities were held in place even during the tenure of Leon Brittan'.[44]

Conclusion

As in the period before 1979 the policy process in broadcasting involved a small group of people in and around the state, who engaged in a series of limited consultations, debates and manoeuvres. The difference was that, under Mrs Thatcher, the assault on the BBC through the licence fee debate, the change of top management and, finally, the reshaping of the broadcasting environment in which it operated, was conducted with a degree of single-mindedness which was unprecedented in post-war history. The critique of the BBC and public service broadcasting which she supported was fed into the complex policy-making process. Part of this process involved establishing the Peacock Committee, a body which set the agenda for subsequent policy in the 1980s. It is to this Committee that we now turn.

6 The Peacock Exercise

The Peacock Committee was set up in March 1985. Its report, published in July 1986, developed a sustained argument in favour of allowing the market to dominate the finance and organisation of radio, television satellite and cable services. Its arguments and recommendations drew on those developed by the advertisers, the IEA and the Adam Smith Institute. They provided the main intellectual justification for the framework within which broadcasting policy developed up to and beyond the 1990 Broadcasting Act. This chapter explores aspects of the Peacock exercise.

Economics and the Peacock Debate

The Peacock report was, above all, an investigation into methods of financing the BBC and other forms of broadcasting. In focusing on the economic aspects of broadcasting policy Peacock broke from previous post-war committees of inquiry into broadcasting. Although interested in finance these committees had been more concerned with the social purpose and organisation of broadcasting. The new focus on economics reflected the agenda of a government that wished to see market disciplines imposed on public services, including health, education and broadcasting.

There had been little sustained academic or national political interest in the technicalities of broadcast economics in the UK until the advent of the Thatcher government. The IEA had published occasional pieces, some of which are outlined in Chapter 2. As we have seen in Chapter 1, the idea that the BBC should take advertising had surfaced before but had never received the political backing it was to receive in the 1980s.[1]

There had never been much material available to the public on the *actual* finances of the BBC and the ITV companies. The published sources were inadequate. They lacked the information needed to construct a detailed picture of the workings of the two systems. This was partly because the Home Office saw its role as one of maintaining and expanding a successful system rather than subjecting broadcasting organisations to detailed financial scrutiny. The House of Commons' Public Accounts Committee had periodically scrutinised the way the Treasury raised an additional tax, or levy, on ITV companies. This tax was imposed in recognition of the fact that these companies enjoyed considerable profits as a result of their monopoly exploitation of a public asset, the airwaves. The IBA was the body which, in effect, determined the amount of the levy to be paid. The Public Accounts Committee had questioned the effectiveness of this system as a way of extracting a fair return from the companies for the Treasury, and by definition the public purse. From the late 1970s onwards the Committee pressed for a system which was less opaque and which would generate more money.

In 1980 Whitelaw announced a review of the levy system. The Home Office did not implement the review until mid-1984, pleading that the changes brought about by the allocation of new ITV franchises in 1981 and the start of Channel 4 in 1982 made such a review untimely. The review involved the Treasury, the Home Office and the IBA. It completed its work in 1985. The inadequacy of the information available to the Public Accounts Committee and the way the review was delayed for four years illustrates some of the problems facing anyone trying to obtain information about how the system worked. The Home Office could allow this situation to continue because the economics of broadcasting was not a major political issue until the mid-1980s and there was little political pressure for the data to be produced and made public. But once this pressure became intense the resources of private research consultancies and academic economists were diverted to the topic.[2]

What did this paucity of data mean? In 1982–3 the BBC recorded a surplus of £73.9 million and in 1984–5 its licence fee income from 18,715,937 licences was £723.1 million. But it was difficult for analysts to discover how the licence fee was used in any detail, and so the BBC's claims about its financial needs were difficult to assess. A fairly detailed attempt, in 1982, to assess the role of broadcasting in the audio and audio visual industries in Greater London was affected by this lack of data. An estimate for the operating expenditure of London network TV production of £241.2 million was qualified by the note that the figure depended 'on a series of assumptions (about purchased programme policy, uniformity of production costs, etc) which cannot be cross-checked from the published BBC accounts'.[3]

Uncertainty about the licence fee settlements was built into the system. Writing in 1970, the BBC's Controller of Finance, Barrie Thorne, commented that 'throughout the sixties there was continued uncertainty of Government action about the timing, and the amount of increases in the licence fees'. Under a government committed to cutting public expenditure it was always likely that demands for increases in the licence fee would provoke a debate which would generate a closer examination of the financial structure of broadcasting organisations. But by the late 1970s the issue of BBC finances was becoming increasingly difficult to resolve. The BBC's income, unlike ITV's, was in part constrained by the number of TV licences issued and renewed each year. The number of new colour TV licences had ceased to grow at a rapid pace, as most UK homes had colour TVs. The BBC could no longer look to an increase in income generated by annual increases in the number of new colour licences bought. So by the early 1980s there was a set of issues surrounding the future finance of broadcasting that needed to be resolved.

In 1982 the BBC and IBA commissioned research into the cost of television to the viewer at a time when the future of broadcasting was being put on the agenda by the debates around cable. The Peat Marwick Mitchell value-for-money audit forced on the BBC by Leon Brittan in July 1984 represented both a short-term response to the political pressures of the day and an attempt by politicians, civil servants and BBC managers to come to terms with the changing nature of broadcasting finance.

There was clearly a need by the early 1980s for a consideration of the medium- to long-term basis on which UK broadcasting would be financed. But none of the factors considered above dictated that the Peacock inquiry should be set up, nor that economics should be at the centre of any inquiry. The fact that the inquiry and subsequent debates were dominated by economics reflected the specific political circumstances of the early to mid-1980s.[4]

Origins of the Peacock Committee

By the late autumn of 1984 it was clear that the BBC was unlikely to get its £65 settlement. In addition the official position of the government was that it was considering, but not committed to, the introduction of advertising. But it was also clear that Mrs Thatcher wanted something radical done about the BBC.

During the winter of 1984–5 the idea of some sort of inquiry was floated by a number of people. In November 1984 Colin Shaw, the Director of Programme Planning at the Independent Television Contractors Association, called for a new public inquiry into broadcasting along the lines of the Annan inquiry of 1974–7. In December the BBC had to deny reports that it supported such an inquiry. The same month the Institute of Practitioners in Advertising called for the government to set up an inquiry into the future funding of the BBC. In January Tim Brinton, Chairman of the Tory Backbench Media Committee, while objecting to 'a new Annan or a royal commission on broadcasting because they take so long' wanted the 'widest public debate about television'. He suggested that the 'Government ... issue a Green Paper to start a discussion for prospective legislation'. At the same time the Home Office denied newspaper speculation that it planned 'a Green Paper on the subject of the BBC or any other area of broadcasting'. In February the idea of a more limited inquiry was clearly under consideration: 'the government is, in fact, likely to look only at the possibility of finding new ways of financing the BBC and ITV'.[5]

Mrs Thatcher wanted swift action and was known to object to lengthy Royal Commissions. Royal Commissions had been devices used by her predecessors to deal with, and sometimes to sideline, complex political issues. But they were not regarded by her as aids to swift decision-making. On the other hand the official government line was not to force advertisements on to the BBC and there did not appear to be, in the wake of the vote on the Ashton Bill in January 1985, a massive groundswell of opinion among Tory MPs in favour of this.

At the same time the Treasury under Lawson was in dispute with the Home Office over the levy review: 'The Home Office, which chairs the review, has been insisting that the object of the exercise is not to increase the tax burden on ITV, but simply to make it more efficient. The Treasury has a less charitable view.'

On ITV, as on the BBC, the Home Office seems to have taken a protective position. The idea of an inquiry into broadcasting finance, rather than a full-scale Royal Commission into broadcasting, won the day. It fitted well with Mrs Thatcher's interest in pressurising the BBC into a more commercially orientated outlook and with Lawson's policy of promoting the deregulation of markets and industries. The inquiry clearly suited Leon Brittan. He did not want to have to force the BBC to take advertisements, something which the inquiry allowed him to avoid. But according to his brother Samuel, he also saw the inquiry as an opportunity to 'cover more than the narrow question of the licence fee versus advertising, and to probe the aims as well as the finance of broadcasting'. Lawson confirms this: 'As Leon had intended, the Peacock Committee interpreted their brief very widely, and their report emerged as something of a libertarian manifesto.' Thatcher has since written that Peacock 'provided a good opportunity to look at all' matters relating to broadcasting and not just the licence fee issue.[6]

The Composition of the Committee

Alan Peacock, the Chairman of the Committee, was an economist who had been handpicked by Downing Street. The Home Office was responsible for selecting the rest of the Committee. It took over a month before the Home Office was able to announce its composition – arguably a sign of division within government about its purpose.[7]

Alan Peacock was a supporter of the Institute of Economic Affairs and had been a Vice-Chancellor of the UK's first private university, the University of Buckingham.[8] Samuel Brittan was a journalist on the *Financial Times* and a friend of Nigel Lawson. At the *Financial Times* in the 1960s and 1970s he had given publicity to the monetarist economic ideas associated with Milton Friedman. By the early 1980s these had become the orthodoxy of government economic policy. Peter Jay as economics editor of *The Times* acted similarly. Samuel Brittan wrote that, 'Peacock and myself ... were inclined towards market provision of goods and services and ... had been stimulated by Peter Jay's writings.' In 1973 Brittan had looked to the future of broadcasting in terms similar to those advocated by Jay which also underpinned the vision for broadcasting advocated by the Committee in its report:

> there may in future no longer be any physical need to limit broadcasting to a small number of channels. Instead there could be an indefinite number of services among which consumers could select and pay for directly. The distinction between publishing and broadcasting would then largely disappear with a consequent extension of cultural diversity and freedom.

Peacock and Brittan were accurately described by Milne as 'free marketeers'.[9]

Alastair Hetherington had been editor of the *Guardian* between 1956 and 1975 and had survived a 'fraught' brief period as controller of BBC Radio Scotland between 1975 and 1978. At the time of his appointment he was Research Professor of Media Studies at the University of Stirling. He appears to have been appointed to balance the politics of Peacock and Brittan and to provide some inside experience of broadcasting management. According to Samuel Brittan, Hetherington, 'who had felt the rough side of BBC authoritarianism in his period as Scottish Controller was – as his interest in subscription showed – far from a dug-in-defender of the status quo'. This seems a fair assessment. In spite of Hetherington's sharp attacks on some aspects of the Committee's conduct, he did associate himself with most of the Committee's recommendations. His acceptance of the market-based approach advocated by Peacock and Brittan was explained by Brittan in terms of his liberalism:

> Hetherington seemed less antipathetic to a market-based approach if it was founded on the English liberal tradition of freedom of choice and opposition to censorship rather than on textbook reasoning, or econometric crystal gazing.[10]

A similar figure representing balance seems to have been Jeremy Hardie, an economist, accountant and businessman. He was former Deputy Chairman of the Monopolies and Mergers Commission. He had stood as a Parliamentary candidate for the self-proclaimed party of the centre, the Social Democratic Party in 1983 and was a director of Broadland Radio, an ILR station.[11]

Peter Reynolds was Chairman of Rank Hovis McDougal, a company that advertised heavily on commercial television and which in 1983–4 gave £20,000 to Conservative Party funds. He was knighted in Mrs Thatcher's 1985 New Years Honours list.[12] Another Tory connection was philosopher Anthony Quinton, President of Trinity College Oxford, a Conservative peer enobled by Mrs Thatcher in 1982.[13] Judith Chalmers was an experienced television and radio presenter and an active supporter of the Conservative Party. According to Brittan she, like Hetherington, was 'keen to preserve the achievements of British Broadcasting and suspicious of market ideology'.[14]

The Committee contained two individuals, Peacock and Brittan, with clearly defined ideas about economics and broadcasting policy as well as a level of economic expertise which outstripped the rest of the Committee. This alone gave them a great deal of influence. Brittan certainly believed that Hardie, Quinton and Reynolds did not have strongly developed opinions on the topic: they 'were not committed either to the existing institutions or to any recommended alternatives'.

The influence of Brittan and Peacock was also a result of the time they could devote to the Committee's work. Peacock and Hetherington gave between a third and a half of their time and the editor of the *Financial Times* allowed Brittan to take some time off from his normal work. But the 'other four members were much more pressed by their regular commitments although they all took an active part especially in the last hectic weeks'.

The divisions which emerged within the Committee reflected these structural features. Peacock and Brittan shaped the basic analysis, with occasional opposition from Hetherington and Chalmers. The others, who had neither the expertise nor the time, seem to have played a secondary role. The selection of members had provided a built-in Tory bias. The outcome might have been different had there been people appointed with well-developed, alternative views. But the Committee was selected to exclude this. There was no representative from the Labour Party, from the media trade unions or from people with a long track-record of management within broadcasting. Its composition, as with all committees of this sort, was profoundly unrepresentative of society as a whole. It reflected the tendency of all governments to chose members from an extremely narrow social group with an equally narrow range of political opinion and relevant expertise.

Specialist journalists writing at the time echoed a widespread view that the Committee was weighted to ensure the right outcome for the government: 'It seems certain that it will pave the way for advertising on the BBC', wrote one journalist. Another commented, 'The cast list of Professor Peacock's committee of inquiry into the funding of the BBC has done little to dampen doubts that herself intended it to provide the rationale for bringing in ads.'

On the issue of advertising these commentators were proved wrong. But their misgivings reflected a feeling in broadcasting circles that even before it sat, the Committee was intent on producing results which would conform to Mrs Thatcher's vision of how the BBC and broadcasting should develop.[15]

Conduct

The composition of the Committee was announced on 17 May 1985. It conducted the inquiry with great speed. It met for the first time on 29 May and held 20 full meetings. Peacock asserted his domination early and by the time of the first meeting 'had already a research strategy and had contacted consultants'. On 28 May he sent out a consultation document inviting submissions to the Committee by 31 August 1985. This deadline was subsequently changed after protests and submissions after the deadline were allowed. But it was made clear that late submissions would have less chance of influencing the outcome.

The Committee held a one-day conference on 28 November in London to which it invited a very small group of 15 organisations, excluding the media trade unions and a range of other interested parties. It commissioned research on overseas broadcasting systems and on the likely impact of advertising on BBC and ITV finances some of which, on subscription and quality, was initiated by Hetherington. In spite of the short time available and the absence of any really widespread public consultation the Committee received submissions from 843 individuals and organisations.[16]

By Christmas 1985 it was apparent that the weight of the economic evidence was against placing advertisements on the BBC, and the Committee began to show a greater interest in subscription TV. Two thirds of the final document was written up by Peacock from a draft by Committee Secretary Robert Eagle and the remaining third was written by Hetherington and Brittan. Economists Martin Cave, Peter Swann and Cento Veljanovski were called in 'for advice and drafts where necessary'. At this stage even Brittan became critical of the pace at which Peacock was proceeding. He formed, with Hetherington:

> an alliance at the end on the need for a clearly written and unambiguous final chapter, and in protest against the submission of numerous drafts in quick succession which the Committee had not had a proper chance to absorb.

By May there were well-informed leaks in the press outlining the main proposals and hinting at divisions within the Committee. The report went to the Home Secretary in June and was considered by the Cabinet before being published on 3 July 1986.[17]

The Committee covered a complex field in a very short time. This was because Peacock wanted to come up with a report within a year. It was operating under pressure from Downing Street. Hetherington noted: 'Although the committee was told that there were no presumptions about what it might recommend there can be little doubt that the Prime Minister hoped for advertising as the way to finance the BBC in the future.' At one of the early meetings of the Committee Peacock is alleged to have said: 'We are all agreed aren't we, that we are going to take advertising on the BBC?' Hetherington also indicates that this was Peacock's original view. Peacock apparently assumed that all members of the Committee favoured advertisements on the BBC.[18]

Hetherington has illustrated how the pace and the prejudices which drove the Committee impinged on key decisions. For instance, at an early stage in the formulation of the report, Robert Eagle, the Home Office civil servant servicing the Committee, rang Hetherington and asked whether he would go along with a 'master plan' which had not at that stage been discussed. The Committee's decision to recommend the privatisation of BBC Radios 1 and 2 was criticised by Hetherington in a speech in September 1986. Apparently the proposals, 'along with all the Committee's other thoughts on radio, were the outcome of no research, little consultation and half a day's discussion, at the end of which Professor Hetherington and Judith Chalmers dissented'.

The recommendation to give Channel 4 the option of selling its own advertisements is another example. Channel 4 had been funded since 1982 by a levy on ITV contractors refundable through their sale of advertising on the Channel. The recommendation made in the report had not been firmly discussed with Channel 4. Peacock put it forward 'having had dinner with someone at Channel 4'. The level of disagreement stimulated by this kind of process was apparent from Hetherington's comments and from the fact that, on some matters, there was no unanimity. The key proposal to auction ITV franchises was agreed only by majority voting, with four in favour (Peacock, Brittan, Reynolds and Quinton) and three against (Hardie, Chalmers and Hetherington).[19]

In spite of meeting some opposition from within the Committee, Peacock with Brittan succeeded in getting it to recommend a three-stage plan designed to create a market-driven system. Alan Peacock, acknowledging that there were differences of opinion, rightly pointed out that the 'longer-term scenarios for facilitating the introduction of a consumer-driven system of broadcasting were accepted by all members of the Committee'.[20]

On the advertising issue, economic research seems to have overridden any political preference that may have been held by members of the Committee. However, if Hetherington is to be believed, the absence of research in some areas proved no obstacle to the Committee making recommendations designed to promote the dominance of market forces in broadcasting.[21]

Peacock's Remit

Peacock's brief was:

(i) To assess the effects of the introduction of advertising or sponsorship on the BBC's Home Services, either as an alternative or a supplement to the income now received through the licence fee, including

    (a) the financial and other consequences for the BBC, for independent local radio, for the prospective services of cable, independent national radio and direct broadcasting by satellite, for the press and the advertising industry and for the exchequer; and

    (b) the impact on the range and quality of existing broadcasting services; and

    (c) to identify a range of options for the introduction, in varying amounts and on different conditions of advertising or sponsorship on some or all of the BBC's Home Services, with an assessment of the advantages and disadvantages of each option, and

    (d) to consider any proposals for securing income from the consumer other than through the licence fee.[22]

The language of this brief, with its concentration on the economics of broadcasting and on the likely economic consequences of changes to the status quo as well as its definition of the viewers and listeners as consumers, set the tone of the report. It helped to produce a document which redefined matters of social and cultural policy in terms of commodity exchange.[23]

A Review of Some of the Evidence

The drive to push broadcasting further towards the market by restructuring its financial base provoked criticism from a wide range of organisations, the majority of which were concerned about the impact of restructuring on the range and quality of broadcasting. A characteristic response along these lines was the initial submission made by the media union, the ACTT:

We believe that there is absoutely no popular mandate whatsoever for an undermining of our public service broadcasting system and that this should be a primary consideration in investigating alternative means of financing the BBC ...

(a)   The case for separate sources of revenue (ie, the licence fee for BBC; advertising for ITV) remains overwhelming in both economic and cultural grounds;

(b)   extending advertising to the BBC would leave us with a broad-casting system poorer in resources, poorer in programme output and poorer in value for money to viewers.[24]

At the time the report was being written it was clear that there was a substantial body of opinion against advertising on the BBC which included, but went well beyond, the established industry. For instance, a survey by the Broadcasting Research Unit of 29 major submissions found that 'at least 90% of the institutional submissions are opposed to advertising'.[25]

In the end there were at least 160 institutional submissions. But the report gives no sense of the detail, range and weight of opposition in the other 131 submissions. In fact a whole set of organisations ranging across a wide body of opinion were against advertising on the BBC – see Table 6.1.

Table 6.1 Organisations Supporting and Opposing Advertisements on the BBC

FOR
Adam Smith Institute, Institute of Practitioners in Advertising, Incorporated Society of British Advertisers, Mars.

AGAINST
Association of Independent Producers, Association of Independent Radio Contractors, BBC, Cable Association, Harlech TV, IBA, Independent Programme Producers Association in Scotland, Independent Television Contractors Association, Local Radio Association, TUC, Arts Council, British Film Institute, Directors Guild, Equity, NUJ, Newspaper Society, Society of Authors, Fabian Society, Labour Party, Liberal Party, Social Democratic Party, National Consumers Council, General Synod of the Church of England.

Source: Adapted from Broadcasting Research Unit, *Summary of Evidence to the Peacock Committee* (BRU, n.d.)[26]

The arguments used in these submissions frequently stressed the economic damage to broadcasting and the likely reduction in the quality of programming which would follow from introducing advertising to the BBC. The Labour Party argued that: 'the effect of introducing advertising to the BBC would be extremely harmful to other advertising dependent media, notably ILR and some of the smaller ITV stations', and that, 'advertising would have a disastrous cultural effect on the BBC weakening regulatory bodies, lowering standards and threatening diversity'.

In a similar vein the Liberal Party's evidence to the Committee queried the economic consequences of the introduction of advertising because:

it would draw the BBC into competition with the commercial companies for already dwindling resources of advertising revenue … Under those circumstances, the BBC would be forced to compete for the highest numbers of viewers, to attract the advertisers, and its 'minorities' programmes would inevitably suffer, as would some documentary, information and arts programmes.

A similar coupling of issues was at the centre of the evidence of the main BBC union, the Broadcasting and Entertainments Alliance. It argued that in prevailing economic conditions 'the BBC will not be able to take advertising without depriving some existing recipients of some of their present revenue'. There would be cultural consequences: 'The introduction of advertising in the BBC would sooner rather than later destroy the current programming and technical standards in the BBC, in independent television and in radio.'

Likewise the National Union of Journalists was opposed to: 'any move away from public funding for the BBC. The economic argument against this is that it is likely to prove unworkable, and unfair both to the BBC and its competitors.' It also argued that:

commercial funding or part-funding of the BBC through advertising or sponsorship would have a detrimental effect on programme standards, both in the BBC and in independent broadcasting. If both the BBC and Independent companies were chasing the same limited source of revenue, a ratings war would ensue.

Equity, the actors' trade union, did not believe that the BBC should be 'involved in all the developing areas of broadcasting'. Nonetheless it:

could see no justification for risking doing grave damage to a system which, by luck or design has produced some of the best television and the best radio programmes made anywhere in the world. We believe that requiring the BBC to compete with the ITV companies and independent radio companies for commercial revenue, would bring about fundamental changes which could be harmful to all the Broadcasters.[27]

The Association of Independent Radio Contractors argued against the inclusion of some advertising. A majority of AIRC members opposed advertising on the BBC, while a minority were prepared to support it in the context of a restructuring of all radio broadcasting. But AIRC members were

> unified as an industry in the view that *some* advertising on the BBC (a compromise which may have a certain appeal outside Independent Radio) would be the worst possible outcome. It would distort the media market place without substituting for the present dual funding ... a true, single, market-orientated system.[28]

By the beginning of 1986 it was clear that even the economists queuing up to advise the Committee were sceptical about the beneficial effects of introducing advertising:

> There has been a remarkable degree of agreement from academics who rarely agree on anything that natural growth in advertising has limits, is cyclical, that oversupply could force down the rates and commercials only help to fund the BBC at the margins.

By this time the Committee had begun examining in more detail the possibilities of subscription as a 'fall-back' position.[29]

The overwhelming weight of evidence and opinion identified the economic and cultural damage that would result from an immediate introduction of advertisments on the BBC. As a result the Committee rejected this option.

A Version of History

At the end of the report Peacock argues that the 'ideal, standard, and goal' of the report is 'consumer sovereignty'. It is described in the following way:

A satisfactory broadcasting market requires full freedom of entry for programme makers, a transmission system capable of carrying an indefinitely large number of programmes, facilities for pay-per-programme or pay-per-channel and differentiated charges for units of time. Such a system may be called the full broadcasting market akin to that which exists in publishing. The difficulty is, of course, how to move from the present regulated system now under stress to the full broadcast market without having to pass in between through a time of troubles which give us the worst of both worlds and the benefits of neither.[30]

This passage draws a parallel between the ideal state of broadcasting advocated by the report and the situation that 'exists in publishing'. The report takes the view that in publishing there is a free market relatively free from state interference which is governed by consumer preferences.[31]

The use of the publishing industry as a model for broadcasting formed one of the basic assumptions underpinning the document:

Since the early days of publishing had been fettered with constraints from which it had now been emancipated, the point was put to us that perhaps technology would reach a point where regulation of broadcasting would no longer be necessary.

The implication here is that just as printing flourished once it was released from state control so too would broadcasting once the current state controls were lifted. Peacock argued that from its earliest days until the late seventeenth century the printing industry had been subject to censorship, by Acts of Parliament and Royal Proclamation:

Pre-publication censorship came to an end when Parliament refused to renew the Licensing Act in 1694, in part, because of the corrupt practices of the Stationers Company. The abolition of pre-publication censorship was described by Macauley as a greater contribution to liberty and civilisation than either the Magna Carta or the Bill of Rights.

The press historian, Michael Harris, has noted how this perspective, which he describes as 'Whiggish':

is one in which more and more newspapers lead to better and better results. 1695 the year that marked the end of pre-publication censorship is held to represent a starting point for the slow but steady emergence of a free press,which found its apotheosis in the tax repeals of the mid-nineteenth century. Such a view implicitly detracts from the importance of the output of earlier periods, trivialises its character and reduces the publications to the status of 'forerunners'. This 'fourth-estate' view is now collapsing.

Recent scholarship has shown that the lapse of the licensing laws was accidental. After the lapse members of the book trade and the government sought new ways to introduce direct controls. Indirect controls were exerted by policitians over newspapers throughout the eighteenth and nineteenth centuries and the removal of pre-publication censorship by the state was replaced eventually by an equally pervasive form of market control exercised on behalf of the dominant groups in society. A more realistic account of press history would be cautious about implying that the lapse of the licensing laws initiated a steady move towards a free press.

Work on the press in the twentieth century shows that the existing concentration of ownership, limited opportunities for entry, and systematic distortion of news in the newspaper press, is a direct result of the activity, over time, of the relatively unfettered action of market forces on the publishing industry. The failure of the report to incorporate the findings of this kind of work on press history meant that the analogy with publishing which underpins the report's recommendations is based on an inaccurate reading of the development of newspaper and publishing history.[32]

Broadcasting as a Commodity

Running parallel to this analogy is an ahistorical analysis of the nature of public service broadcasting and a redefinition of the concept in economic terms, which strips it of its cultural and social connotations. Early on in the report the Committee discusses the 'public service' principle. It quotes statements defining public service broadcasting from a variety of sources. This is because:

We found there was no simple dictionary definition. This is not surprising since previous committees have also found it difficult to define the concept. The Pilkington Committee (1962) found that 'though its standards exist and are recognisable, broadcasting is more nearly an art than an exact science. It deals in tastes and values and is not precisely definable.'

While the Peacock report acknowledges this problem of definition it does not explore its significance. The report then surveys a series of definitions of public service broadcasting taken from the 1981 Act, the Broadcasting Research Unit, the 1984 Cable and Broadcasting Act and the Annex to the Licence and Agreement of the BBC Charter. The two most inclusive and complex are the definition implied in Section 2 of the 1981 Act and the Broadcasting Research Unit's definition. The Act required the IBA:

(a) to provide the television and local sound broadcasting services as a public service for disseminating information, education and entertainment;

(b) to ensure that the programmes broadcast by the Authority in each area maintain a high general standard in all respects (and in particular in respect of their content and quality), and a proper balance and wide range in their subject matter, having regard both to the programmes as a whole and also to the days of the week on which, and the times of the day at which, the programmes are broadcast; and

(c) to secure a wide showing or (as the case may be) hearing for programmes of merit.

The Broadcasting Research Unit's definition offered a wider perspective on the 'idea' of public service broadcasting. The Unit argued that public service broadcasting had meant a number of things over the years including providing a universal service, catering for the needs of minorities, competing in the area of programmes and not numbers of viewers, and policies which sought to maximise rather than restrict the independence of programme makers.[33]

These definitions include a wide range of obligations and practices. They reflect the fact that public service broadcasting has had a complex history. Its origins lie in part in the ideas about public service held by the Victorian middle classes which became part of the ethos of the early BBC. The changing practices of broadcasters and their interaction with their audiences and political masters shaped both the ideal and the practice of public service broadcasting.

Reith's concept of the purpose of broadcasting in the 1920s and 1930s gradually gave way to a different one by the war years of 1939–45. After the war the ideal and practice of public service broadcasting continued to evolve in the context of the arrival of commercial TV (1954), the social and cultural changes of the post-war period, and the sharp political turmoil of the 1960s and 1970s.[34] In fact the definitions, or rather descriptions, provided by the 1981 Act and the Broadcasting Research Unit, are inadequate because they do not, and are not meant to, give an account of the evolving nature of public service broadcasting.

The report fails to acknowledge the complexity of the definitions it cites in paragraphs 28–35, either by accounting for them historically or by querying their nature and the extent to which they related to practice. The definitions referred to in paragraphs 28–35 are, in effect, left standing at the start of the report, and are then almost completely forgotten. Near the end of the report the idea of public service broadcasting is reviewed again and a new definition proposed in paragragph 580:

> The best operational definition of public service is simply any major modification of purely commercial provision resulting from public policy. Defined in this way the scope of public service will vary with the state of broadcasting. If a full broadcasting market is eventually achieved, in which viewers and listeners can express preferences directly, the main role of public service could turn out to be the collective provision … of programmes which viewers and listeners are willing to support in their capacity of taxpayers and voters, but not directly as consumers. These would include programmes of a more demanding kind with a high content of knowledge, culture, education and experiment (including entertainment).

This definition asserts that broadcasting should be 'purely commercial' and that public service broadcasting is that which offers programmes not supplied by the market. The social and cultural goals which had been at the centre of the evolution of public service broadcasting are thereby relegated to the edge of a system, at the centre of which are 'purely commercial' considerations.

In this definition public service broadcasting is described as an appropriate economic response by 'taxpayers' to a market failure. Public service broadcasting is stripped of its history and the words, but not the meanings they have carried, are forced into the service of an ideal held by the Committee, one in which 'purely commercial' considerations rule. This new definition is an almost complete rejection of the goals and achievements of public service broadcasting as it had developed since the 1920s.

Competition and Consumer Sovereignty

The Committee took the concepts of duopoly, competition and consumer sovereignty from economics and applied them to broadcasting. Chapter 4 of the report is devoted to analysing 'The comfortable duopoly'. Here the BBC and ITV system is described as a duopoly which restricts access to the market by other producers, limits consumer choice and keeps costs within the industry high. The duopoly is contrasted with the features characteristic of a competitive market place:

> In highly competitive industries firms will have relatively little control except possibly in the short run over prices of both the products they supply and of the inputs of labour, raw materials and capital which they use in supplying them. There are no barriers to entry into the industry erected by the existing suppliers or by government regulation though there may be economic risks which act as a deterrent to new entrants. Producers will try to increase their market share by 'differentiating their product', ie by competing through service and quality. Broadly speaking, consumer choice determines the size of the industry in which the number of competing firms is large.

This is an idealistic account of how markets work and of the role of consumer choice. For instance, it does not accord with the economics of the US media industry nor the UK newspaper industry. But, in a sense, the reality of this account is irrelevant. It is the method used which is significant. This method proceeds by taking a preferred concept – duopoly, competitive markets – and applying it to a problem, in this case broadcasting. The way in which it is applied suggests that the concepts are not only appropriate to the subject matter under discussion but, by the simple device of excluding others, they are the best way of discussing the subject. This procedure limits the nature of the debate and the likely range of reasonable conclusions that can be drawn.[35]

So in Chapter 4 of the report broadcasting is discussed as if it were always meant to behave like a competitive market. Once this assumption is accepted the rest follows: television is a duopoly, which is a bad thing because a duopoly is not a competitive market. Broadcasters are self-regarding and insufficiently cost conscious, and so on. A similar process is at work in the use of the idea of the consumer. Again an economic concept is used as if it were appropriate and, in its very application, shapes the debate and points towards the possible conclusions. Once this concept is applied the people who watch TV or listen to radio are described not as people, or 'the public', or 'different publics', or 'citizens' or 'viewers' but as consumers. As consumers they behave as ideal consumers do in economic theory: they are driven by the desire to consume – not to think, excel, reflect, enjoy, select, reject, rejoice or weep, but to consume television and radio programmes.

Of course, people are more than just consumers and there is no such thing as a perfect market or consumer sovereignty. These concepts are tools which are useful when applied in some types of narrow economic analysis, but are of limited value when applied to broadcasting. In the UK broadcasting was never viewed as being an embodiment of free market theory. It is completely misleading to judge its goals, achievements and future in the light of that theory. Broadcasting emerged and evolved to meet a much more complex range of needs than reading Peacock would suggest. And so we could go on.[36]

The report then builds its recommendations on a combination of a misreading of the history of the publishing and broadcasting industries and an inappropriate application of concepts from the field of economics to broadcasting. In this way it redefines the industry as a branch of the capitalist market economy which should be judged by the criteria which determine success in that economy. We now consider these recommendations.

Recommendations

The core recommendation redefines broadcasting as a purely commercial activity and relegates public service broadcasting to the margins of the system:

> Our own conclusion is that British broadcasting should move towards a sophisticated system based on consumer sovereignty. That is a system which recognises that viewers and listeners are the best ultimate judges of their own interests,which they can best satisfy if they have the option of purchasing the broadcasting services they require from as many alternative sources of supply as possible. There will always be a need to supplement the direct consumer market by public finance for programmes of a public service kind ... supported by people

in their capacity as citizens and voters but unlikely to be commercially self-supporting in the view of broadcasting entrepreneurs.

Public service broadcasting would ideally involve: 'a multiplicity of programmes which could in principle be provided by programme makers who would make contracts with some statutory body to implement public service obligations in return for grants'.

However, the report acknowledges that the goal of consumer sovereignty to which public service broadcasting must be subordinated is not realisable:

> Our consumer sovereignty model is, of course, a standard and a goal; not a fully specified mechanism to be pulled off the shelf tomorrow by a trigger-happy central planner. A satisfactory broadcasting market requires full freedom of entry for programme makers, a transmission system capable of carrying an indefinitely large number of programmes, facilities for pay-per-programme or pay-per-channel and differentiated charges for units of time. Such a system may be called the full broadcasting market akin to that which exists in publishing. The difficulty is, of course, how to move from the present regulated system now under stress to the full broadcasting market without having to pass in between through a time of troubles which could give us the worst of both worlds and the benefits of neither.[37]

Here it highlights the idealism which underpins its method and the difficulty it sees in reaching its goal. In order to make the passage from the present to the ideal future as smooth as possible the report proposes that broadcasting should move through three stages towards a full broadcasting market. Stage 1 would see the development of satellite and cable services while most viewers and listeners relied on existing services. During this stage the BBC licence fee would be indexed to the retail price index. This would lay the foundation for Stage 2 during which there would be a proliferation of broadcasting systems, channels and methods of payment. This shift would allow subscription to replace the 'main part of the licence fee'. In Stage 3 where there would be an indefinite number of channels and methods of payment including pay-per-programme and pay-per-channel during which technological advance would reduce the costs of channel diversity and of the charging system. This stage would be characterised by a multiplicity of choice leading to a full broadcasting market. A 'Public Service provision', it asserted, would continue through all three stages. The idealism in the recommendations is self-evident, as is the reduction of public service broadcasting to a marginalised 'provision' within the evolving system.[38]

The Committee made 18 recommendations for implementation in Stage 1. These combined the strategic with the ad hoc, and the realisable and the unrealistic. Here we list each one, commenting on its purpose and, where appropriate, its subsequent history.

> Recommendation 1: All new television sets sold or rented in the UK market should be required from the earliest convenient date, and in any case not later that 1 January 1988, to have a peritelevision socket and associated equipment which will interface with a decoder to deal with encrypted signals.

This reflected the Committee's desire to achieve a market in broadcasting through the mechanism of subscription and in one sense contradicted the spirit of the report. The goal, a market free of government interference, was to be achieved by a major act of government intervention in industrial policy. If effected, this would force costly peritelevision sockets on consumers who would have no choice in the matter. The recommendation was not acted on by the government.

> Recommendation 2: BBC television should not be obliged to finance its operations by advertising while the present organisation and regulation of broadcasting remain in being.

The Committee recommended this because: 'So long as the present duoploy remains in being and competition is limited to a fringe of satellite and cable services, the introduction of advertising on television is likely to reduce consumer choice and welfare.'

The case against advertising had been won. Advertising finance for the BBC was only ruled out, however, as long as the current broadcasting structures remained in place.

> Recommendation 3: the licence fee should be indexed on an annual basis to the general rate of inflation.

Indexation to the RPI was a way of forcing the BBC to accept the criticism that it was insufficiently market-orientated, inefficient and over-stretched, criticisms which had featured prominently in the period leading up to Peacock. This was because inflation in the broadcasting industry ran ahead of the general rate of inflation. Indexing the licence fee to this general rate was designed to: 'put some pressure on the BBC to exploit its revenue-earning potential more forcefully and to think more carefully before embarking on peripheral activities far removed from its core obligations'.

The government accepted this proposal. Indexing proved to be a key factor in generating cuts in BBC activities in subsequent years.

> Recommendation 4: to permit the BBC to be the managing agent in the collection of the licence fee, the Post Office should be released from its responsibility as agent to the Home Office for collection and enforcement procedures associated with the licence fee. The BBC should become responsible for inviting proposals for collection and enforcement procedures and for identifying the most efficient and economic collection and enforcement system.

This uncontroversial measure had an economic rationale. The Post Office charged the BBC for collecting the fee. The BBC would be able to cut the costs of this charge if it put the collection of the fee out to tender – a device widely favoured by advocates of the marketisation of public services. The BBC became responsible for collecting the licence fee in 1991.

> Recommendation 5: On the understanding that the proceeds would be used to reduce the cost of the television licence and not to increase the total sum available for broadcasting a separate licence fee of not less than £10 should be charged for car radios.

This was never implemented. It would have proved politically unpopular and would have been difficult to enforce.

> Recommendation 6: Pensioners drawing supplementary pension in households wholly dependent on a pension should be exempt from the licence fee.

This recommendation was a response to the widespread view that the fee was too expensive for many pensioners. The Committee deliberately narrowed the number of pensioners who could benefit and argued that the income raised by Recommendation 5 would cover the cost of this move. The recommendation proved far too radical for the Thatcher government.

> Recommendation 7: The BBC should have the option to privatise Radios 1, 2 and local radio in whole or in part. IBA regulation of radio should be replaced by a looser regime.

In addition five of us go further:-

Recommendation 7a: Radio 1 and Radio 2 should be privatised and financed by advertising. Subject to the Government's existing commitments to community radio, any further radio frequencies becoming available should be auctioned to the highest bidder. IBA regulation of radio should be replaced by a looser regime.

This recommendation exposed divisions within the Committee. Hetherington and Chalmers felt that Recommendation 7a would damage the BBC's remaining services and 'cripple a number of ILR companies'. This was one of the proposals that Hetherington later revealed had not been properly discussed.[39] Even so he and Chalmers did accept Recommendation 7.

The arguments about loosening the IBA's control over radio and promoting more stations were derived indirectly from the Omega Report and directly from a submission to the Home Secretary in January 1986 by the Association of Independent Radio Contractors (para 639). The difference between the proposals 7 and 7a was one of degree not substance. The government's response was to accept the arguments of the AIRC which it embodied in the Green Paper on Radio in 1987. However it left the issue of BBC radio in the hands of the new management regime of Checkland, Hussey and Birt.

'Recommendation 8: The BBC and ITV should be required over a ten year period to increase to not less than 40% the proportion of programmes supplied by independent producers.' This was designed 'to increase competition and multiply sources of supply'. To prevent competition being stifled by the independent sector's becoming concentrated in a few companies, the report suggested that 'provisions against concentration in that industry along the lines which the Fair Trading Act 1973 provides for newspapers' should be brought into force.

This recommendation reflected the view that independent production was a means of opening up the duopoly, promoting efficiency and greater diversity of programme supply. The success of Channel 4's experiment with independent production influenced this proposal. The problem with the recommendation was that the 1973 Fair Trading Act had not prevented concentration in the newspaper industry. Concentration had proceeded apace in the 1980s, often because of the political links between media companies and ministers and in spite of the provisions of the Act. The report makes no reference to this political factor when discussing concentration.

The main aim of Recommendation 8 was, like Recommendations 3 and 7, to promote the spread of market forces into the public service broadcasting system on a massive scale without introducing advertising. The government was happy to use independent production companies to exert market pressures on the industry, promote entrepreneurs, and help to destabilise and casualise the broadcasting workforce. It acted swiftly. From November 1986 onwards it put pressure on the BBC and ITV companies to increase the amount of product they took from the independents. It also placed a requirement that they take up to 25 per cent of their output from independents into the 1990 Act.

'Recommendation 9: The non-occupied night-time hours (1.00am to 6.00am) of the BBC and ITV television wavelengths should be sold for broadcasting purposes.' This idea of dealing with frequency allocation through auctions owed its origins to the IEA and was introduced in order to bring an element of pure market forces into the system. It was not accompanied by a detailed justification or any assessment of the likely audience for programmes transmitted at that time. This proposal was opposed by the established broadcasters and was not implemented.

> Recommendation 10: Franchise contracts for ITV contractors should be put to competitive tender. Should the IBA decide to award a franchise to a contractor other than the one making the highest bid it should be required to make a full, public and detailed statement of its reasons.

This recommendation was also taken directly from the IEA. It proved very controversial at the time, and was included in a modified form in the 1990 Act. It provided the framework in which franchises were re-advertised in 1991. Auctions were, in theory, meant to minimise the arbitrary nature of franchise allocation by introducing an objective mechanism, the bid, into the process. There had been widespread dissatisfaction with the opaque way the IBA had allocated ITV franchises in the early 1980s.

In addition the Treasury saw auctions as a way of obtaining higher returns from the ITV companies than had been the case with the levy. It was a view endorsed by Thatcher who wrote that Peacock's proposal 'had the merit of openness and simplicity as well as maximizing revenue for the Treasury'. As Chalmers, Hetherington and Hardie pointed out in dissenting from the proposal, the operation of the bid was not likely to be any less arbitary than the system by which the IBA reached its decisions because 'it would be very hard for the IBA to choose between a high cash bid and a bid which offered less money but a better chance of high quality public service broadcasting.'

In fact the recommendation implicitly acknowledged the difficulty of promoting market forces while at the same time seeking to maintain high standards. The Committee recommended that any bid should allow for the cost of a range of stringent public service broadcasting requirement 'which we would expect to include all the requirements of the 1981 Broadcasting Act Section 2'. In making this recommendation the Committee acknowledged that a simple bidding process could not deliver high quality programmes and that the operation of the market had to be modified. The proposal was a half-way house between the existing system and the ideal. It was designed, in harmony with the overall objective of Stage 1, to increase commercial pressures within the system.

> Recommendation 11: Franchises should be awarded on a rolling review basis. There would be a formal annual review of the contractor's performance by the Authority.

> Recommendation 12: Consideration should be given to extending the franchise periods, perhaps up to 10 years.

These were relatively uncontroversial proposals.

> Recommendation 13: DBS franchises should be put to competitive tender.

This recommendation was not implemented immediately. By this stage the IBA had embarked on the process of establishing a DBS operator using its normal practices based on the consideration of the proposals of applicants, not auctions.

> Recommendation 14: Channel 4 should be given the option of selling its own advertising time and would then no longer be funded by a subscription from ITV companies.

This proposal was intended to increase competition for revenue within the ITV system, because 'Channel 4 is now at a point where its costs are of a similar order to the revenue from advertising'. There was no detailed consideration of this within the report. It appeared, according to Hetherington, without any proper discussion with Channel 4 and as a result of a personal contact made by Peacock with someone at the Channel.

The problem with the proposal was that by making Channel 4 compete with ITV for the same source of revenue the Channel might be forced to erode its commitment to distinctive programming and schedule material which would compete head on with the programmes on ITV for audiences and advertising revenue.[40] This proposal was accepted by the government and incorporated in the 1990 Act.

Recommendation 15: National telecommunications systems (eg British Teelcom and any subsequent entrants) should be permitted to act as common carriers with a view to the provision of a full range of service, including delivery of television programmes.

This was designed to set the stage for the multichannel delivery service needed to provide a full broadcasting market. The demand impinged too closely on the complex telecoms policy area then being worked through by the government and was not implemented.

Recommendation 16: The restriction of cable franchises to EEC-owned operators should be removed.

The government eventually accepted this recommendation, thereby opening up the UK market to companies from the US.

Recommendation 17: All restrictions for both Pay-Per-Channel and Pay-Per-Programme as options should be removed, not only for cable but also for terrestrial and DBS operations.

The restrictions then in place prevented the BBC and ITV from entering the subscription market and prevented some kinds of cable programmes from being subject to this payment regime. This recommendation was a logical extension of the demand to promote a subscription-based system.

Recommendation 18: as regulation is phased out the normal laws of the land relating to obscenity, defamation, blasphemy, sedition and other similar matters should be extended to cover the broadcasting media and any present exemptions should be removed.

This recommendation reflected the libertarian stance on social issues taken by the Committee which proved irreconcilable with the views held by Mrs Thatcher. Mrs Thatcher's position won the day. The 1990 Act effectively represented a rejection of Recommendation 18. It reversed broadcasters' immunity from prosecution under the Obscene Publications Act 1959 and imposed a host of other measures designed to limit the freedom of broadcasters on matters relating to the coverage of sex and politically controversial issues.[41]

In Stage 2 the whole BBC system would become subscription based while ITV would continue to take its revenue from advertising. Public service broadcasting, according to Peacock, would then become 'those programmes of merit which would not survive in a market where audience ratings was the sole criterion'. Public service broadcasting would no longer remain a responsibility of the BBC but would be organised by a new Public Service Broadcasting Council (PSBC) which:

would be responsible, in Stage Two, for the secure funding of Radios 3 and 4, local and regional radio and public service television programmes on any channel. Whenever a PSBC grant was given, the PSBC would have the right to stipulate where programmes should be broadcast, and these should be broadcast in non-encrypted form. The external services would continue to be provided by the BBC and funded as at present. A new charter for this newly defined BBC would be required.

The PSBC could be financed by a licence fee or by a levy of sorts on ITV companies.[42]

In Stage 2 the regulation of programme content would gradually be lifted, once a PSBC had been established and a political judgement made that 'sufficient diversity had been introduced into programme sources and payment methods'. This would lead to 'the abolition of prepublication censorship or vetting of any kind of broadcasting'. With broadcasting, like the press, subject to the law of the land and 'censorship' ended, this:

> would be a sign that broadcasting had come to age, like publishing three centuries ago. Prepublication censorship, whether of printed material, plays, films, broadcasting or other creative activities or expressions of opinion, has no place in a free society and we would advise Government and Parliament to embark forthwith on a phased programme for ending it.

Here, in Stage 2, a number of chickens came home to roost. Public service broadcasting is defined narrowly and negatively as programmes the market will not sustain. This is the consequence of the reasoning outlined earlier in this chapter. Once this has been done it becomes possible to reduce public service broadcasting to the margins of the system.

Stage 2 also reproduces the Whig version of press history which underpins the report and assumes that 1695 saw the end of prepublication censorship. This is not true. Prepublication censorship has remained a feature of the UK press ever since. It is true that prepublication censorship now rarely takes the form of overt state vetting, leaving aside the 'D' notice system and the Official Secrets Act. But it has been replaced by government news management, the censorship of the press exercised by proprietors and editors, and gagging writs issued by rich people to prevent the publication of embarrassing material.

Stage 2 also equated the public service broadcasting obligations of the BBC and ITV with prepublication censorship and vetting. True these bodies did, and do, engage in these activities to a greater or lesser extent. But so too does the press. Yet the public service broadcasting regulations were not simply negative. They required broadcasters to act positively in the public interest.[43]

According to the Committee, Stage 3 would be a period when the owners of all transmission equipment would allow freedom of market entry to programme-makers, when viewers would pay directly for services and when there would be a policy to 'prevent monopolistic concentration among programme channellers or producers'. The report argued that this system could be achieved without tying broadcasters to any one delivery system.

Antitrust laws in the US and Fair Trading legislation in the UK have not prevented the growth of oligopoly within the media industries. What then led the writers of this report to believe that things would be different for broadcasting? History suggests that were a government to introduce policies designed to prevent concentration in the new broadcasting market, they would be either marginal to the operation of market forces or they would be circumvented by proprietors and governments.

Conclusion

Alan Peacock was clearly aware that there were powerful forces pressing for advertising in 1984 and 1985. Yet the Committee did not find in favour of placing advertisements on the BBC?

The lobby for advertising was a prominent part of the pressure for change, but even in 1984 this represented only one strand of a wider body of thought which which was pressing for a major reorientation of broadcasting towards the market. This was represented in the work of the IEA and the ASI as well as the ILR companies, who wanted a lighter regulatory regime. There were also those like Murdoch who wanted change but did not want advertisements on the BBC except in the context of a broader restructuring of the industry. From the early 1980s the Home Office had been, in a sense, gradually and very slowly accepting the need for a radical rethink of the situation, even if it was not sympathetic to all the solutions that were on offer.

Thatcher was not politically strong enough to force advertising on the BBC. She faced opposition from the Home Office and from her most senior Cabinet colleague, Whitelaw. By accepting the idea of an inquiry she had implicitly moved towards a compromise on the issue. But the inquiry had a pronounced IEA influence, in the form of Peacock and Brittan. This meant that, from the outset, the Committee was being led by people who shared her general perspectives on the role of markets in the economy and who could draw on an established intellectual framework for analysing broadcasting associated with the IEA.

The forces in place in early 1985 may have appeared to imply that the Committee was going to opt for advertising, but the reality was, arguably, that it was expected by both Thatcher and the Home Office to look much further afield. The terms of reference set for the Committee, in directing its attention to the range of ways in which the BBC could be financed and to assessing the likely impact of this on the whole system, opened the door to wider considerations.

The economic evidence produced for the Committee clearly indicated that introducing advertising would have detrimental effects on the whole system. This was decisive in framing Peacock's recommendations. But equally decisive was Peacock's and Brittan's predisposition for promoting IEA-type ideas about consumer sovereignty in broadcasting. In a sense, the committee was able to reject advertising, not only because the evidence was against it, but because it was driven by a set of ideas which were far more radical in the long term.

The answer to the question why the Committee did not favour advertising lies in the complexity of the issues it was called upon to consider. This complexity was recognised by most of the key participants even before the Committee was set up. Advertising was an important, but not the only, issue which was being debated in government at that time. There were considerable pressures exerted from inside and outside government for a wholesale reappraisal of broadcasting policy, which is what Peacock delivered. Advertising on the BBC was both the occasion which allowed this debate to go public and the centrepiece of the public debate. But the key participants in the process – Thatcher, the Brittans, Peacock, the Home Office, and even Murdoch – were well aware that it raised much broader issues.

The Peacock report emerged from the political climate of the first and second Thatcher administrations. It resulted in a reprieve for the BBC's licence fee. Yet it also established the framework for subsequent discussions around broadcasting policy in the government. This framework placed profit and business at the centre of policy, and eased public service ideals to the margins.

The strategy at the heart of the report – shifting broadcasting further towards the full, capitalist dominated, market – along with many of the 18 Stage 1 recomendations, was adopted by the government after 1986. In policy terms this meant laying the economic and managerial foundations for restructuring the BBC, deregulating ITV and ILR and creating new openings for market-driven cable and satellite-delivered services.

Peacock was the centrepiece of UK broadcasting strategy during the 1980s. It was produced by a government broadly united on strategy and partly divided on tactics. It provided the strategy around which the government could, with some minor differences, unite. Samuel Brittan was well aware of this when he wrote: 'The worth of the report ... lies in the fact that it planted the idea of a broadcasting market akin to publishing, which will flower in time.' And so too was Alan Peacock, who says the final report: 'In fact ... offered revolutionary proposals designed to alter the whole system of broadcasting finance.'[45]

7 The Policy Framework after Peacock

This chapter analyses the framework in which broadcasting policy developed after 1986. It describes how policy was influenced by the Peacock report and how it was implemented within the context of policy differences between the Home Office under Douglas Hurd on the one side and Mrs Thatcher and the DTI on the other. It places developments in policy towards the BBC in the wider context of broadcasting policy as whole.

The Launch

Peacock was launched at a press conference on 3 July 1986 where a tone of confusion was set concerning the impact and significance of the report which was to characterise its initial reception. The splits within the Committee, which have been described in Chapter 6, were made public at the launch in the form of disputes between members of the Committee involving Hardie, Brittan and Hetherington.[1] The *Today* newspaper, which at this time was not owned by News International, felt that the proposals were 'deeply flawed' and should be treated by the government with 'extreme caution'. The *Guardian* suggested that the proposals did not make sense. The *Financial Times* criticised the recommendation to auction ITV franchises, the proposals on subscription television and Peacock's understanding of the pace and nature of technical change:

> While Peacock offers cogent analysis and some useful practical suggestions the likely trend of technological developments needs to become much clearer before any firm judgement can be made on its prescriptions for the longer term.

This view could almost have been based on a Home Office briefing.[2]

Another response was to praise the report and suggest it had not gone far enough. *The Times* argued that Peacock 'can hardly fail to exercise a strong influence on thinking and policy about broadcasting'. It went on to restate the case for advertisements on the BBC. The *Daily Express* did not approve of the retention of the licence fee, which it saw as 'misguided', and referred to the BBC's 'arrogance and extravagance' arguing for a quick introduction of pay-per-view.[3]

The divisions of opinion in the Committee and the press were mirrored by rumours of disputes among Cabinet ministers. The *Daily Telegraph* argued that the Home Office had attempted to blunt or sideline the report. Government philosophy was, according to the *Daily Telegraph*, 'as offensive to the ethos of the Home Office as to that of the BBC' and alleged that the BBC's 'friends at the Home Office' were pigeon-holing the report. The *Daily Mail*'s comments reflected the view that Peacock had fallen victim to uncertainty and division at the centre of government, and said the handling of the report showed a government 'unsure of what to do'.[4]

The BBC's response was cautious. It welcomed the decision on advertising, criticised the RPI linkage, commented on the 'unrealistically high' figure of 40 per cent for independents, and drew attention to the potential dangers of overeager deregulation. Under Milne the BBC did not give a ringing endorsement to the report. The ITCA criticised the auctioning proposals. The trade journal *Broadcast*, reflecting a commonly held view within the industry, commended the recommendation on independents because broadcasting 'should encourage access and diversity and there is a need for plurality in our system'.

Peacock felt that there had been: ' a set of unfortunate leaks, unfortunate because they took particular recommendations, such as the rejection of advertising by the BBC, out of context'. In November 1986 he reportedly 'accused broadcasters of failing to report his committee's work on financing the BBC'. In March 1987 he complained that:

> at the time of writing no programme has appeared, so far as I am aware, where the issues raised by the Committee have been properly presented and discussed. It is not so much biased reporting as covert censorship.

But by then a view had emerged among broadcasters which identified the significance of the report for the commercial system: 'it is Peacock's recommendations about ITV, rather than the BBC, which look like having the more immediate and significant effect'.[5]

The Cabinet and Peacock

There was clearly 'dissension within the Cabinet' over the nature of the response to the report. This was reflected in the fact that the government did not give wholehearted endorsement to the report's recommendations. Samuel Brittan was critical of what he saw as the Home Office's less than satisfactory handling of prepublication publicity. Home Secretary Douglas Hurd was not as firm an advocate of long-term deregulation, the core of the report, as his predecessor Leon Brittan. Hurd reportedly communicated his reservations to his colleagues. But an agreement was reached at Cabinet level. Ministers agreed to establish a Cabinet Committee to examine the proposals before adopting them in full, an approach which was essentially in harmony with the Home Office's attitude to change.

It is arguable that this agreement was only possible because of a combination of factors. The rejection of advertising had undermined the Prime Minister's publicly stated preference and the complexity of the area which the report revealed made it easier to argue for a slower response to its recommendations. The imminence of a general election and the relative weakness of the Prime Minister's position within the Cabinet after the Westland and Libyan bombing affairs may also have contributed to the muted response. Nigel Lawson was in no doubt about the damage inflicted by Westland on Thatcher's authority in Cabinet and within the Parliamentary Conservative Party: 'back benchers ... felt that they had been badly let down by the Cabinet ... and wanted blood'. In his view the affair, 'left Margaret herself so badly wounded that at one point it looked mortal'.

Part of this process seems to have been to let the Prime Minister 'win' or appear to win, on the issue of increasing rather than, as the report recommended, decreasing the opportunities for censoring the political and moral content of broadcasting. Alan Peacock encountered what appears to be evidence of this when he went to the Home Office after publication of the report. The anti-libertarian line was presented to him before anything else was discussed:

> I have never quite recovered from the fact that the first meeting I had with the Home Secretary after the publication of the Peacock Report began with the expression of his doubts about our libertarian position on programme content.

Under pressure from Mrs Thatcher the Home Office acquiesced in the establishment of a Broadcasting Standards Council which was widely perceived as a new sex and violence watchdog. Thatcher records how she 'insisted, against Home Office resistance, that our 1987 general election manifesto should contain a firm commitment' to this project.[6]

The official position was summed up by Hurd in a speech to the Royal Television Society on 8 November 1986. There he hinted that the sheer complexity of the report, and its departure from its remit, provided grounds for delay:

> The Peacock Committee was given relatively restricted terms of reference, but understandably, being a lively set of people, they overflowed their terms of reference and produced a report which touched on most of the possibilities for the future. The members of the Committee would I think agree that they set an agenda rather than worked out full conclusions.

The initial response by the government and the press to the report was coloured by the Home Office line. Thereafter the framework shifted. The election victory of June 1987 boosted Thatcher's authority. This enabled the DTI which, with its predecessor the Department of Industry, had been a centre of pressure for the privatisation of state-controlled industries under Thatcher, to play a much more overt role in the development of broadcasting policy and in implementing proposals in the report.

The government's initial hesitant response to the report was only a temporary phase prompted largely by factors external to broadcasting policy. Thereafter policy developed under the auspices of a special Cabinet Committee, the members of which included Thatcher, the Home Secretary, the Secretary of State at the DTI and the Chancellor of the Exchequer. Nigel Lawson noted how this Committee 'occupied a surprising amount of my time in 1987'. Thatcher ceded to Lawson the chairing of meetings of key ministers between full meetings of the Committee. Neither Lawson, nor his friend Samuel Brittan, were in any doubt about the importance of the Peacock report for policy development. Lawson felt that:

> The main long term impact of Peacock was to give a push to technological developments already in train. In terms of immediate policy, its two most important recommendations concerned the licence fee and access to the viewing public for independent programme makers.

Brittan considered that the report's immediate influence was felt in the establishment of the Cabinet Committee, the publication of the Green Paper on radio, the extension of ITV franchises to 1992 to allow for legislation, the DTI review of cable policy and the Home Office-commissioned report on subscription. Both Lawson and Brittan had a close and firm grasp of the report's significance for policy development and their general point, that the report was not sidelined and did have a major influence on policy is essentially correct.[7]

The DTI and the Home Office

The development of policy after Peacock continued to be affected by divisions within the state over the nature and pace of change. These divisions manifested themselves in the form of differences between politicians, Hurd against Thatcher, Young and Tebbit, as well as between politicians and civil servants in different departments. From 1979 Thatcher had used her power of appointment to develop a departmental counterweight to the traditionalism of the Home Office – witness her use of the Department of Industry in the promotion of cable in the early 1980s. After the 1987 election she intensified this process by appointing David Young as Secretary of State at the DTI where he used his position to battle against Home Office traditionalism and promote free-market policy options for broadcasting.

The tensions this move generated provided the context in which policy developed at Cabinet level. The Treasury's role was important. Lawson sat on the Cabinet Committee and chaired meetings of ministers on the subject. This reflected the role of the Treasury in guarding its departmental interest in the economic implications of any changes in the structure of broadcasting. In addition Lawson was clearly sympathetic to the broad direction of Peacock's proposals and was critical of Home Office traditionalism. But policy details were the remit of the Home Office and the DTI. The role of Thatcher and Lawson on the Committee seems to have been to reinforce pressure exerted by the DTI on Home Office ministers and civil servants to come up with market-orientated policies. None of the participants in this process, including Hurd, ever expressed publicly the view that market forces should not be allowed increasingly to shape broadcasting policy. What we are tracking here are differences on pace and degree, not of principle. In the end politicians and civil servants were all prepared to see broadcasting gradually swamped by a sea of market forces.[8]

After the 1979 general election Keith Joseph, a key figure in the development of what later became know as Thatcherite policy, was appointed to the Department of Industry. According to Lawson:

> Keith was the founder-member of the group of Tory radicals which, under Margaret's leadership, were the Government's driving force during the first two Thatcher parliaments. The only other full members of that group were Geoffrey Howe, Norman Tebbit and myself.

Soon after David Young was appointed as an unpaid, part-time industrial adviser to Joseph who tried to educate his civil servants into thinking the way he did on economic policy. Young has described Joseph's method:

> I was not really there at the beginning when Keith Joseph first handed down his reading list of about a dozen books. They went from Adam Smith and De Tocqueville to Sam Brittan and Keith himself. Peter Jay was included ... that was the method that Keith chose to ensure that his civil servants made policy suggestions along lines that were likely to be acceptable to him and his colleagues.

The Department of Industry was the seat of radical Thatcherite industrial policy in the early 1980s. In 1983 it merged with the Department of Trade to become the Department of Trade and Industry. The DTI nurtured the ministerial careers of three of Thatcher's closest allies, Cecil Parkinson, Norman Tebbit and David Young. Tebbit replaced Parkinson as Secretary of State in October 1983 when Parkinson resigned and held the post until 1985. He was succeeded by Leon Brittan who held the post until he was forced to resign over the Westland affair in 1986. David Young was appointed after the June 1987 election. Once in place Young appointed his long-time associate, Jeffrey Sterling of P&O ferries, as a special adviser.[9]

The 1983 White Paper on cable was seen at the time as evidence that the 'free market sentiments which, for the most part, informed the Hunt Report have overridden Home Office caution'. The Department of Industry played a key role in this area developing policy on information technology, cable and satellite. In 1983 Home Office control over spectrum management was ceded to the Department of Industry. In January 1988 the IT division of the DTI was given 'an overall brief for broadcasting as an industry'. The Department of Industry and its

successor the DTI played an increasingly important role in shaping broadcasting policy as the decade proceeded. This became even more apparent
after 1987 and in the development of policy for the 1988 White Paper
on broadcasting.[10]

Tensions between the Home Office and the Department of Industry
surfaced early. In 1981 the Department of Industry's Minister for IT,
Kenneth Baker, pressed the BBC to become involved in satellite broadcasting, a move which the Home Secretary at the time, Whitelaw, advised
the BBC against. In 1982, when Baker wanted to arrange a Downing
Street seminar on computing and electronic communications: 'The Prime
Minister was keen, but I had to square the Home Office, which had
responsibility for broadcasting and guarded this fiefdom jealously.'

By 1983 a large number of illegal pirate radio stations were transmitting. The IBA, the BBC and the Home Office wanted the DTI to
use its powers to close them down. But the DTI was not keen to do
this. In August 1984 the AIRC's Director, Brian West, reported that
Kenneth Baker had told the IBA, the AIRC and the Home Office that
the DTI had no enthusiasm for using its powers to crack down on the
pirates through its specialist Radio Communications division. West
pointed out that, although the Home Office wanted a crack down, Hurd,
then a junior minister, had indicated that 'the Home Office only has
words; the DTI has troops'.

In November a couple of reports revealed the underlying reason for
the delay in closing down the pirates. Norman Tebbit, a supporter of
the deregulation of radio, was, as Secretary of State at the DTI, putting
pressure on the Home Office:

> Mr Leon Brittan, Home Secretary and barrister, is believed to be
> concerned at the DTI's apparent lack of urgency in tackling the issue.
> Mr Norman Tebbit, Trade and Industry Secretary, is known to be
> a supporter of neighbourhood radio and free competition.

Even the Attorney General, Sir Michael Havers, was believed by some
ILR executives, the IBA and Leon Brittan to be 'puzzled by the DTI's
lack of despatch in dealing with pirates'.[11]

Young was appointed to the DTI in 1987 and his brief clearly
included pressing for a more commercially orientated broadcasting
policy. As one commentator suggested, it 'was probably for that reason
that Margaret Thatcher positioned him as a counter to Mr Hurd, whom
she would suspect of less commercially rigorous tendencies'.

The period after the 1987 election until the announcement of the White Paper on broadcasting in November 1988 was one in which the Home Office under Hurd and the DTI under Young negotiated over the details of broadcasting policy.

According to Thatcher when it came to the issue of the quota of independent productions on the BBC and ITV:

> there was a sharp division between those of us like Nigel Lawson and David Young who believed that the BBC and ITV would use every opportunity to resist this and Douglas Hurd and Willie Whitelaw who thought that they could be persuaded without legislation. Douglas was to enter into discussion with the broadcasters and report back. In the end we had to legislate to secure it.

She stated that she 'would have liked to privatize' Channel 4, 'though Douglas Hurd disagreed'. She was also:

> pressing for the phasing out of the BBC licence fee altogether to be announced in that document [the White Paper]. But Douglas was against this and a powerful lobby on behalf of the BBC built up. In the end I agreed to drop my insistence on it and on the privatization of Channel 4.

In January 1988 Young's hand was strengthened when the Information Technology division of the DTI was given 'an overall brief for broadcasting as an industry'. It was Young's long-standing business associate and special adviser, Jeffrey Sterling, who organised the series of breakfast discussions on broadcasting policy with interested parties such as Rupert Murdoch. In June 1988 Young and Hurd in a 'hastily-summoned meeting' with Chairman of the IBA Lord Thomson and Maramaduke Hussey, unveiled plans to move Channel 4 and BBC2 onto satellite. The initiative, it appears, was Young's and in the end came to nothing. But, in the eyes of one observer, it helped 'to explain the hasty announcement' made in May 'delaying plans for a White Paper on Broadcasting from this summer until the autumn'. It was an expression of the pressure Young was exerting on Hurd and his officials to make the White Paper a radical set of proposals. Hurd, it appears, gave way under this pressure. According to one source, 'There came a point when Douglas pulled away from his officials, and realised that they were living in a world of the past.'

In the agreement reached in the Cabinet Committee, Hurd obtained a commitment on safeguarding the quality of programmes and on limiting cross-ownership. Young, among other things, achieved auctioning for the ITV franchises and less protection for Channel 4 – both recommended by Peacock. Hurd and Young agreed that the licence fee should be phased out.

This account over simplifies a complex process in which other people, notably Lawson and Thatcher, played key roles. But it illustrates how tensions within the government and between civil servants in different departments had an impact on policy development. Young confirms this, although he plays down his differences with Hurd:

> I sat in the committee dealing with the future of broadcasting for over a year. It was a very amicable committee, although I kept reading in the papers about the battles that I was fighting with Douglas Hurd, the then Home Secretary. Once again the reality was very different. All the papers assumed that I would be violently against the BBC, quite forgetting that Stuart had been Chairman. If I did have a difference with Douglas we would meet and agree a way through in minutes. Our officials, on the other hand, did fight considerable turf battles. DTI was there because we were responsible for the radio spectrum, the Home Office because they were responsible for broad-casting. In any more sensible world we would have exchanged responsibilities, or else both would have been with the DTI, for the Home Office knew little of the commercial realities of television and radio. In the end we reached a sensible compromise, although the existing television companies did not think so at the time.[12]

After Peacock: a World Fit for Money

The decisions taken after 1986 gradually reshaped the whole framework of broadcasting policy. Changes in policy towards commercial broad-casting affected the BBC by altering the environment in which the Corporation had to operate. Here we focus on the decisions which had implications for the BBC. In Chapter 8 we describe how policy related to developments within the BBC.

The Peat Marwick Mitchell report had been commissioned by Leon Brittan to meet two objectives: to placate colleagues who were critical of the BBC and to establish a benchmark for the development of policy towards the BBC. The policy which emerged seems to have been based on an understanding that the BBC would take on board the criticisms in the Peat Marwick Mitchell report in return for a broad Home Office defence of the licence fee. For the BBC this meant acknowledging Peat Marwick's criticisms of the Corporations's lack of clear policy objectives and of the way it ran its ancillary services (catering, transport, design and graphics). It also meant accepting the need to promote cost-cutting and efficiency and to start contracting out some of its in-house activities.

This strategy was reasserted by Hurd in the run up to the publication of Peacock. It basically sought to promote internal, market-driven reforms while eschewing rapid changes in the basic structure and finance of the organisation. This was the position adopted by the Home Office and in essence by the government after the Peacock inquiry. It was modified by pressure from Thatcher, Tebbit and the right who pressed for a new set of managers in the BBC to implement change. The Home Office acknowledged the need to change and hawks in and around the government won some significant alterations at the BBC. At the same time the Home Office moved more quickly to reform commercial broadcasting. This had major implications for the BBC.[13]

The Home Office still sought to modify the pace and direction of some of the changes and struggled, in the face of pressure from Downing Street and the DTI, to maintain its leading role in the process. Home Office's activity in the run up to publication of the Peacock report illustrates this. It clearly saw its role as dampening public and political expectations around the report. In the run up to publication, according to Milne, there were 'leaks of every kind, most of them uncomplimentary, about the report from Government sources. It was thoroughly rubbished.'

One consequence of the establishment of the Cabinet Committee to explore Peacock was the decision, announced in late June 1986, to cancel the community radio experiment set up in 1985 by Leon Brittan. The Home Office had not been keen on allowing the pirates to flourish. The package around Peacock, which involved looking at the whole field of deregulation in commercial broadcasting, gave the Home Office the opportunity to press for the cancellation of the experiment pending discussions in Committee. On 1 July Hurd told the AIRC that the community radio experiment would be dropped and the future of radio considered in the light of the recommendations in the Peacock report. This was welcomed by the AIRC which had lobbied against the experiment on the grounds that the new, under regulated stations, would provide unfair competition.[14]

In the House of Commons Hurd struck the same cautious note. He welcomed Peacock's findings on advertising but asserted that 'before reaching any conclusions the Government would welcome comments on the committee's analysis', and that it would 'reach final views on the report only in the light of parliamentary and public reaction'.

He announced that the government would discuss auctioning ITV franchises with the IBA, but that the forthcoming DBS contract would not, as Peacock recommended, be allocated by tender. Echoing Thatcher's known position he rejected out of hand proposals to lift controls on programme content because 'the peculiarly intrusive nature of broadcasting and in particular television, continue to require special regulatory arrangement to ensure standards in broadcast services'. Peacock's recommendations on radio would be looked at in the light of a consultative Green Paper which would examine further services at national, local and community level as well as 'the future of BBC radio services and ... those provided by the IBA'. He recognised 'merit' in many of Peacock's Stage 1 short-term recommendations and singled out 'the recommendation to increase the proportion of television programmes supplied by independent producers. The best way of achieving this will need careful consideration.'

These were the only points he chose to extract from the report. In questions he indicated that the government had not agreed to Peacock's proposal to link the licence fee to the RPI, but would 'look carefully at the question of subscription'. In his comments he outlined the basis of the compromise agreed at Cabinet. While the report's overall analysis fitted well into 'our philosophy' and would be looked 'back on as the necessary stimulus to the next stage of British Broadcasting', the government would review its recommendations in the light of further analysis. The centre of policy-making, he signalled, would shift from the BBC to the commercial sector, and to policies affecting the overall structure of broadcasting.[15]

Thereafter Home Office ministers Shaw and Hurd had to repeat that, contrary to Press speculation, the report's recommendations had not been shelved.[16] However, the intial briefing issued by the Home Office had the effect of signalling that far-reaching decisions would not be reached speedily. As we have seen, a committee of ministers was set up to review the future of broadcasting and, in addition, a committee of senior civil servants met to discuss Peacock. The plans for a Green Paper on radio had been announced and a report into subscription television was commissioned by the Home Office. By August 1986 it was clear that the Home Office was moving towards accepting the recommendation in Peacock on indexing the licence fee to the RPI.[17]

On 20 November Hurd announced to the House of Commons that the licence fee would remain at £58 until April 1988. This extended the March 1985 decision by one year, tightened the financial squeeze on the BBC and postponed a rerun of the debate over the licence fee until after the general election which was expected in 1987. He expressed sympathy for the idea of indexing the licence fee to the RPI. In addition he stated that he would enter into discussions with the BBC and the IBA about their plans to move towards accepting 25 per cent of their programmes from independent producers – a policy advocated by the DTI.[18] This announcement coincided with the assault on BBC management led by Tebbit discussed in Chapter 4.

A further decision on the licence fee was announced in January 1987. The fee was to be increased in line with movements in the RPI for three years from 1 April 1988. This tightened the squeeze on the BBC, as broadcasting inflation ran ahead of inflation in the economy as a whole. That same month the Green Paper on radio was issued. It contained proposals to expand commercial radio leaving the BBC system ostensibly intact. But the proposed changes were designed to result in a massive increase in the number of commercial stations which would make it harder for the BBC to justify its continued presence in local and national radio.[19] By the end of January Milne had been sacked. The two main strands of government policy on the BBC after Peacock, a financial squeeze and a change in the BBC's management team were now established.

After the 1987 election the main focus of activity was the preparation of legislation for commercial broadcasting. In March 1988 the government announced an inquiry into alleged restrictive practices by trades unions in the film and TV industry. This move was prompted, in part, by Mrs Thatcher's antipathy towards trades unions and the need to put pressure on ITV managers and unions in the run up to changing the system. It put trades unions in the BBC under added pressure at a time when they were having to respond to a growing assault by managers on their members' pay, conditions of service and job security. In May 1988 Hurd formally announced that a new body – the Broadcasting Standards Council – would be established to monitor standards in broadcasting. This seemed to be designed to decrease the autonomy of broadcasters, the BBC Governors and the IBA in programming matters.[20]

Communications Studies and Planning International, the consultants employed by the Home Office, issued their report on *Subscription Television* in May 1988. The Peacock report's long-term recommendations on subscription were not based on any detailed or systematic research. The CSP report rejected the idea of the BBC's becoming a pay-per-view service immediately, on the grounds that it would not be cost effective. But the CSP report argued that subscription should be gradually introduced on terrestrial services.[21]

The Home Affairs Select Committee

In December 1987 the Conservative-dominated Home Affairs Select Committee initiated a study on the future of broadcasting. Its report was published in July 1988. The tone of this report reflected a commitment to phased deregulation, along the lines advocated by the Home Office, but deregulation nonetheless. The comments on the BBC in the report reflected the position adopted by the government. The new management at the BBC had 'adopted a positive stance towards the expanding competitive television market'. This orientation meant that the Corporation's managers, unlike the regime under Milne, were more modest in their aspirations:

> In contrast to the recent past, the BBC now accepts that its current remit to operate two channels of television as well as four radio networks and regional and local radio is a sufficient contribution to broadcasting although it welcomes the opportunity to exploit sales of programmes skills, and other resources to new services. We welcome this realistic approach ...

On top of this the Committee implicitly acknowledged that the post-Milne shake-out led by Hussey should be given time to work: 'The Governors have only recently appointed a new Director General and his changes in the administrative structure of the Corporation are still working through.'

Given all this, it considered that 'subject to some detailed proposals made below, we recommend no change in the basic role and regulatory function of the BBC'. This, in effect, endorsed government policy on the BBC.[22]

The more cautious approach of the Home Office was evident in some of the other recommendations. In advocating that 'public service broadcasting should be an integral part of the new broadcasting environment' the Committee was pushing the concept back to the centre from the margins where it had been relegated by Peacock. In recommending that a 'prerequisite of any financial and institutional arrangements must be that the British Television industry can continue to sustain and develop its programme-making capacity' it was asserting a principle of protectionism at odds with the philosophy of Peacock, the DTI and the government. It openly criticised the proposal, promoted by Lord Young, to put BBC2 and Channel 4 onto satellite, concluding that there were 'good reasons to doubt the prospects of obtaining wide coverage of BBC 2 and Channel 4 on satellite'.

Yet the Committee was happy to endorse proposals which promoted a more market-orientated, commercially conscious broadcasting system. It supported 'the target of 25 per cent of programmes made by independent producers shown on the BBC and ITV to be achieved by 1992', a move which in reality meant a further squeeze on costs and jobs at the BBC. Its recommendation that in 'the medium term, at least, the BBC should continue to be financed by means of the licence fee indexed to the retail price index' was yet another endorsement of this freeze. Hurd gave a spin to this recommendation and to the report's generally favourable attitude to subscription by announcing on the day the report was published that he wanted to see the BBC move towards subscription in the 1990s. The Committee also accepted, implicitly, the case for making the BBC less dependent on the licence fee by supporting the 'responsible introduction of sponsorship of BBC programmes in the field of arts and sport'.[23]

The report reflected the divisions in policy discussed above. It reproduced strong versions of traditionalist concerns about quality, public service broadcasting and UK production capacity. At the same time it endorsed government policy on the BBC and moves towards a more market-orientated broadcasting system. The report gave a parliamentary stamp of approval to policy as it had developed since 1986 and showed little evidence of the coherence or independence of thought needed to do anything else. One major function of the report was to provide Hurd and others with material they could use to support the proposals made in the White Paper later that year.

The White Paper 1988

In the run up to the production of the White Paper, tensions over the BBC resurfaced among ministers preparing the document. As a result of pressures on the Home Office from the Treasury the White Paper contained references to the BBC's taking subscription services. The original draft of the government publication hardly mentioned the BBC, but the final document is likely to emphasise the need for the BBC to find alternative sources of income and to repeat the warning delivered by Mr Douglas Hurd, Home Secretary, that the current licence fee is not 'immortal'.

According to one report this reflected a wider set of concessions by Hurd who, under pressure from Young, had 'gradually overcome the reluctance of his Home Office officials to open the broadcasting world to greater competition'.[24]

The White Paper, *Broadcasting in the '90s: Competition Choice and Quality*, was published on 7 November 1988. The proposals reflected a major shift towards allowing the market to shape the development of broadcasting. The proposed new regulatory environment would clearly exert pressure on BBC audiences and income once in place. Moreover, in time, it would call the licence fee and the BBC's interpretation of public service broadcasting into question:

> The government agrees with the Home Affairs Committee that the BBC 'is still, and will remain for the foreseeable future, the cornerstone of British broadcasting' ... This does not mean that the BBC has to involve itself in every aspect of broadcasting, or that it should be insulated from change.

On efficiency the White Paper commended Peacock's observations and, like the Home Affairs Select Committee, endorsed the government policy of encouraging internal reform in the BBC:

> The Corporation has started on a process of tightening its management structure and shifting resources into programme improvements through savings elsewhere. There is scope for further progress. The BBC's pursuit of efficiency has been reinforced by the Government's decision, described in Chapter X, to refer possible restrictive labour practices in television and film production to the Monopolies and Mergers Commission.

The White Paper boasted about the 'squeeze' provoked by the government's decision to index link the licence fee to the RPI.

> In effect the Government has applied a double squeeze. Inflation in the broadcasting industry has generally run ahead of the RPI; and

the notional base figure on which the 1988 licence fee was calculated represented less than the actual level of spending for which the BBC had budgeted. This squeeze has encouraged the BBC to target its activities more effectively.

On subscription the government broadly endorsed Peacock's position:

The Government intends to encourage the progressive introduction of subscription on the BBC's television services … The Government accordingly proposes to authorise the BBC to encrypt its services so that it can raise money through subscription … the BBC will have in mind the objective of replacing the licence fee. To provide a financial incentive the Government intends after April 1991 to agree licence fee increases of less than the RPI increase in a way which takes account of the BBC's capacity to generate income from subscription.

While the White Paper rejected Peacock's proposal that all the BBC's night hours should be sold off it did so on the assumption that the BBC would use the channels it retained 'as fully as possible for developing subscription services'. It remained reluctant to accept the Peacock and the Home Affairs Select Committee's recommendation that all new television sets should have peritelevision sockets fitted. It preferred that the industry should fit 'suitable connectors as standard equipment without the need for compulsion; but it will keep the question of a mandatory requirement under review'.

The White Paper recognised the BBC's acceptance of the government's independent programme target and viewed this acceptance as a 'further stimulus for change'. It stated that the BBC would be covered by the new Broadcasting Standards Council and the provisions of the 1959 Obscene Publications Act. The BBC had, 'after discussions' with the government, agreed to 'less restrictive arrangements for the broadcast coverage of sponsored events, such as arts and sports events'. The BBC and the IBA's transmission facilities were to be privatised.

The White Paper repeated the details of the by then well established strategy of internal reform adopted by the government in 1986; new management, efficiency savings, cuts in licence fee income and a push towards subscription. It also redefined the BBC as the only major provider of public service broadcasting within a new framework of intensified commercial competition.[25]

Alasdair Milne felt that the White Paper bore 'all the hallmarks of the continuing struggle between the Department of Trade and Industry

and the Home Office that has characterised this government's approach
to broadcasting'. He noted the 'gleeful' tone of the White Paper's
reference to a 'double squeeze' and that the government had rejected
'the advice of its own consultant, who argued cogently that the licence
fee should not be replaced by subscription'. He felt the White Paper
'bids fair to do a demolition job on public service broadcasting in this
country'.[26]

In the debate on the White Paper in February 1989 Hurd repeated
the assertion made in the document that 'the BBC will ... remain the
cornerstone of public sector broadcasting'. But he pushed forward by
five years some of the big questions such as the BBC's ability to raise
money by subscription and the future of BBC radio to the debate on
the renewal of the BBC's Charter, which expired in 1996. It was a view
former Labour Home Secretary Merlyn Rees challenged: 'It is hard to
accept that the Home Secretary is speaking in good faith when he says
that the BBC is the "cornerstone" of broadcasting, because, by his actions
he clearly intends to demolish it.' He argued that pushing the BBC down
the road of subscription and other commercial-revenue-generating
activities could 'never be more than a useful top-up of revenues if the
BBC's role as the "cornerstone" of broadcasting is to be secured'.[27]

The Broadcasting Bill was published in December 1989 and, in its
proposals on the BBC, did not differ from the policy established in the
White Paper. Hurd had by then been replaced by David Waddington
in a reshuffle precipitated by the resignation of Thatcher's Chancellor,
Nigel Lawson. Renton had been replaced by Mellor as Minister of State
responsible for broadcasting.[28]

The 1990 Broadcasting Act recast the environment in which the BBC
had to operate. It created a relatively deregulated commercial TV,
satellite, cable and radio sector. One effect of this new environment
would be the erosion of the BBC's audience share. It left the BBC and
Channel 4 as the only mainstream broadcasters with the sort of public
service broadcasting obligations which had been embodied in the 1981
Broadcasting Act and which previously had been imposed on all TV
and radio organisations. It placed the BBC's internal organisation under
pressure by formalising, in law, the obligation to take 25 per cent of its
output from independent producers. The government had left the
BBC organisationally intact, but on the understanding that the changes
already under way in the BBC and those which flowed from the Act
would radically transform the Corporation's size and role in the future.
The government placed a further squeeze on the BBC in October 1990.
It announced it would be moving from a system (1988–91) of tying

the licence fee to the RPI to one, from April 1991, of setting the fee below the RPI – just as the White Paper had predicted.[29]

In November 1990 Mrs Thatcher fell from power as result of an internal coup in the Parliamentary Conservative Party, provoked by a combination of popular discontent with her policies, especially the popular revolt over the Poll Tax, dissatisfaction with her style of government, and her policy on Europe. The government under John Major which succeeded her inherited her Broadcasting Bill as well as the regime of management and the policy on the BBC. By November 1990 her government had established the direction of change for the BBC. The major debates around the BBC and government policy as they emerged in the early stages of the debate on the renewal of the BBC Charter in 1991 and 1992 were shaped by the developments outlined in this book.[30]

The basic agenda for broadcasting policy after 1986 was set by the Peacock report. The policy was developed within the context of minor divisions between ministers and their departments which reflected different perspectives on the nature and pace, but not the direction, of change. The often conflicting signals coming from government after 1986 reflected ongoing differences over aspects of that change. Overall, pressure on the BBC was intensified by the imposition of management changes, a financial squeeze, the imposition of the 25 per cent quota and the changes in the commercial sector embodied in the 1990 Act.

This process of external pressure on the BBC had begun before 1986 but was intensified from the summer of that year. This is the framework in which policy towards the BBC developed between 1979 and 1992. What were the impacts of these policies during these years?

8 The BBC under Thatcher

This chapter traces some of the key developments within the BBC between 1979 and 1992. It describes the way the BBC responded to an increasingly hostile government and the way that government gradually replaced the Governors and senior managers of the Corporation in order to alter the politics and goals of the organisation.

The Governors

The 1981 Royal Charter which came into force on 1 August 1981 specified that there should be twelve governors including a Chair and Vice Chair. The relationship between the Governors, the government and BBC managers had often been the subject of internal and external controversy. The rights and duties of the governors have, in practice, been interpreted differently at different periods in the history of the Corporation. Governors had always been chosen from the people who supported the political and economic disposition of power in society and who were usually from very privileged backgrounds which were thoroughly unrepresentative of society as a whole. Between 1970 and 1989, 79 per cent of BBC governors were men, 56 per cent had been privately educated and 49 per cent had attended Oxford or Cambridge.[1] During the period 1981 to 1990 the Governors became a powerful force in changing the face of the BBC.

George Howard, a friend of Whitelaw, was Chairman of the Board of Governors from August 1980 until August 1983. He had been appointed a Governor in 1972 by the Heath government and was a product of an appointments system which had traditionally honoured parliamentary political divisions and had, in that narrow sense, been bipartisan. Regardless of the political party in power, appointments to the Board of Governors had always been calculated to maintain a balance of party political interests on the Board. This convention was breached under Mrs Thatcher.

The decision on who was to succeed Howard was taken in 1982 while Whitelaw was still at the Home Office. In retrospect it seems that the successor was chosen to balance the interests of the Home Office, the BBC and Mrs Thatcher. The man chosen was Stuart Young, an accountant from Mrs Thatcher's North London constituency and brother of her close political ally, David Young. Young had been appointed a governor from 1 August 1981 and on appointment had allegedly criticised the licence fee. But he had grown attached to the organisation. His brother, David Young, commenting on Stuart's career as Chairman, reports how he 'loved the BBC with a passion that fulfilled his days'.

George Howard became 'keen that … Stuart take over from him' and there was support for Young from senior managers at the BBC. By March 1983, a matter of months before the general election, Whitelaw offered Young the post. It was a shrewd move. Whatever his attachments to the Prime Minister, Young proved to be a staunch defender of the BBC's traditional position during his period as Chairman from 1983 until his premature death in 1986. It was alleged at the time that Downing Street believed Young had been captured by the BBC. Young's appointment was made at a time when the authority of Whitelaw as Home Secretary ensured a degree of continuity in the succession. All Home Secretaries after Whitelaw owed their advance primarily to Thatcher and this meant that when the issue of a successor to Young came up in 1986 the appointment reflected to a much greater extent Mrs Thatcher's personal preferences.[2]

There was tension between Hurd and Thatcher over Young's successor. Reports circulated that Mrs Thatcher wanted her ally, businessman Lord King, while Hurd wanted a more emollient character. Mrs Thatcher's stamp was on the final choice. Marmaduke Hussey came from outside the BBC. He had worked as Managing Director of Thomson newspapers, owners of *The Times*, from 1971 to 1980, and as a Director of Times Newspapers under Rupert Murdoch from 1982 to 1986. He was a friend of William Rees-Mogg, Deputy Chairman of the Governors from 1981 to 1986, with whom he had worked at *The Times*. A source in Norman Tebbit's office said at the time that Hussey's role at the BBC would be to 'sort it out'. Although the appointment of controversial figures to this post was not without precedent, the appointment came at a time of major crisis in BBC–government relations when senior Cabinet members were clearly bent on changing the style, if not the personnel, of BBC management.

It also came after seven years in which Downing Street-driven appointments to governorships had broken with convention, stacking the deck with people seen to be on the right of the political spectrum. There had been a growing estrangement between senior BBC managers and the Board during this period.[3]

There is no doubt that the relationship between the BBC Board of Governors and its senior managers deteriorated seriously in the years 1982–6. Rees-Mogg commented in 1986, shortly after his term on the Board had ended: 'The BBC is a nonsense held together by tradition … The main fault is the relationship between the Governors and the management.' This view was shared, from a different perspective, by one of Milne's senior executives, Brian Wenham:

> Milne, in his memoirs rather played down the appalling atmosphere of these times … The unvarnished truth was that a sizeable faction of the board wanted rid of Milne and his chief editorial associates but could not bring themselves to strike. So they merely wounded, damagingly so for the BBC, whose wounds were then further exposed to the turning of the Tory knife.[4]

This deterioration was a result of the range of policies pursued at government level against the BBC. One of these was to place on the BBC Board of Governors people deemed to be politically acceptable to Mrs Thatcher, breaking with the convention of bipartisan appointments. There was no breach with the practice of appointing governors secretly, in an undemocratic fashion from a list of people deemed acceptable to the government and civil service. But those appointed, in the eyes of many, tended to reflect right-of-centre Toryism. As one writer put it in 1986:

> It is no coincidence that the Board of governors has been lately unbalanced by appointees with Right of Centre sympathies … Although governors are officially nominated by the Home Secretary, it is no secret that recent appointments have been vetoed by No 10.

The result of this, according to Milne, was that the Governors grew apart from their managers whom they saw as a 'liberal elite who dominated the news and, particularly, the current affairs output'.[5]

Table 8.1 BBC Governors at 31 March 1982 and 31 March 1985, with Dates of Appointment

1982

George Howard	(as Governor)	Feb. 1972
	(as Chairman)	Aug. 1980
Sir William Rees-Mogg		Aug. 1981
	Vice Chairman	
Lady Faulkner		Oct. 1978
Dr Roger Young		Oct. 1979
Alwyn Roberts		Oct. 1979
Lord Allen of Fallowfield		Dec. 1976
Baroness Serota of Hampstead		Aug. 1981
Sir John Johnston		Dec. 1978
Prof. Christopher Longuet-Higgins		Aug. 1979
Miss Jocelyn Barrow		Feb. 1981
Mr Stuart Young		Aug. 1981
Mr Peter Moores		Aug. 1981

1985

Stuart Young	Chairman from	Aug. 1983
Sir W. Rees-Mogg		Aug. 1981
	Vice Chairman	
Lady Faulkner *a*		Oct. 1978
Alwyn Roberts		Oct. 1979
Watson Peat		Aug. 1984
Sir J. Johnston *a*		Dec. 1978
Jocelyn Barrow		Feb. 1981
Daphne Park		Aug. 1982
Sir John Boyd		Nov. 1982
Malcolm McAlpine		Aug. 1983
Lady Parkes JP		Aug. 1984
Earl of Harwood		Jan. 1985

a Faulkner and Johnson retired on 31 July 1985.
Source: Adapted from BBC, *Annual Report and Handbook 1983* (BBC, 1982), p. xii; and *Annual Report and Handbook 1986* (BBC, 1985), p. viii.

The Board of 31 March 1982 already had a majority of appointments made under the post-1979 Thatcher administration. One survived from the Heath government of 1970–4, four from the Labour government of 1974–9 and seven from Mrs Thatcher. By 1985 all but two of the governors had been appointed under Mrs Thatcher. The nature of some of these appointments were controversial. Sir John Boyd although a trades unionist was recognised as being on the right of the movement. Daphne Park, a governor who wanted to suppress both the *Real Lives* and *Zircon* programmes, had been a senior officer in the secretive, highly controversial and unaccountable government spying agency MI6. In the same period Thatcher is reported to have vetoed candidates whom she did not consider politically suitable. Writing in 1992 Milne criticised the failure of the Thatcher governments to appoint a wider spectrum of opinion on the board:

Not that there was much balance in the selection by Mrs Thatcher's Government. When you end up with people like the late Sir John Boyd, Lord Barnett and Bill Jordan, purporting to represent left-of-centre views, the board's political hue needs urgent attention.[6]

William Rees-Mogg played a pivotal role as a known Conservative supporter and Vice Chairman from 1981 to 1986. As editor of *The Times* he had played a role in giving the ideas of the IEA a wide hearing in the 1960s and 1970s. Milne believed that Mogg was 'at times factious against the management'. There can be little doubt that Mogg was highly critical of BBC management. In 1986, after he had retired as Vice Chairman he attacked the BBC using language reminiscent of the attack made on the BBC by D'Arcy MacManus Masius in 1984. It echoed the rhetoric of 'enterprise' so central to the Thatcher administrations: 'The large BBC bureaucracy lacks anything one could call an enterprise culture. Indeed it has a bias against commercialism, except in terms of the quasi commercial pursuit of television ratings.'

Under Thatcher then, the Board was stacked to the right. Liberal Peer Lord Bonham Carter was a governor of the BBC in the 1970s. His view of what happened in the 1980s was unequivocal:

Of course, I was a political person. But in those days things were different: appointments had to be consensual. There was balanced politicization. Now, it's unbalanced politicization. What was unique about the BBC governors in the eighties was that you had Rees-Mogg as vice-chairman and Stuart Young as chairman – two open, committed supporters of the present Government. That had never ever happened in the whole history of the Corporation. They had simply abandoned balance.

But Stuart Young did become opposed to aspects of Thatcher's approach to the BBC and, towards the end of his life, wanted appointments to the Board to be less controversial. David Young recounts how in 1986 Stuart 'was very concerned to remove the BBC from the political arena' and wanted a figure associated with Labour to fill the position vacated by Mogg. The person he wanted, according to his brother, was Joel Barnett, a former Labour Cabinet minister.[7]

Satellites

The shifting political climate in which the BBC operated from 1979 can be illustrated by an examination of the relationship between the Corporation and the government over the issue of Direct Broadcasting by Satellite (DBS). This story shows how government policy towards the BBC's expansion into satellite gradually changed between 1981 and 1985. Between 1981 and 1983 it supported the expansion of the BBC into satellite, although on terms partly dictated by commercial considerations. After 1983 policy hardened towards the BBC in general and this had an impact on its involvement in DBS. The BBC's involvement in DBS fed the growing public criticism of the Corporation after 1983, provoking attacks in the national press which accused the BBC of expansion for expansion's sake. The Corporation's failure to become involved in satellite at this point was due, ultimately, to the government's growing reluctance to fund public service broadcasting's expansion into satellite.

In 1977 [8] the World Administrative Radio Conference allocated the UK five channels which could be used for DBS broadcast systems. A Home Office study group was set up in March 1980 to investigate the subject, a clear indication that the initiative lay with the Home Office. The IBA showed an interest in these developments from the outset and in January 1982 made a bid to the Home Office to provide some of these services. But in 1981 Kenneth Baker, then at the Department of Industry, invited the BBC to bid for a stake. Whitelaw privately urged caution on Howard. The BBC's new Charter of 1981 'had been brought up to date in a way which authorises the BBC's fullest participation in all the possibilities opened up by the advent of new communications technology'.

According to Milne the BBC needed to be involved in the new technology of satellite because it would one day replace terrestrial transmission allowing the BBC to deliver 'different programme opportunities' and to provide, through subscription or pay-per-view, 'additional money that might help to reduce the necessary increments in the licence fee which seemed to be a growing political worry'. So with a Charter allowing it, a management in support of the move, and a sponsoring department guiding developments as well as the support of a minister in the Thatcherite Department of Industry, there appeared to be every reason for the BBC to get involved.[9]

In March 1982 Whitelaw announced that the first of five DBS channels would go to the BBC. The service was planned to start in 1986. The remaining three channels were to be allocated 'as and when demand justified it'. The BBC's Charter allowed the Corporation to participate in DBS while the 1981 Broadcasting Act only empowered the IBA to provide terrestrial services. The capital costs of the satellite system were to be raised from the private sector. This decision, that the costs were to be met by the market, represented a break with previous practice in which the capital costs of BBC TV and radio had been met from the licence fee. This represented a stiff dose of Thatcherite economics which had been inserted into the Home Office. The IBA continued to lobby for the allocation of the remaining three DBS channels.

Early in 1983 the BBC signed up with United Satellites (Unisat), a consortium of UK firms including BT, British Aerospace and Marconi. Unisat was to lease space (two transponders) on its satellite to the BBC for seven years at a cost of £24 million. By the summer of 1983 the BBC was considering dropping its plans to use a British-built satellite in favour of a cheaper American one. Stuart Young had reportedly told the Board of Governors that if the BBC were to continue it would have to press for government finance. The victory of Mrs Thatcher in the June 1983 election had strengthened her position generally and made it less likely that any funding would be forthcoming, especially when cable policy was being ostentatiously promoted as a private sector affair. Whitelaw's replacement at the Home Office, Brittan, was also prepared to listen to pleas from the commercial TV companies that they should be allowed to take part.[10]

Just as the 1983 general election signalled a shift in policy away from open support for the licence fee, so it became increasingly clear that the BBC would have difficulty justifying continuing with a risky project for which it needed to go cap-in-hand to a hostile government. In September

1983 Brittan announced that the IBA would be allowed to issue one or more DBS franchises. In December the government proposed provisions to the Cable and Broadcasting Bill which would have enabled the IBA to appoint DBS programme contractors. This inevitably put a shaky BBC proposition under pressure from prospective intense competition, and it appears that the possibility of a joint IBA–BBC deal on satellite was being proposed to Milne by the autumn of 1983. In December the BBC, according to the IBA, 'after re-evaluation of the economics of the DBS project, approached Government and the IBA to explore possibilities of co-operation'. The BBC needed its licence fee, it had lost Whitelaw at the Home Office and, if it were to remain involved, would have to accept a commercially funded solution.[11]

A period of negotiations followed. In January 1984 a working group was set up comprising the ITCA, the IBA and the BBC. The ITV companies pressed for an extension of their franchise from eight to 15 years as a condition for accepting the joint venture. Within their own camp the ITV companies had difficulty in agreeing. Their reluctance was apparently overcome after the direct intervention of Mrs Thatcher. The deal was reached by 8 May 1984 when the Cable and Broadcasting Bill had its second reading. At this point Brittan announced amendments setting up a consortium under a joint BBC and IBA board, which would negotiate a deal with Unisat. The BBC would have a 50 per cent share, and the ITV companies and other private sector participants would have the other 50 per cent. The channels were to be funded by subscription or, possibly, advertising. The ITV companies were promised that their franchises would not necessarily be readvertised in 1989.[12]

In May 1984 applicants were invited for potential third party involvement in the project. The five successful applicants were announced on 31 July, by which time the BBC was reported to be under pressure from the IBA to reduce its 50 per cent share. The DBS consortium met in August under Milne's chairmanship and, by late October, Leon Brittan had established a Satellite Broadcasting Board to start discussions with the DBS consortium. The SBS had three members each from the BBC and the IBA including Young and Thomson.[13]

A business plan produced for Brittan by the consortium in December 1984 raised doubts about the viability of the project. It recommended that the consortium should not be restricted to purchasing the Unisat system and that the DBS franchise should run for 15 years. The Unisat system was too costly. In March 1985 Milne stressed the financial difficulties posed by the project, arguing that it would be virtually impossible for the BBC to go ahead with the project if the Corporation did not receive an adequate licence fee settlement. In fact the financial obstacles were exacerbated by problems of finalising the technical standards and by the government's desire not to become involved. As Milne put it:

> They would not put one penny of public money towards this kind of venture which they saw as purely commercial ... They did not like the thought that it might fail, but they were not to be harried into a change of policy by the prospect of failure.

In June the project collapsed. The consortium, or Club of 21 as it was known, decided they could not carry on. Lord Thomson laid the blame firmly at the feet of the government's contradictory policies. On the one hand the government refused to provide public money for the project and on the other it intervened and insisted on a particular form of UK satellite technology. He stated that:

> the financial sums did not add up to a viable enterprise. This, I believe, was largely because of two fundamentally contradictory conditions the Government insisted on for this version of a British DBS system. The first was that its financing must be entirely from the private sector, without any element of public funding, unlike almost every other European country. The second was that a particular British consortium set up with Government encouragement should supply the satellite system, and this proved too costly in comparison with the international market place, and too costly for a profitable operation.

The project collapsed, and with it the BBC's direct involvement in UK DBS services. Milne regarded this as 'one of the chief failures in my time as Director General of the BBC'.[14] The UK involvement in DBS was then handed over to the IBA which, in February 1986, was authorised to advertise for programme providers for three DBS services. This process led to a consortium, British Satellite Broadcasting, winning the contract.

The BBC was no longer at the centre of this process. The shift from 1981, when the government encouraged BBC participation, to the 1985 collapse of the Club of 21 had a number of causes. First, the government, Thomson argued, wanted to tie the hands of the consortium by intervening to influence the choice of satellite while at the same time refusing to intervene to help to fund the project. This underlying contradiction had been embedded in the process from the start.

Second, the government's position on the BBC and the role of commerce in broadcasting was hardening between 1981 and 1985. In 1981, although critical of aspects of the BBC and ITV, Thatcher had not developed a general, publicly expressed policy of hostility to the BBC or to public service broadcasting. But by the end of her first term the policy on cable and the beginnings of a reassessment of the BBC were in place. This developed into the orchestrated anti-BBC campaign of 1984. By this time it was politically impossible for the Thatcher government to sanction requests from the BBC and IBA for funding for DBS when its overall stance on the BBC and public service broadcasting had hardened into one of open warfare. If the second Thatcher term had not been characterised by this attack, it is possible that a solution to the funding of the DBS initiative might have been found.

But an additional factor was at work in 1983. This was the move by Rupert Murdoch into cable and satellite. The exact nature of the relationship between Murdoch's activities and the government's cooling towards BBC involvement in DBS is not clear and requires more detailed investigation. However, by 1983 Rupert Murdoch had become involved in the Sky satellite channel and by 1985 he had access to just under 3 million homes in Europe using cable technology. In May 1985 the government relaxed controls on the operation of Satellite Master Antennae TV systems. This allowed blocks of flats, hotels, and groups of houses to erect satellite receiving dishes. The SMATV decision opened up new possibilities for expanding Murdoch's UK market. By 1985 it was clear that the government had created conditions which would allow non-public service operators to establish themselves in the satellite market using low-power, low-cost technology. This could only be at the expense of the Club of 21 and IBA initiatives. The BBC's independent involvement in satellite, had it succeeded, would have provided damaging competition for Murdoch. His papers openly attacked the BBC at a time when his companies were seeking a foothold in satellite. The fact that the government was not prepared to encourage the BBC involvement in DBS after 1983 was consistent with its established support for Murdoch's commercial interests in the media and the intense campaign by Thatcher and Murdoch against the Corporation. The Murdoch factor then, so important in the licence fee debate, may also have played a role in the demise of the Club of 21 and the BBC's involvement in high-powered DBS satellite developments.[15]

BBC Management and the Government 1982–7

It may be that if the leading personalities in the conflict between the BBC and the government had been different then the outcome would also have been different. Milne, although he was 'the first TV professional to become DG', was viewed by Robin Day as someone lacking 'the qualities required in leadership. He was not a natural communicator, he was impatient of slower minds opposed to his, and his political antennae were not sufficiently sensitive.' Similar uncomplimentary things have been said about Mrs Thatcher. Milne may have fared better if he had been a different person but he was faced very early in his tenure of office with a set of hostile political circumstances that would have been almost impossible for any Director General to surmount.[16]

Using the Media

Soon after the 1983 general election BBC managers generated stories for the media stressing the importance of a satisfactory licence fee settlement for the maintenance of BBC services and emphasising the determination of BBC management to retain the licence fee. In October 1983 the head of transmission planning said that the BBC was unlikely to complete moves to all-day broadcasting until the licence fee had been renegotiated in 1985. In March 1984 Milne asserted that the licence fee would be retained because there was neither government intention nor Treasury commitment to change. Later in the year, in July, Milne's special adviser, Stephen Hearst, warned broadcasters, at the annual Radio Festival, of potential cuts in BBC2 and Radio 2 if the licence fee was negotiated at less than £60. As the debate intensified the BBC's house journal *Ariel* was used to provide information to staff in support of the management line.[17]

From October 1984 to March 1985 Milne and Young led a vigorous campaign to defend their bid for a licence fee. It was a high-profile campaign using BBC facilities, interviews with national and trade papers, specially commissioned research, speeches at industry gatherings and private lobbying of civil servants and MPs. Milne defended the BBC fiercely, attacking many of the ideas held by the advocates of change in a manner which cannot have endeared him to Mrs Thatcher.

In October, in an article in *Marketing Week*, Milne replied to the D'Arcy MacManus Masius report and dismissed the case for advertising on the BBC. In November Stuart Young defended the BBC in an interview in *The Times* and the *Observer* reported that the Saatchi report had provoked 'fury and embarrassment within the top echelons of the BBC'. That same month Young attacked the D'Arcy and Saatchi reports in *Ariel*. In December a BBC-supported report was published, *The Funding of BBC*, by AS Ehrenberg of the London Business School. This argued that the 'licence fee remains excellent value for money' and that the fee had to be raised 'to take account of inflation, rising production standards, and the decreasing numbers of conversions to colour'. On matters of cost it asserted that:

> For the country as a whole, the licence fees add up to some £500 million a year (excluding the cost of radio). We spend 50 times that much on motoring and drink, some £25 billion. For the individual viewer, watching BBC TV costs just over 2p an hour or almost 25p a week. So spending a bit more would generally not be the major issue it is often said to be, as long as we still got something for it, like more good programmes.

The report suggested that in the medium term subscription might be an option, but meanwhile 'it is important that the current licence fee income should not lag too far behind ITV's'.[18]

By mid-December Milne was doing a series of radio phone-ins defending the BBC. Between December 1984 and February 1985 the BBC's magazine, *Radio Times*, carried a series of interviews with senior figures like Young, Bill Cotton the Managing Director of television and Dick Francis the Managing Director of radio, broadly putting the BBC's case. In January 1985 BBC Radio 4 mounted a debate on the advertising issue in which Young took part with Rodney Harris of D'Arcy MacManus Masius and Tim Brinton among others. Also that month the BBC announced scheduling changes in an attempt to win back audiences from ITV.[19]

By this time the BBC was 'complaining of an unfair press and an ill-informed Parliament'. Milne hit out publicly against the way *The Times* had been covering the licence fee debate, questioning the motives of the paper's proprietor, Rupert Murdoch. In February Milne addressed the Broadcasting Press Guild and warned of cuts in production if the settlement was inadequate in what was described as 'a last-ditch attempt by him to persuade the assembled ranks of Fleet-Street of the wisdom of the BBC's case in the licence fee argument'. At this time senior BBC figures were lobbying MPs at the House of Commons and at weekly lunches with journalists. They were also discussing the issues with civil servants. It was a period of intense lobbying in which the resources of the BBC were thrown behind an attempt to steer opinion-makers in Parliament and the press away from the agenda set by the BBC's critics. In the short term, from the BBC's point of view, all this effort had an unsatisfactory outcome. As Milne has put it:

> we waited for the Home Secretary to deliver his judgement. Alarm bells rang in a small way when a senior civil servant, at a party in Broadcasting House was overheard to say, '£65? You've got your figures the wrong way round.'

The announcement of a £58 rather than a £65 settlement for two not three years and of the setting up of the Peacock Committee was a defeat for the BBC's strategy. Management had insisted on a £65 fee and no advertising. The government had delivered an effective cut in income and had left a question mark over the fee. Publicly management remained bullish. Young appeared on television a matter of days after the announcement and made it clear that the BBC, if necessary, would fight hard for advertising. This was clearly a way of signalling to the ITV sector that advertising on the BBC would severely damage its income. Steps were taken by management to assess the implications of the settlement and to deal with Peacock. A group under Brian Wenham was established to draft material for submission to Peacock which included Stephen Hearst, Janet Morgan and Andrew Ehrenburg. Milne also established a working party to examine BBC expenditure over the next three years, under the Director of Finance Gerald Buck. This group included Michael Checkland.[21]

During the first five months of 1985 relations between Milne and the Governors deteriorated rapidly. A series of incidents occurred which, according to Milne, 'gravely disturbed the working relationship between the Board and the management'. These included: problems relating to the cost of the purchase of new premises for the Corporation; the criticism provoked by the rescheduling of the long-running popular science fiction programme, *Dr Who*; the management of a libel action against the BBC; the failure to transmit the Pope's Easter message; and a row over the unauthorised transmission of an interview with a member of the royal family. In March 1985 Milne had lunch with Young and Rees-Mogg and 'they explained the Board's sensitivities and how some of the newer Governors were finding relationships with management uneasy'. In his memoirs Milne is particularly critical of Rees-Mogg's role in these developments.

The Board moved against Milne on 1 May demanding that he demote his Assistant Director General, Alan Protheroe, and appoint Michael Checkland, an accountant who was Director of Resources for Television, as Deputy DG in charge of resources. Milne initially resisted the changes, which implied a clear criticism of his performance. But in the end he agreed to a modification of Protheroe's role and to the appointment of Checkland as Deputy. The period leading up to the public announcement of the changes was accompanied by rumours that Milne was to be sacked. It was clear that by early 1985 Milne was out of tune with both the politicians and many of the Governors.[22]

In the summer of 1985 the BBC announced a package of cuts totalling £65 million. A committee was established by Checkland to coordinate them. The BBC wanted to be seen to be being efficient. At the same time Wenham's group was commissioning research into likely revenue from subscription and programme sponsorship and by August had submitted the BBC's initial response to Peacock.[23]

The submission combined an assertion of the BBC's long-term commitment to efficiency with a defence of the licence fee and an indication that it was prepared to explore alternative sources of revenue. The BBC had set in train 'a thorough review of the services it should in future provide for the public' as a result of the £58 award 'and against the background of a potentially much larger programme provision from non-BBC services'. It challenged the idea that 'the BBC's partial immunity from the disciplines of the market place must make it either profligate or inefficient or both'. It cited the Peat Marwick Mitchell report in its defence as 'the most recent of successive inquiries into the BBC's finances and operations'. The report had identified areas where 'some' improvements in efficiency might be made, and had approved

> the BBC's own rolling programme of activity reviews. These, coupled with the BBC's current reassessment of its scope and overall objectives … are a crucial part of the Corporation's constant monitoring of its mechanisms for efficient and effective management.

The submission asserted the simple truth that the reality of BBC finances and management was very different from the one portrayed in the press. On the matter of the licence fee the submission noted that:

> Political unease, fed by newspaper commentary, has stimulated argument about the existing system. Accordingly, the BBC is both

re-examining the methods for assessment and collection of the licence fee, and exploring other ways by which its income might be boosted.

These 'other ways' included commissioning studies of the potential revenue from advertising, of sponsorship in the United Kingdom, and of subscription techniques. These also covered participation in a working party with the Home Office and the Post Office 'to examine whether full advantage is being taken by the public of the schemes currently available for spreading the cost of their television licence over the year'. But this did not stop it asserting that,

> Our basic objection to advertising in the BBC is rooted in the belief that the competition for income would progressively threaten the range and quality of programmes. This would also diminish the work the BBC could place with actors, writers, musicians and other contributors throughout the United Kingdom.

This was a vigorous defence of the status quo. It asserted the view that the Corporation was efficient and subject to constant internal scrutiny. It argued the case for the retention of the licence fee system with confidence. In substance it made few, if any, concessions to the arguments used against it the previous year.[24]

The submission was produced just as the *Real Lives* affair blew up. As outlined in Chapter 4 this provoked a major internal row between the Governors and Milne's management team reflecting deep divisions between the two parties. Rumours that Milne had tendered his resignation fed a general atmosphere which questioned the quality of BBC management. This occurred at a time when the Corporation should have been presenting a united front to the Peacock Committee. The public impression generated by the affair was one of division and inadequacy at the highest levels of the Corporation. An editorial in *Media Week* summed up the mood:

> There is also a cravenness and favour currying at the highest levels of the BBC. The spectre of Peacock stalks the corridors. Having decided to go ahead with the Real Lives programme, the Corporation should have seen it through and defended it on the ground of public interest and awaited the judgement. Can a Director-General so manifestly supine to Government and Governors now honourably remain?

Since then, Milne has described the BBC's response to the *Real Lives* incident as 'plain craven'. Internally the row marked a turning point. Milne's relationship with the Board of Governors and the government thereafter deteriorated progressively in spite of what appeared to be a successfully conducted campaign around Peacock.[25]

In January 1986 BBC managers met members of the Peacock Committee, in February it submitted written answers to the Committee and in March met members of the Committee again at the Home Office. The BBC's findings on the future of advertising spending called into question some of the more optimistic projections in circulation at the time and contributed to the growing body of economic evidence which undermined the case for advertising on the BBC. The systematic efforts mounted by BBC management to present a clear case to the Committee contributed to the report's findings. But it did nothing to dispel the hostility of the Committee to the idea of the long-term survival of public service as the mainstay of the broadcasting system. Indeed the Peacock Committee, in its final report, made no secret of its low opinion of BBC management's inability to explain what they meant by public service broadcasting:

> BBC spokesmen have not always been as effective as they might have been in explaining it, either because they have been too vague or because they have claimed too much. For instance, some statements of the BBC Director General Alasdair Milne risk giving the impression that the viewer's or listener's main function is to react to a set of choices determined by the broadcasting institutions.

In March 1987 Alan Peacock made a much fuller and more serious attack on the BBC under Milne:

> Instead of taking the lead in a full discussion of the financing options available and how these might relate to criteria for policy, the BBC brushed aside any suggestion that change was necessary ... It relied on the weight of its authority and its past experiences and not on a properly structured economic analysis which considered how far past experience would remain relevant. The attacks on the Committee's views on subscription and Pay-TV made in their name, once the report had appeared, were embarrassing in the crudity of their language and speciousness of economic arguments.

The BBC, in a sense, won the battle but lost the war.[26]

The Peacock report left major question marks over the future of public service broadcasting and of the BBC in particular. This uncertainty was reflected, or rather echoed, in the intensification of the internal and external debate over the adequacy of BBC management. By May 1986, before Peacock was published, it was widely known that the Governors and Young were critical of Milne's performance. As we have seen, the Governors were by then forcing management changes on Milne against his will.[27] In October Rees-Mogg, who had by then retired as Vice Chairman of the Governors, attacked the 'unsatisfactory' structure of BBC management and the culture of BBC management. This attack was deemed sufficiently serious by Milne to merit a reply by his special adviser Stephen Hearst.[28]

The autumn and winter of 1986 saw tensions mount inside the BBC over a series of incidents: the handling of the Panorama case, the furore over Tebbit's attack on the BBC coverage of the UK-backed bombings of Libya and the conflict between the government and the BBC over the *Secret Society* programmes. These incidents exacerbated conflicts which existed between Milne's management team and the Governors. The arrival of two new governors in the summer and autumn of 1986 plus the intensity of the pressures outlined above brought matters to a head. Joel Barnett took over as Vice Chairman of the Governors in August 1986 and Hussey's appointment was announced in October. Tebbit makes it clear that in his mind, and those of other senior Conservatives including the Prime Minister, Hussey's job was to sort out top management, something which by implication meant getting rid of Milne. Referring to the publication of the Conservative Central Office report on the BBC's bombing of Libya he comments:

> Some of my critics on the Conservative side felt that the timing of my blast would make it more difficult for the incoming BBC Chairman Marmaduke ('Duke') Hussey to make the changes he might think necessary. Naturally it was a point considered before the Prime Minister agreed that I should publish my dossier. I would have thought that the reverse was true. Indeed it was not to be long before both the Director General, Mr Milne, and his Assistant Director General Mr Protheroe, left.[29]

Milne may have been aware of the gathering storm but, by his own account, only realised late in the day what was afoot. Whilst Barnet and Hussey were determining his fate with what appears to have been the support of Tebbit and the Prime Minister, Milne and his team were fighting hard to maintain their position. At the height of the row over the *Maggie's Militant Tendency* libel case, in October 1986, a confidential memo to the Board of Management was leaked to the press. This justified the decision to pull out of the libel case by citing:

> at least 13 instances in which potential witnesses were alleged to have been contacted about the case before it began. Two Conservative MPs and a senior party aide are among seven people said by the memo to have either changed or dropped evidence against the two MPs during legal proceedings.

At the same time the Corporation reacted strongly and in detail to the Central Office report, refuting allegations made by Tebbit. In a statement on 30 October, responding to the allegations, Milne attacked the report in a confrontational style which can have won him few friends in government: 'There is, however, the genuine worry that the complaint itself and the manner of its delivery could suggest that the Conservative Party is attempting to intimidate the BBC.' He noted also that the attack 'comes at a time when the future of broadcasting is being considered by a Cabinet Committee'. On 5 November 1986, the day that the BBC's detailed response was issued, Tebbit and Milne lunched at the BBC and Tebbit's judgement was damning: 'I would say only that the meeting underlined to me that Mr Milne was a very weak man unlikely to be capable of imposing decent standards within the Corporation.' Milne had clearly failed to alter Tebbit's opinion of him.[30]

The row over the *Secret Society* series can now be seen as the straw which broke the camel's back. The decision by Thatcher to launch a high-profile assault on the BBC involving raids on BBC premises on the grounds of protecting national security provided a further set of reasons why Milne had to go. On 29 January 1987 Milne was forced to resign against his will. On 30 January Hurd asserted, rather disingenuously it might be argued, that the government was not behind Milne's dismissal. This point was repeated the same day by Hussey when he also let it be known that, in future, the powers of the Director General would be curbed.[31]

What does all this tell us? Milne's role as a manager of the BBC awaits detailed assessment. His personal qualities, so frequently alluded to by critics, may have contributed to the destabilisation of his position. But it is clear that his main crime was to be in charge of an organisation which was the focus of intense government criticism at Cabinet level. He and his team of managers mobilised BBC resources to tackle the assault on the BBC's finances and programming and the very vigour and limited success of this clearly made him a marked man. His task was made harder by a Board of Governors increasingly packed with figures apparently hostile to much of what the BBC was and by sections of the national press intent on destabilising the BBC.

In retrospect it would have been very surprising if Milne had survived any longer than he did. Only the passage of time and the detailed analysis of the records will make possible a more conclusive judgement. But it is fair to say that the only thing that would have saved Milne and his team in these turbulent years was if he had signalled clearly from 1983 onwards that he would give in to the demands coming from government, the lobbyists and the press for a more commercially orientated BBC. His unwillingness to do this is one the rare instances in broadcasting history where a senior manager has stood out consistently and publicly against government interference.

The BBC after Milne: Hussey, Checkland and Birt

Milne's departure signalled a major change in direction for the BBC. He was succeeded on 26 February by Michael Checkland who, as far as Hussey was concerned, it seems was a compromise. A Deputy Director General, John Birt, was appointed in March 1987 apparently at Hussey's insistence. There were tensions between Hussey and Checkland which culminated, by the end of 1991, in Hussey's engineering the virtual dismissal of Checkland and his replacement by Birt. Nevertheless the team of three embarked on reorganising the management culture, the journalism and the finances of the BBC in a spirit which, with occasional exceptions, harmonised with the new enterprise culture which the government was seeking to impose on broadcasting.[32] This section traces some of the key developments in the BBC between 1987 and 1992 and argues that by the publication of the Green Paper in November 1992 the future direction of the BBC had been mapped out in accordance with the spirit, if not the letter, of the Peacock report.

The New Vision at the BBC

Of course, one could do so much by changing the framework of the system: as always, it was the people who operated within it who were the key. The appointment of Duke Hussey as Chairman of the BBC in 1986 and later of John Birt as Deputy Director-General represented an improvement in every respect. When I met Duke Hussey and Joel Barnett – his deputy – in September 1988 I told them how much I supported the new approach being taken.

Margaret Thatcher's comments, quoted here, reflect the major change in attitude by her government to top management at the BBC in the wake of Milne's departure. Friction did not disappear but from early 1987 onwards there were no repeats of the fierce clashes between government and the BBC that had characterised the tenure of Stuart Young and Alasdair Milne. By the end of August 1987 two key figures in Milne's team, Protheroe and Wenham, had departed. Public statements by BBC managers adopted the free-market rhetoric so beloved of the Thatcher administration. In an address to staff in March 1987 Checkland, stressing the need to put all the Corporation's energy into programme-making and the need to make up a projected £30-million shortfall by a 1 per cent increase in productivity, presented a view of the BBC and its future which was far removed from the one projected by Milne:

> We must be seen less as an elderly institution and certainly never as a senile bureaucracy, but more as a modern £1,000 million company, adapting to competition and change as many other organisations and companies have had to do in this country, and doing it with enthusiasm and not with regret for the passing of our imperial role.[33]

This was a vision which matched the prejudices of the Thatcher government. As an article in *Management Today* put it:

> Checkland shared the views of the board of governors and of chairman Marmaduke Hussey, that the BBC needed to retrench, and that it was possible to achieve this without jeopardizing the Corporation's world class reputation as a broadcaster ... One gain is that, with his acceptance of Mrs Thatcher's brand of economics, the BBC at least appears to be off the political agenda.

But Checkland did not have a thoroughly harmonious relationship with Hussey. As Roger Bolton, a trade union official for BECTU, noted in 1991 after the announcement that Checkland was to be replaced by Birt:

Checkland, during his time as Director General has had to manage a relationship with a Chairman whose mission in life was to introduce Thatcherite policies into the BBC and who for his part saw Checkland as an obstacle to the introduction of these policies. That is why he bullied the Board of Governors into replacing Checkland with Birt.[34]

But, in 1987, this was in the future. The new team under Checkland, Hussey and Birt embarked upon restructuring BBC internal management and imposing cuts in jobs. It also showed a marked reluctance to challenge the government on programme issues, but more importantly on matters of broadcasting policy generally. Here we detail some of these developments and argue that BBC management from 1987 onwards accepted that public service broadcasting would no longer shape UK broadcasting policy and that the BBC should accept a role as provider of a reduced range of services to smaller audiences.

Tebbit noted a change in the BBC after the row over the Libyan bombing: 'Despite a continuing fixation with South African politics I think the Corporation's news coverage has improved. The lack of balance in the drama department and parts of current affairs remains a challenge.' Indeed the new regime trod cautiously. Early in 1987 Checkland stalled on running the *Secret Society* programmes which had triggered Milne's sacking. Birt's appointment at the end of March was a prelude to a restructuring of news and current affairs under one direc-torate with Birt asserting the need for BBC journalism to be more 'authoritative'. Birt, a friend of Peter Jay, whose career had been in commercial television, had early on signalled his criticisms of the BBC's attitude to authority. In 1988 one journalist wrote that:

Birt has identified the Old BBC values as 'crudely, thoughtlessly anti-Establishment'. He seeks to insert a culture which uses thought, ideas and rigorous analysis to enlighten current events, deferring neither to authority nor to anti-authority. In doing so, he has already courted the charge that he is acting solely in the interests of the presently established power.

The 'tough, hands-on line' of Birt and Checkland, 'proved unsettling for journalists'. In practice these developments signalled that the new management was taking a cautious line on controversial issues and that a new era of tight controls over the journalistic output of the BBC had begun.[35]

In May 1987 the BBC cancelled a radio programme on the Cold War experience of British servicemen after the Ministry of Defence sent 'a letter threatening prosecution under the Official Secrets Act'. During the general election campaign of 1987 Mrs Thatcher recorded an interview at 10am on the eve of the poll in which she was asked,

> why she did not show more sympathy for the unemployed and the underprivileged. What mattered, she responded, was what you did rather than what you said ... And she summed up with a phrase that produced by far the most revealing exchange of the whole election campaign: 'But please, if people just drool and drivel that they care, I turn around and say, "Right, I also look to see what you actually do".'

She and Tebbit were 'concerned that the BBC would make the most of it ... But the management decided to keep the interview in the can for as long as possible to minimize its impact.' The interview was not run on the lunchtime or early evening news but appeared at the end of the 9pm news: 'Mrs Thatcher ... was delighted. It seemed that the browbeating of the past year had worked.' Also during the campaign Tebbit intervened directly in the BBC's *Breakfast Time* programme by ringing up Hussey and ensuring that Cecil Parkinson appeared as a guest on the next morning's programme, even though the staff had decided to drop him in favour of another guest.[36]

This caution was paralleled by concerns generated by the reorganisation of news and current affairs. At a meeting in July 1987 of the 'newly combined news and current affairs group for television and radio' Birt told his senior editors about his plans to pool resources into the four specialist areas of politics, economics, finance and industry and foreign affairs. The new caution towards the government surfaced at the meeting where it emerged that:

> Among areas under study will be the editorial supervision of difficult programmes and, particularly, the use made of legal advice. This is aimed at avoiding such recent embarrassing controversies as the Panorama libel case involving Conservative MPs.

There was discontent in the ranks of BBC journalists, some of whom felt that Birt's authoritative journalism, 'his oft-quoted "mission to explain"' would result in 'over-scripted stories, explaining rather than entertaining, which make boring television'. The air of caution was sustained by the decision in August 1987 to drop a *Panorama* programme on the controversial *Spycatcher* affair. Birt's style seems to have solved two major problems at once: first, by signalling a new centralised, politically cautious management regime, and second by starting to define the BBC's role as a provider of high quality services which the market could not provide. As one commentator put it:

> As the BBC moved towards the more competitive broadcasting environment of the 1990s, with cable and satellite offering consumers greater choice, it decided it needed to consolidate its reputation as a public service broadcaster with heavyweight news and current affairs programmes.[37]

New Managers

The changes in senior management throughout the Corporation after Milne's dismissal in 1987 reflected these two broad aims. In June Checkland restructured the organisation. The three managing directors of TV, radio and external services were replaced by five managing directors of TV, regional broadcasting, radio, external services and BBC Enterprises. In this reshuffle two of Milne's top managers, Brian Wenham and Alan Protheroe, went. By October the BBC had in place two individuals known for their close personal links with the government. Tim Bell continued as a PR consultant. Lord Young's special adviser, Howell James, was appointed Director of Corporate affairs at the BBC. James had worked in commercial broadcasting, for Capital Radio and TVAM and had been appointed special adviser to Young on the strength of a recommendation from Bell. Young felt that, in making the appointment, the BBC was acting in a very far-sighted way. By November Michael Grade had gone. The new team was clearly constructed with half an eye, at least, to appeasing the occupant of Number 10, a fact which prompted criticism from the Labour Party.

The new team contained many people with no experience of the broadcasting industry. Writing in March 1992, Roger Bolton of BECTU commented that:

> It is interesting to note the number of senior posts to which individuals from outside the BBC, with no broadcasting experience, are being appointed. In fairness it must be said that many of those joining the ranks of senior management are experienced in marketing, retail

and accounting ... consider the background of some of the leading lights ... Director of Resources, Televison (ex-British Coal), Director of Finance (ex-London Transport), Director of Personnel (ex-Burton's Group).[38]

Cuts, Cuts and More Cuts

Checkland and Hussey lost no time in looking for other changes. Checkland promised that from 1 April 1987 £4 million extra would be made available to fund an additional one hundred hours of independent production in 1987-8, out of a target of 200 hours. The plan was to raise the figure to 600 hours by 1991. This was responding positively and swiftly to the government's demand that independents should get 25 per cent of the production in BBC and ITV. Checkland 'played down the implications for staff'. But John Foster, the broadcasting organiser of the NUJ, was clear that these changes would lead to an erosion in the terms and conditions of permanent staff at the BBC.[39]

The new, commercially orientated, spirit permeated management pronouncements. The General Manager of BBC radio engineering suggested the BBC might be willing to rent out its national network radio transmission facilities to the planned commercial Independent National Radio. In October Checkland published his strategy, *The Next Five Years*, which outlined policy up to 1993. The plan included a 1 per cent a year reduction in staff costs between 1988 and 1993. One estimate put the number of jobs this threatened at 5,000 on top of the 2,000 or so lost between 1985 and 1987. The plan was to achieve the 25 per cent target by 1992. At the centre of the plan was the policy of devolving managerial and budgeting responsibilities 'to operational levels'.

This plan was a calculated, high-profile response to the attacks in the early 1980s on BBC mismanagement. Checkland was acutely aware of the need to be seen to be managing in a new style which was responsive to the critiques mounted since 1983. Interviewed in 1988 he commented:

> The BBC had to be seen to be well-managed. Some of its difficulties in the past have been when it has been perceived, for whatever reason, as not being well managed as an operation – as being too big, too cumbersome and fragmented in its approach. I want to take the pressure off the organisation by having it well managed, and that will give much more freedom to programme makers to operate.

The signals sent out in the first year of the Checkland regime were unequivocal. Thereafter the BBC moved along the lines laid out in that year in the context of a government policy which was, as has been shown, focused almost exclusively on reregulating commercial television. The new management gradually steered the BBC on a new course.[40]

Timidity

The apparent unwillingness of the BBC to maintain a critical stand towards the government after 1987 did not pass unnoticed. A Granada TV programme criticising the management changes, called *Taming the Beeb*, was broadcast in March 1988. Its themes figured in an article in *The Listener* by Bob Woffinden which asked 'Has BBC journalism lost its spirit of inquiry?' Although both Lord Thomson and Hussey wrote to Hurd in May 1988 objecting to the proposed Broadcasting Standards Council as unnecessary, Hussey did agree to have his views on the proposed BSC canvassed by the Chairman designate of the BSC, Rees-Mogg, in the summer of 1988. Birt and other TV executives met Rees-Mogg in the autumn. This cautious approach to the widely criticised BSC initiative had echoes in the Corporation's decision to delay the transmission of a sensitive programme on the SAS in early October. It was also seen in the Corporation's timid response to the ban on broadcasting the words of legal political parties based in Northern Ireland which was imposed by Hurd on behalf of the government at the end of October.[41]

The White Paper and the Broadcasting Bill

Hussey welcomed the new competition proposed in the 1988 White Paper and although Checkland raised some minor points of detail no serious critical response emerged from the Corporation. The BBC, according to one observer, seemed to be let off the hook by the proposals in the White Paper because 'it had in any case been tamed by the Hussey/Checkland/Birt axis'. A *Sunday Times* journalist noted the 'BBC's great escape' attributing it in part to the fact that: 'With Milne gone, the BBC converted to Thatcherite doctrines of efficiency and economy and news output under the new management of John Birt, the healing process seems firmly underway.'[42]

The Broadcasting Bill was published in December 1989 and Checkland and Hussey kept a low profile during the ensuing debate. They criticised the proposals to allow independents to use spare BBC signal capacity, the plans to end the universal access by viewers to national events, and the intention to give the Office of Fair Trading a role in monitoring the 25 per cent quota. But there was no sustained attack from the BBC on the implications of the Bill for public service broadcasting. This relative silence was combined with a rolling programme of job cuts.[43]

Commercialism, Independents and More Cuts

At the end of 1988 one of the BBC's commercial competitors, Sky TV, decided to place its advertising account with Lowe Howard Spink. Lowe Bell Communications, LHS's holding company, was Tim Bell's company, the BBC's PR consultant. Instead of pulling out of its relationship with Bell, the Corporation promised to review the situation if it presented a conflict of interests. By January 1989 the BBC had agreed, in a document responding to the White Paper, to consider a night time subscription service provided its night time frequencies were not sold to private companies. Checkland issued his plans for the night time pay-per-view service along with renewed commitments to efficiency and to independents in early February. This was just in advance of a parliamentary debate on the White Paper. In May 1990 Tim Renton announced that government had agreed, in principle, to the service.[44]

The pressure from the government on the BBC and ITV to reach the 25 per cent target was supplemented by pressure from the Independent Programme Producers Association who complained in July 1989 that they were being excluded from tendering for news and current affairs programmes. The IPPA lobbied the Prime Minister and as a result, trading agreements between the Independents, the BBC and the ITV companies were submitted to the Office of Fair Trading for scrutiny. In October Checkland, still anxious to cooperate with the independents, announced that a firm of external consultants, Ernst & Young, would be employed to report on the relationship between the Corporation and the independents. The report issued in August 1990 suggested that independents were neither more efficient nor cheaper. But nevertheless Checkland committed the BBC to 25 per cent or 1,400 hours for 1993. In February 1990 management reaffirmed its commitment to more commercialism by entering an agreement with Lloyds Bank in which the bank provided

£1.3 million to sponsor a BBC programme, the 'Young Musician of the Year'.[45]

Some Consequences on the Ground

Figures for job losses and the precise effects of cuts are difficult to find and to evaluate. There is no doubt that there were significant job losses at the BBC after 1987. In its evidence to the Monopolies and Mergers Inquiry into labour practices in TV and film-making the BBC claimed that from 1 April 1985 until the end of March 1989:

> 2,000 posts were shed and savings of £32 million were achieved principally by withdrawing from certain specialist activity and where, on a more limited scale, following the evaluation of competitive tenders, it was found that external provision of supporting services was cost effective.

In April 1988 Checkland announced plans to shed an additional 1,500 jobs over a five-year period between 1988 and 1993. According to one estimate there was to an 8 per cent staff reduction in TV and Radio from 25,378 in 1986 to 23,307 by the end of 1989 by which time a review of corporation activity under Ian Philips had been set up to explore more cuts.[46]

How did this work out on the ground? Again this is difficult to clarify. But some indication can be gleaned from trades union descriptions of the cuts flowing into London Television for the period 1990–1: one estimated that there had been a loss of over 119 jobs in programme departments, design and scenic services, studio production resources, film production resources, post production resources, outside broadcasting production resources and film laboratories. The union identified management plans to introduce, between 1990 and 1993, competitive tendering in cleaning and services, security, catering and mail services. In cleaning and security alone a total of 258 full- and part-time posts were at risk. These cuts, as one BECTU official, Ernie Johnston, pointed out had a serious human dimension:

> It is clear that the BBC's policy of meekly accepting the dictates of this Government has led directly to the disastrous position we presently find ourselves in. None of the sanctimonious words of the director

general referring to dealing with cuts on a humane basis have any foundation in fact. If he had actually taken the trouble of talking to those threatened with the loss of their jobs he would realise their fear, despair and anger.[47]

The fundamental threat this posed to the trades unions within the BBC led to strike action and the development of an intense critique of management strategy. BETA's 1986 annual conference had committed the union to 'take whatever action necessary, including industrial action' to protect jobs, pay and conditions in the BBC. BBC local radio journalists held a 24-hour strike in July 1988 in protest against the proposed 10 per cent cut in local radio budgets and in the summer of 1989 BETA, the NUJ and the ACTT were engaged in a protracted pay dispute with management.

It was during this dispute, in June 1989, that the Phillips Committee was set up to: 'recommend ways of releasing resources for a more competitive pay structure whilst retaining the range and quality of our existing programme services in radio and television'.

The recommendations of the Phillips Committee became known as 'Funding the Future' which, according to BETA, was 'a package of cuts and job losses which led to 100s of redundancies in Weekly Paid areas. The money released by decreasing staff numbers was to be spent in enhancing pay for monthly staff.' The monthly increases were to be accompanied by changes in the conditions of service for monthly paid staff. The accountants Peat Marwick McClintock were called in and produced a set of proposals designed 'to introduce more flexibility into work patterns, and remove many of the financial rewards currently earned for working long, irregular and anti-social hours'.[49]

Producer Choice

In 1991 management announced plans to introduce an internal market into the BBC, called Producer Choice. By 1993 Producer Choice had become the centrepiece of John Birt's strategy for the BBC. It was meant to refit the BBC for the new wave of intense competition which would come with the proliferation of cable and satellite, as well as to persuade the government that the BBC should have its Charter renewed. It was also an intensification of the policies of retrenchment and withdrawal from the centre stage of broadcasting which had been initiated after Milne's sacking.

The plan was to turn BBC departments into cost centres with zero budgeting procedures. Each centre had to buy in services from other BBC centres or external sources, whichever was the most cost effective. Producer Choice came into effect in April 1993. The plan was clearly based on ideas introduced in other public services during the 1980s, notably the health service. It was aimed, like previous initiatives by BBC managers after Milne's departure, at producing a BBC more fully integrated into the market. Producer Choice had serious implications for the future of the BBC as a major in-house producer of programmes. The logic was that where BBC departments could not compete with the market, they would close down. This in turn would mean an erosion of the overall production base of the BBC, a point acknowledged and welcomed by John Birt soon after he took over as Director General in February 1993 at a meeting with the broadcasting unions:

> According to the minutes of that meeting – produced and authorised by BBC management – John Birt said that: so far as both resource provision and programme making was concerned, he would be concerned if the proportion provided by the BBC in-house fell below at least 50 percent of the total.

According to Roger Bolton of BECTU when Birt made this statement BBC in-house work was operating at 35 per cent lower than it had been in 1987. Add Birt's estimate to this and the implication was that he would allow the production base of the BBC to slide to around 33 per cent of the level it had been in 1987 before he would become 'concerned'. Even if these figures are not strictly accurate, the analysis is.[49]

Conclusion

The evidence presented in this chapter supports the view that there was a major break in management at the BBC from 1987. Between 1982 and 1987 the management team, led by Milne, were confronted with hostile governors, hostile lobbyists, a hostile press and a hostile government. That government was led by a Prime Minister intent on taking on the BBC. Milne's reaction was to combat the attacks and use the resources of the Corporation to do so. On the issue of the licence fee he clearly had the support of Stuart Young. But on other matters

Young's support, and certainly that of the governors, became increasingly uncertain. By resisting the pressure for change so vigorously Milne became a target.

All the evidence shows that after Milne's dismissal the new managers towed a distinctly Thatcherite line cutting jobs, introducing tendering and, through Producer Choice, embarking on a strategy of making every key decision in the Corporation subordinate to market forces. Peacock had recommended a diminished role for the BBC and a marginalised public service component in the new, market-driven system. In doing this the report echoed the orthodoxy which was established by the work of the lobbyists, the Murdoch press and senior politicians from 1983 onwards. The managers at the BBC after 1987 responded positively to the ideas developed by the critics of the BBC in the early 1980s and, in effect, pushed the BBC down the road advocated in the Peacock report.

The BBC was not at the centre of the 1988 White Paper nor of the Broadcasting Act of 1990 because it had already been dealt with by the government. The 1990 Act certainly pushed commercial broadcasting down the road of subordination to the market and provided a context in which this would happen for the BBC. But this was only a context. The BBC had set off down that road in early 1987.

9   The Erosion of Autonomy: Concluding Observations

We know from historians that hardline Tory ministers like Churchill thought the BBC dangerously soft. But strikers could see it was outrageously dependent on right wing sources for its information, it amounted to a strike-breaking device. [Harry Wicks]

The contribution of political economy to this debate is to analyse how and in what ways the relation between the media and the state has consequences for the range of expression and ideas in the public arena. [P. Golding and G. Murdock][1]

Harry Wicks was a lifelong revolutionary socialist, active in the national and international labour movement. For Harry Wicks the consequences of state control of the BBC during the general strike of 1926 were clear. The BBC acted as 'a strike-breaking device'. This book has shown, as have other studies, that the BBC was not a directly subordinate arm of the UK state in the way implied by Harry Wicks. In the 1980s it was seen by many Tory politicians as being 'outrageously dangerous' as Churchill had allegedly believed.

The BBC has existed within a set of relationships with the UK state which have shifted over time. Although this book does not claim to be a study of the political economy of broadcasting in the 1980s it has sought to 'analyse how and in what ways the relation between the media and the state has consequences for the range of expression and ideas in the public arena'. It has also sought to chart the 'shifts in the balance between commercial and public enterprise' in the field of broadcasting.[2] In charting these shifts its purpose has been one of record. I have tried to provide an historical account of the changes which occurred in the 1980s, to present them at a level of detail which has not, to date, been done and in a way which will, it is hoped, prompt more investigation and debate.

This voyage through the events and issues of the 1980s has prompted a series of conclusions which, I hope, will clarify the reasons why broadcasting policy developed in the way it did during the 1980s. These are presented in the first part of this chapter. The voyage has also prompted some observations about aspects of the relationship between the capitalist economy, broadcasting and the state. These observations form the second and concluding part of this chapter. The basic argument in this second part is that the changes in broadcasting in the 1980s have eroded its relative autonomy from the political and economic imperatives of the capitalist economy. An additional point is that this process was accompanied by a parallel one in which the state sought to increase the range of sanctions it could deploy against recalcitrant broadcasters.

The Outcome

When the BBC approached the last Charter negotiations at the end of the seventies, the broadcasting landscape was very different. The BBC had two television channels, ITV one. There was no Channel 4 and no cable. There had been talk about satellite broadcasting but none existed. The BBC's four radio networks were, in their respective ways, dominant. BBC local radio had been in operation for 10 years, competing with independent stations. But competition in today's terms was far off. It was the new Conservative government, led by the largely unknown Margaret Thatcher, which settled the 1980 charter ... From that perspective, the BBC's position today looks much less secure. Competition has greatly increased and been encouraged as an act of policy. Its own competitive position, particularly in television, has worsened. Its funding has been shrunk, again as an act of government policy.

Alasdair Milne's summary, written in 1992, indicates the range of changes which occurred between 1979 and 1992. But they went deeper and wider than this. In 1979 the direction of broadcasting policy was shaped within a public service framework. Most of the major participants in policy-making anticipated change, but change achieved through a process of modifying the existing system. By 1992, as a result of what has been described in this book, this perspective no longer held the centre of the policy-making process. Policy-making retained an element of the older, public service, tradition, but it was shaped more sharply than before by a committment to allowing market forces to shape broadcasting.

Peacock may have rejected advertising, but the report provided the intellectual justification and framework for this shift. It was a framework which drew on the ideas associated with the IEA. Peacock's proposals met with opposition from the Home Office and broadcasters and not all of them were implemented. But a surprising number of the Stage 1 recommendations had been implemented in one way or another by 1992. These included: rejecting advertising; indexing the licence fee; getting the BBC to manage the collection of the fee; lifting regulations from commercial radio; imposing the independent production quota and a version of the TV franchise auctions; changing the basis of Channel 4 funding; and facilitating pay-per-view TV.

More significantly, Peacock's goal of creating more competition was placed at the very centre of policy-making. So, too, was the definition of public service broadcasting as just one element in the system, rather than the concept which shaped the system as a whole. Its positive approach to commercially driven cable and satellite services had been endorsed and acted on by the government.

By 1992 the commercial broadcasting companies were operating within the framework of the 1990 Broadcasting Act which, in turn, had been heavily influenced by Peacock. Commercial concerns had begun to dominate independent radio and television as competition intensified, programming responded to reflect that change, and companies merged in response to commercial pressures. Satellite TV, in the shape of Murdoch's Sky channel, was establishing a major foothold in the UK broadcasting system. These changes owed much to Peacock's vision and recommendations.

The attack on the BBC had, in part, triggered this reorientation of policy. By 1992 the BBC had suffered a loss of income, a dramatic change of management, and a change in, what could be called, corporate culture at the top. Its new managers after 1987 largely accepted the new framework established after Peacock. Through a process of internal restructuring, job cuts and the introduction of Producer Choice, they mapped out a completely new role for the BBC which was radically different from its role in 1979. As an organisation it was reconciled to being a provider of public service programmes in a predominately market-driven environment, and a smaller provider at that. Producer Choice had subjected the Corporation to the pressure of market forces and raised questions about whether the BBC would continue into the twenty-first century as a major programme producer.

At times in the 1980s some people believed that the BBC might not survive the decade. It did, but only as a radically different outfit. It was now orientated, internally and externally, towards the market in ways which had never been considered up to 1979. This had been achieved by the changes in management and in the broadcasting environment in which it operated.

There can be little doubt that the changes in the assumptions under-pinning policy development in the UK had shifted dramatically in the 1980s. After the fall of Mrs Thatcher in 1990, the verities she adhered to receded from the public rhetoric of the government led by John Major. But Major's administration remained committed to the framework of policy embodied in the 1990 Act and to the changes being pushed through at the BBC.

Changes of this sort were going on throughout Europe in the 1980s. Competition had increased, public service institutions were weakened and national structures for regulating the media had lost power in the face of transnational broadcasting throughout Europe. It will take time, and a good deal of detailed study, to determine the different effects these are having and will have on different, national, communications systems. It is not the purpose of this book to make these comparisons, but it is important, in order to make them, that we gain a greater understand-ing of what has been happening in the UK. This book has tried to make a contribution to that process.[3]

The Attack

Why did the BBC become the focus of so much intense political activity after 1979? The answer is complex. Changes in the economics of the media industries, at a global level, were at work during the 1970s encouraging trends towards conglomeration and the erosion of national, legal barriers to the accumulation of profit. These trends have not been analysed in this book because they have been discussed in detail elsewhere.[4] In the UK the trends took, in part, the form of key industrial actors pressing the government for change: I have focused on the activities of sections of the newspaper and advertising industries. There were clear economic benefits awaiting those who could break into the UK's protected broadcasting market or who, if already in, could modify the rules or environment in their favour.

The pace of technological change was clearly a significant factor which favoured these pressures. Implementing new cable and satellite tech-nologies would inevitably have called for some modification of the regulations governing broadcasting. Equally the cost of implementing these changes favoured those industrial actors with money to invest at a time when the UK state was increasingly keen to offload the cost of major infrastructural development onto the private sector.

In addition the political changes of 1979, the election of the Thatcher administration, was decisive. Mrs Thatcher wanted to allow private media corporations the space to compete with public service broadcasters. This was partly because she and her supporters in government had personal links with those sections of the media industries which wanted change and drew heavily on them for political support. It was also because they were advocates of a particular set of ideas about *how* the economy should be run – ideas which contained the seeds of hostility to selective public enterprises such as health, education, social services and broadcasting, but not the armed services, the police or the security services. They also shared, with a wider section of the Conservative Party, a critical view of the politics of public service broadcasting, one which identified broadcasting with the promotion of an anti-enterprise, anti-authority, left-of-centre culture.

Other parts of the state system, notably sections of the governing Tory party and civil service, did not share the views on broadcasting espoused by Mrs Thatcher and mounted resistance. The convergence of pressure from powerful media interests and from the dominant section of the governing party proved enough to win the day. The BBC was subdued and broadcasting policy reshaped.

How was this Achieved?

It would be wrong to say that the Prime Minister, her Policy Unit, ministers and advisers in and out of government were clear about what they wanted for broadcasting as early as 1981 or 1982. They developed and refined a critique of public service broadcasting drawing on a range of sources. Mrs Thatcher contributed the political will needed to keep the issue at, or near, the centre of the political agenda. In this she drew on the ideas and support of the groups discussed in this book.

The process was complex and the outcome never a foregone conclusion. There were too many obstacles to make any outcome inevitable: foreseen (Home Office, broadcasters, Whitelaw) and unforeseen (Westland, the shifting balance of power in the Conservative Party, the potential outcome of major conflicts such as the Falklands, the coal dispute etc), on top of the inherent complexity and sensitivity of the area.

The exact origins of the decision to go for the BBC are unclear, but a range of forces pushing for reform had gone public by early 1984.

These were people linked by shared ideological perspectives and sometimes, as in the case of Murdoch and Thatcher, by common material interests. They were participants within overlapping networks of personal and organisational affiliation. Some, like Murdoch or the Saatchis, were by occupation capitalists. Others – such as those associated with the Adam Smith Institute and the Institute of Economic Affairs – are best understood as ideologues driven by a desire to promote the virtues of capitalism. Still others were politicians with close links to both industry and the ideologues. Some of these politicians, like Young and Tebbit, were in government. These networks acted as an informal coalition of interest on the issue of broadcasting, a coalition which operated inside and outside the formal state system linking the world of business to the world of policy-making.

The techniques used were various. Pressure groups produced ideas which favoured the material interests of the commercial media operators and chimed with the free market prejudices of the dominant part of the governing party. Sections of the national press were used to amplify these views and to set the agenda of debate among MPs, BBC Governors and within the broadcasting industry. Timing was important. The attack was launched at a time when, through the process of the discussions over the licence fee renewal, the BBC was up for scrutiny. Parliament was used by the lobbyists and by Cabinet ministers as an arena in which to amplify and legitimate their ideas and policies.

The political leadership of Thatcher, Tebbit, Lawson and Young in this process was very important. Political power was used at the centre, by Thatcher or with her approval, to publicise the anti-BBC line, to create regulatory conditions favourable to some industrial actors, and to pressurise the BBC into change by influencing the composition of the Board of Governors and of senior management. Thatcher also used her power to set one department, the Home Office, against another, the DTI. She forced the pace of the debate by appealing over the head of Cabinet, through the press to a wider public. She was also engaged in a more general process of shifting key personnel within the civil service around to ensure people with outlooks more supportive of hers were given influential positions.

Opposition

There was opposition to these ideas and the mobilisation against the BBC and public service broadcasting. It was within and without the state. It came from broadcasting unions, cultural workers, churches, educationalists and community and media pressure groups. It was also within the Tory Party and the civil service. This opposition succeeded in slowing the pace of change and modifying some fundamental aspects of the early attack. The BBC was not broken up in the mid-1980s, the licence fee was retained and the government was forced onto the defensive on issues of accountability and quality.

But, as in so many other areas of public policy, the Thatcher governments succeeded in spite of this opposition. Although the 1980s saw waves of resistance at grass roots level to aspects of Thatcher's policies, this resistance was never generalised sufficiently beyond key industries to generate the political pressure needed to force a general retreat on a range of policy fronts. Only the massive, generalised, popular opposition to the poll tax forced the Tories into a major tactical retreat. The use of unemployment and harsh industrial relations legislation, plus changes in the management of public services, increases in the powers and resources behind the police, and a new aggressive style of management fed this situation. It is not the purpose of this book to explain the nature of opposition to the Tory governments of the 1980s, but it is important to note that broadcasting politics was bound up with the general balance of political forces in the country. The failure of opposition to Tory broadcasting policy was, in part, linked to the general absence of sustained, generalised, opposition to the Tories in these years.

But other factors were at work. Broadcasting is not a popular political issue. The issues are complex and have not been the subject of the kind of popular political debate that centred around other subjects such as education, employment and health. Politicians have not generally made a name for themselves by being an expert in this field. Although there never was a parliamentary majority among Conservative MPs for dismantling the BBC in the mid-1980s the issue was never significant enough to prompt concerted opposition to government policy from Tory backbenchers.

While many media workers in the BBC and ITV actively opposed the changes their numbers were never large enough to achieve significant changes in policy. Most workers in the industry were concerned but, for one reason or another, felt unable to mount any serious large-scale resistance. Miliband's analysis of media workers is, perhaps, accurate: the 'most numerous' among them are, like most other workers, those 'whose political commitments are fairly blurred, and who wish to avoid "trouble". In effect such people occupy one part or other of the spectrum of conformity and can accommodate themselves fairly easily to the requirements of their employers.'[5] In this media workers were no different from other workers. Their political commitments aside, they were subject to the real pressures of keeping a job, paying the rent or mortgage and vulnerable to the barrage of pressure and propaganda coming from management and politicians on the issue of broadcasting. In this respect they were like workers in all the other public services which were attacked under Thatcher: occasionally they took action, but the taking of action in such a harsh climate was a very risky business and one which was, understandably, reluctantly undertaken.

At the top of the BBC, the IBA and commercial broadcasting companies were people who had made a career of conforming to the requirements imposed on the media by the state and who were connected by social and professional links to the political establishment. The manipulation of the appointment to the BBC Board of Governors discussed in Chapter 8 was an aberration from the norm only in so far as it intensified the degree of potential conformity at the top of the BBC. The people who ran broadcasting were not, by definition, likely to make a song and dance about opposing the government. Those individuals who openly opposed the changes such as Milne could, and in some cases did, pay a heavy price for their opposition.

Within the state system opposition existed but it rarely went public. Whitelaw steadfastly opposed key changes, but never saw it as an issue on which to move beyond threats and resign. Civil servants seem to have opposed changes but in the end collapsed under the pressure for change. The sheer weight of the economic and political forces behind the changes made opposition inside and outside the state very difficult.

So, after 1979, in a dynamic process involving coalitions within and outside of the state, the governing party actively pursued a policy of radically altering the basis on which broadcasting operated. The evidence presented in this book goes some way, I hope, towards establishing that this policy largely succeeded.

Capitalism, Broadcasting and the State

For the first step in that analysis is to note the obvious but fundamental fact that this class is involved in a relationship with the state, which cannot be assumed, in the political conditions which are typical of advanced capitalism, to be that of principal to agent.[6]

This concluding section makes some observations on the relationship between capitalism, the state and broadcasting in the light of the material surveyed in this book. It argues that the relationship between these three elements is a dynamic one. To paraphrase Miliband, the relationship cannot be assumed and consequently it should be the subject of regular scrutiny and evaluation. This section also argues that, under the governments led by Margaret Thatcher, the state succeeded in redrawing the framework within which the BBC and UK broadcasters operated in the interests of capitalist accumulation. It sought, through changes in the top personnel at the BBC and in the general legal framework within which broadcasters operated, to intensify direct, formal control over aspects of broadcasting practice.

The State

Although the relationship between the state and the BBC is often referred to in academic work on the media, it has not been the subject of sustained critical analysis in recent years. The broad field of media studies in the UK was dominated, in the 1980s at least, by an interest in the conditions under which media texts are consumed. Recent work has begun, with great clarity and insight, to focus on the conditions of production and to track the various conditions under which news is produced, including the influence of the state system on news production. Yet the state does not figure as a discrete topic in two of the very best media readers produced in 1982 and 1991.[7] Some writers have addressed the issue. Ralph Miliband has defined the state system thus:

> These are the institutions – the government, the administration, the military and the police, the judicial branch, sub-central government and parliamentary assemblies – which make up 'the state', and whose interrelationship shapes the form of the state system. It is these institutions in which 'state power' lies, and it is through them that this power is wielded in its different manifestations by the people who occupy the leading positions in each of these institutions – presidents, prime ministers and their ministerial colleagues; high civil servants and other state administrators; top military men; judges of the higher courts; some at least of the leading members of parliamentary assemblies, though these are often the same men as the senior members of the political executive; and, a long way behind, particularly in unitary states, the political and administrative leaders of the sub-central units of the state. These are the people who constitute what may be described as the state elite.

Of course, the state system is not synonymous with the political system. The latter includes many institutions, for instance parties and pressure groups, which are of major importance in the political process, and which vitally affect the operation of the state system. And so do many other institutions which are not 'political' at all, for instance giant corporations, Churches, the mass media, etc. Obviously the men who head these institutions may wield considerable power and influence, which must be integrated in the analysis of political power in advanced capitalist societies.

This then is the state system, according to Miliband. He goes on to relate it to the capitalist economic system:

> it is the capitalist context of generalised inequality in which the state operates which basically determines its policies and actions ... The state in these class societies is primarily and inevitably the guardian and protector of the economic interests which are dominant in them. Its 'real' purpose is to ensure their continued predominance, not to prevent it.

Within this framework the media are not seen as part of the state system. They are part of the political system of a country and the people who run the media are not 'the actual repositories of state power'. Some of these people, like Rupert Murdoch in the period covered in this book, may be capitalists, who although not formally part of the state system do wield immense power over the state's policy through their personal and political connections, a power that is based upon their economic strength. Miliband sees the BBC as an organisation which is an '"official" institution and as such is much more susceptible than newspapers to a variety of pressures'.

There can be little dispute that the state in the UK functions as the 'guardian and protector' of the dominant economic interests in the country. Miliband has since refined this model by arguing that:

> an accurate and realistic 'model' of the relationship between the dominant class in advanced capitalism and the state is one of part-nership between two different, separate forces, linked to each other by many threads, yet each having its own separate sphere of concerns. The terms of that partnership are not fixed but constantly shifting ... the notion makes allowance for all the space which political and state action obviously has in practice; but it also acknowledges a capitalist

context which profoundly affects everything the state does, particularly in economic matters where capitalist interests are directly
involved.

Neither Miliband nor I imply that this relationship excludes conflict
between capitalists and the state, or that elements within the state
system do not hold different views about what measures are best suited
to sustaining a healthy capitalist economy. In fact, as the literature
produced by the ASI and the IEA indicates, many of the ideologues
for the system believed that the state contained elements of people and
practices which inhibited the promotion of capitalism in the UK.
Similarly, as this book indicates, the relationship between the state,
capitalism and broadcasters was never without conflict, of varying
degrees of seriousness.[8]

Much of this is relatively uncontroversial. Commentators have,
however, sought to comment on or specify the nature of the relationship between the state and broadcasters. Some, like Howard Davies,
have pointed out that, 'It would be strange indeed if the major instru-
ments of social communications did not exist in parallel and interlocking
relationship with other institutions.' Raymond Williams has argued, in
the context of a discussion of broadcasting, that because the UK had
'an unusually compact ruling class' this allowed 'much of the effective
state life of this country ... to be delegated to public appointed authorities which have a certain measure of autonomy'. James Curran has
pointed out that this autonomy has not been given by the state to broadcasters without a fight: 'Broadcasters have gained, nevertheless, a genuine
autonomy from political parties and individual administrations as a
result of an extended historical process of negotiation and resistance.'[9]

Thus the relationship of capitalism, the state and broadcasting in the
UK has been one in which the legal framework and the practices built
up over the years gave broadcasters a degree of real autonomy from the
state and in the case of the BBC, a degree of autonomy from the direct
operation of market forces on their activities. This was a fundamental,
and positive aspect of broadcasting in the UK, on which many of the
achievements of the system rested.

In this model, as can be inferred, the links between the state and broadcasting were only partly formal. Broadcasters operated within a set of
shared assumptions and practices based on the social, political and
economic relationships of the people who were at the top of the institutions of capitalism, the state and broadcasting. At times these

relationships changed and as a result shifted the nature of the relationship between broadcasters, the state and capitalism.

Nicholas Garnham has commented on the way a specific set of relationships shaped the early BBC in stressing the need to pay attention to:

> The balance of forces between capital and the State's assessment of both economic and strategic requirement. Thus at the foundation of the BBC we see an interaction between the needs of the nascent British electronic industry, which the State wished to foster both for strategic and economic reasons, and the industry itself, which was interested only in the sales of hardware, and was able to shift the expense and ideological problems of production onto the State. Furthermore, the State needed to take account both of the economically and politically powerful British press, which was opposed to competition for advertising and of a culturally conservative and elitist ruling-class fraction.

These factors produced a system in which the BBC was regulated by the state, for the reasons outlined by Garnham, but also, partly, insulated from the full workings of market relations. This was not to last for ever because, from the early days, pressures existed to draw broadcasting closer to the market. The success of that pressure depended upon shifts in the social, economic and political forces which shaped broadcasting.

Margaret Gallagher has also noted how changing social forces led up to the introduction of commercial broadcasting in the early 1950s. The early BBC was:

> supported by the governing party, the bureaucracy and other media, [and] the form and output of the organisation reflected the social forces which had brought it into being. Subsequent changes in the arrangement of these forces (beginning after World War II) were fed into parallel changes in the structure of British broadcasting and its programming.[9]

This book has provided an initial description of the most recent phase in these changing relationships. It has described the way in which – complex and conflict ridden as it was – commodity relations were pushed into the heart of the public service broadcasting system with an intensity and sense of purpose which superseded similar developments such as the introduction of commercial TV (1954) and commercial radio

(1971). Nicholas Garnham has drawn attention to the general context in which what has been described in this book occurred:

> We are witnessing merely the latest phase in a process integral to the capitalist mode of production ... It is a development that goes back at least 150 years in Britain, part of a process by which commodity exchange invades wider and wider areas of social life and the private sphere expands at the expense of the public sphere, driven by capital's relentless search for new areas in which to realize surplus value, thus introducing the 'dull compulsion of economic relations' to more and more spheres of social life.[11]

There can be little doubt that what happened to the BBC in the 1980s was part of this process. Maintaining a sea of public broadcasting in a world where electronic communications were becoming increasingly commodified would have required concerted action at national and international level. At the UK level the dominant part of the Tory party was not only against this, it took concrete steps to accelerate the commodification of broadcasting.

Of course Mrs Thatcher and her supporters never put it quite like this. But, I hope there is sufficient evidence in this book to show that this was the direction in which they were moving. In fact much of the language they used suggested that the next step for broadcasting was to turn it into a market-dominated commodity.

What does all this say about the evolving relationship between the state, capitalism and broadcasting in the UK in the period after 1979? The period witnessed an erosion of the relative autonomy of broadcasting from capitalist economic pressures. The developments described in this book will, in time, call for a thoroughgoing reconsideration of the formulations about the relationship between broadcasting and the state outlined in this section in so far as they now need to take account of the intensification of capitalist control over the workings of the UK broadcasting system which stems from the changes of the 1980s.

The relative autonomy from the relations of the market afforded by the state's use of law and the body of practice built up around public service broadcasting – the insistence that broadcasting should be run as a public service, with no advertising or carefully regulated advertising and positive programming obligations – has been eroded. Broadcasters in the UK are now formally subordinated to the economic imperatives of capitalist accumulation in ways they have never been before. This book has described the mechanisms which have been used to achieve this. This will have major consequences for the content of broadcast output as these imperatives begin to exert a determining pressure on programme production.

The state has in one sense withdrawn from broadcasting and allowed the market a bigger foothold. But it has only withdrawn to allow a stricter form of control. It is inconceivable that, under the general political conditions of the 1980s, the UK state would have regulated broadcasting away from the market and towards popular forms of democratic control in the 1980s because this could, potentially, have produced a broadcasting system which challenged capitalist social and economic relations. It was not inconceivable, as it turned out, to consider passing increasing amounts of power in broadcasting over to businessmen whose wealth and power depends on the successful perpetuation of the capitalist system. So, what we witness in the 1980s was, in a sense, an exchange of responsibilities, but one which tied the broadcasters more closely to the economic system which the state exists to guarantee.

There is an additional point. The state was not prepared to adopt the libertarian policy on matters of content advocated by Samuel Brittan through the final recommendation in the Peacock report. In fact a succession of steps were taken by the Tory governments of the 1980s which resulted in an intensification, not of the formal day-to-day control of the state over broadcasters, but of the panoply of sanctions which the state could use to keep broadcasters in line. These included the direct manipulation of appointments to the Governors and managers of the BBC, the use of the police to raid BBC premises, the imposition of the 1988 Broadcasting Ban, rigid control of BBC finances through the RPI linkage of the licence fee, the establishment of the Broadcasting Standards Council, and the imposition of clauses relating to impartiality, obscenity, police powers over broadcasters, as well as control over satellite communications in the 1990 Broadcasting Act. No capitalist state can afford to relinquish all power over communications. To do so would be to cede vital powers to manage affairs in times of crisis. The particular form that the intensification of sanctions took under Thatcher reflected the particular concerns of the people in power at that time.

None of this is that puzzling. The UK press is a loyal part of the capitalist system, using its powers regularly to trumpet the virtues of that system and to attempt to marginalise or crush dissent. But it too can act in unpredictable ways and come into conflict with the state and politicians. It has therefore always been hedged around by a variety of laws and regulations. The state to paraphrase Miliband is the guarantor of the system, not individual capitalists, and it is in the state, not the wider political system, that formal power over society rests under capitalism. The nature of the direct powers held by the state over press and broadcasting has changed over time, but at no stage in its history has the UK state relinquished its right to exercise sanctions over the media. In the 1980s it ceded an important degree of economic and cultural power but retained key sanctions and in doing so was acting in a manner consistent with well-established practice.

The issues discussed here have a direct bearing on the nature of democracy. The imperfect public service broadcasting system in place in 1979 had, at its centre, the idea that the public had collective rights over mass, electronic communications. This idea, with others, gave birth to the rich, complex, often contradictory system which contributed positively to democratic culture in the UK. It definitely needed improving – with the introduction of direct democratic accountability and representative structures – but it did not need transforming into a system in which commercial priorities drove the system.

The result of this transformation, if unchecked, will be a mass communication system in which citizens are reduced to consumers with the right to buy an increasing number of media products with an ever-narrowing range of content and social, cultural and political debate. This will suit those for whom mass communications is about making money and promoting their particular brand of politics and culture, and these will be a powerful, rich minority. It will not suit the maintenance, development and survival of a diverse democratic culture, which needs a wide range of universally accessible information.

This book has tried to describe an important process of change which has a direct bearing on the health of the political and cultural life of the country. It has tried to detail how change occurred and to explain that change within a wider conceptual and historical framework. Why spend so many hours and so much ink on all of this? Well, broadcasting is the most important form of mass communications in the world, a form through which power relations are mediated globally. Understanding how the system relates to wider structures of power is a necessary preliminary to devising strategies for altering those relations. The matter was of some urgency for Harry Wicks and his fellow strikers in 1926. It remains so for those of us living in the last years of this century.

Notes and References

Introduction

1. C. Seymour-Ure, *The British Press and Broadcasting since 1945* (Blackwell, 1991), pp. 80, 89.
2. Seymour-Ure, *The British Press*, pp. 71, 78, 137–8.
3. R. Collins, *Broadcasting and Audio-Visual Policy in the European Single Market* (John Libbey, 1994), p. 12.
4. Seymour-Ure, *The British Press*, p. 145.
5. P. Scannell, 'Public Service Broadcasting and Modern Public Life' in P. Scannell, P. Schlesinger, C. Sparks, eds, *Culture and Power* (Sage, 1992), p. 318.
6. P. Scannell, 'Public Service Broadcasting', p. 318.
7. For different sides of this debate, see S. Koss, *The Rise and Fall of the Political Press in Britain* (Fontana, 1990) and J. Curran and J. Seaton, *Power without Responsibility* (4th edn, Routledge, 1991).

Chapter 1: Some Background

1. Seymour-Ure, *The British Press*, p. 216.
2. P. Scannell and D. Cardiff, *A Social History of British Broadcasting Volume One 1922–1939* (Blackwell, 1991), p. 4.
3. Seymour-Ure, *The British Press*, Chapter 8; R. Crossman, *The Diaries of a Cabinet Minister. Volume Three. Secretary of State for Social Services 1968–70* (Book Club Associates with Hamish Hamilton and Jonathan Cape, 1978), 28 May 1968, 27 February 1969. For a readable survey of the relationship between Prime Ministers and TV, see M. Cockerell, *Live from Number 10: the Inside Story of Prime Ministers and Television*, 2nd edn (Faber and Faber, 1989).
4. Scannell and Cardiff, *Social History*, p. 18.
5. On Pilkington, see Seymour-Ure, *The British Press*; Robin Day, a political broadcaster whose career spanned the 1950s to the 1990s, dates the growing distrust between senior politicians of all parties

and the BBC from the days of Greene's directorship. Robin Day, *Grand Inquisitor* (Pan, 1990), pp. 196–7; A. Briggs, 'Obituary: Lord Swann', *Guardian*, 24 September 1990.

6. N. Garnham, 'The Future of Public Service Broadcasting in Britain in Historical Perspective', in C. Shaw, ed., *Rethinking Governance and Accountability* (BFI, 1993), pp. 16–31; Day, *Grand Inquisitor*, pp. 191, 203, 279–80.

7. H.H. Wilson, *Pressure Group* (London, 1961); Local Radio Workshop, *Capital: Local Radio and Private Profit* (Comedia, 1983), Chapter 1, for a survey of the lobby for commercial radio.

8. T. Benn, *Out of the Wilderness. Diaries 1963–67* (Hutchinson, 1987), 20 November 1964. Between 1975 and 1985 the BBC received six increases in its licence fee. Using 1975 figures as the base, the cost of a monochrome licence increased by 125 per cent and of the colour licence by 222 per cent in this period. These increases were partly due to inflation in the economy as a whole. Between 1971 and 1986 the benefits which accrued to the BBC from the switch to colour licences tailed off: between 1971 and 1976 the increase in the number of colour licences issued was some 1316 per cent, between 1976 and 1981 the percentage increase was 59.5 per cent, and between 1981 and 1986 it was only 16.3 per cent: *Report of the Committee on Financing the BBC* (CMND 9824, HMSO 1986), paras 2.8, 2.9.

9. For discussions of the policy process, see J. Tunstall, *The Media in Britain* (Constable, 1983), Chapter 3 and Seymour-Ure, *The British Press*, Chapter 9; Crossman, *Diaries Vol. III*, 14 May 1970.

10. See A. King, 'Margaret Thatcher as a Political Leader' and K. Minogue, 'The Emergence of the New Right', in R. Skidelsky, ed., *Thatcherism* (Basil Blackwell, 1990), pp. 51–64, 125–42.

11. For aspects of policy on these issues in the early 1980s, see: S. Lambert, *Channel Four: Television with a Difference?* (BFI, 1982); the material on IT policy and cable draws directly on T. Hollins, *Beyond Broadcasting: into the Cable Age* (BFI, 1984), Chapter 4. The evidence for the chronological account which follows is given in subsequent chapters.

12. A. Ehrenberg and T.P. Barwise, *How Much Does UK Television Cost?* (London Business School, 1982); Hollins, *Beyond Broadcasting*, Chapter 4.

13. T. Douglas, 'Should Auntie Go Commercial'?, *The Times*, 17 December 1984; Seymour-Ure, *The British Press*, p. 16; J. Miller and A. Sutherland, 'How a "Dead Duck" Started a TV Big Bang',

Sunday Times, 13 November 1988; A. Hetherington, 'The Mass Media', in D. Kavanagh and A. Seldon, eds, *The Thatcher Effect: a Decade of Change* (Oxford University Press, 1989), pp. 297–8; J. Tunstall, 'Coming up for Air', *Times Higher Education Supplement*, 22 January 1988; J. Curran and J. Seaton, *Power without Responsibility*, 4th edn (Routledge, 1991), p. 369; J. Tunstall and M. Palmer, *Media Moguls* (Routledge, 1992), pp. 36, 207.

Chapter 2: Arguing for the Market

1. C. Velanjovski, 'Preface', in C. Veljanovski, ed., *Freedom in Broadcasting* (Institute of Economic Affairs, 1989), p. vii. For a discussion of the relationship between technology and society, R. Williams, *Television: Technology and Cultural Form* (Fontana, 1974).
2. N. Lawson, *The View From No 11: Memoirs of a Tory Radical* (Bantam Press, 1992), p. 721; M. Thatcher, *The Downing Street Years* (Harper Collins, 1993), p. 635; House of Lords Debates, 13 December 1988, col. 838, quoted in W. Stevenson and N. Smedley, eds, *Responses to the White Paper* (BFI, 1989), p. 6.
3. B. Winston, 'The Illusion of Revolution', in T. Forester, ed., *Computers in the Human Context* (Basil Blackwell, 1989), pp. 71–81 deals with these kinds of arguments. See also the debates on these themes covered in D. MacKenzie and J. Wajcman, eds, *The Social Shaping of Technology* (Open University Press, 1988).
4. L. Forgan quoted in G. Hodgson, 'Now is the Time for All Right-thinking Men …', *Sunday Times Magazine*, 4 March 1984, p. 44. Forgan ended the 1980s by arguing that her 'experience of dealing with a regulator such as the IBA has turned me into an extreme libertarian. We now have to face up to the question of whether all this control is worth the erosion of freedom of expression'; quoted in N. Fraser, 'IBA Looks Forward to Life after Death', *Observer*, 10 December 1989. This echoed the equation of public regulation with censorship that is made in the Peacock report and used to justify dismantling public service broadcasting – see Chapter 6 below. Forgan was appointed by John Birt to a senior management position at the BBC in 1993.
5. These comments draw on D. Edgar et al., *The New Right and the Church* (Jubilee Group, 1985); D. Kavanagh, *Thatcherism and British Politics: The End of Consensus*, 2nd edn (Oxford University Press, 1990), Chapters 3, 4.

6. Kavanagh, *Thatcherism*, p. 121.

7. Kavanagh, *Thatcherism*, pp. 89–91; K. Baker, *The Turbulent Years: My Life in Politics* (Faber and Faber, 1993), p. 56; A. Sherman, 'Why the BBC Needs its own Monitors', *Guardian*, 8 December 1986. For a fuller account of the CPS, see R. Desai, 'Second-Hand Dealers in Ideas: Think Tanks and Thatcherite Hegemony', *New Left Review* (no.203, 1994), pp. 50–9.

8. Kavanagh, *Thatcherism*, p. 96; P. Stothard, 'Who Thinks for Mrs Thatcher?', *The Times*, 31 January 1983.

9. Kavanagh, *Thatcherism*, pp. 80–4; Lord Young, *The Enterprise Years: a Businessman in the Cabinet* (Headline, 1991), p. 205; J. Paxman, *Friends in High Places: Who Runs Britain?* (Penguin, 1991), pp. 181–2; S. Castle, 'Manifesto Bid by Radical Right', *Independent on Sunday*, 8 July 1990. See Desai, 'Second-Hand Dealers', pp. 29, 47–9.

10. C. Velanjovski, 'Preface', in Velanjovski, ed., *Freedom in Broadcasting*, pp. vii–ix.

11. C. Veljanovski and W. Bishop, *Choice by Cable* (Institute of Economic Affairs, February 1983), pp. 57–8, 111–12.

12. Veljanovski, ed., *Freedom in Broadcasting*, pp. vii, ix, 262; P. Fiddick, 'Pleas to Safeguard ITV Profits', *Guardian*, 28 November 1988; C. Velanjovski, 'Time for a Redefined Image', *Sunday Times*, 14 May 1989.

13. Kavanagh, *Thatcherism*, p. 87.

14. R. Oakely, 'Privatized Policy-making for the Tory Right', *The Times*, 17 February 1989; Kavanagh, *Thatcherism*, p. 87; report on Commons debate on BBC in *Television Weekly*, 4 January 1985; *Hansard*, 22 March 1985; D. Barker, 'BBC "Must Look to Costs"', *Guardian*, 30 April 1985; S. Castle, 'Manifesto Bid by Radical Right', *Independent on Sunday*, 8 July 1990; D. Graham, 'De-regulation – the Only Path to Freedom', *Stage and Television Today*, 2 May 1985, and 'Broadcasting Market forces', *New Statesman*, 24 May 1985. The Adam Smith Institute's ideas on the BBC got sympathetically quoted in G. Levy, 'Big Spender with the Begging Bowl', *Daily Express*, 20 October 1984.

15. Adam Smith Institute, *Omega Report: Communications* (London, ASI, May 1984), pp. 38–42.

16. Desai, 'Second-hand Dealers', p. 31. On the relationship between public opinion and Mrs Thatcher's policies, see I. Crewe, 'Has the Electorate become Thatcherite?', in Skidelsky, ed., *Thatcherism*, pp. 25–49.

17. T. Douglas, 'Should Auntie Go Commercial?', *The Times*, 17 December 1984.

18. Local Radio Workshop, *Capital*, Chapter 1; Wilson, *Pressure Group*; S. Barnard, *On Radio: Music Radio in Britain* (Open University Press, 1989); Lambert, *Channel 4*; Tunstall and Palmer, *Media Moguls*, Chapter 2; Collins, *Broadcasting and Audio-Visual Policy*, p. 57.

19. Anon, 'Doubts about BBC £10 Car Radio Fee', *Broadcast*, 9 November 1984; NH, 'Would Ad Finance Plan Aid the BBC?', *Broadcast*, 5 October 1984; N. Stavely, 'Advertising on the BBC: Sundry Empires Strike Back', *Admap*, June 1985.

20. Editorial, *Admap*, December 1984; Editorial, 'No Time to Submit', *Media Week*, 5 July 1985; 'Update', *Broadcast*, 26 July 1985.

21. D'Arcy MacManus Masius, *Funding the BBC from Advertising* (DMM, September 1984), pp. 1–7.

22. NH, 'Would Ad Finances Aid the BBC?', *Broadcast*, 5 October 1984; T. Brooks, 'ISBA Presses Hard for Adverts on the BBC', *Media Week*, 5 July 1985; SC, 'Public Poll Prefers Ads to Licence Increase', *Broadcast*, 30 November 1984. For the BRU's critique of these polls, see D. Morrison, *Invisible Citizens: British Public Opinion and the Future of Broadcasting* (John Libbey, 1986).

23. Saatchi and Saatchi, *Funding The BBC – the Case for Allowing Advertising* (Saatchi and Saatchi, October 1984), summary, pp. 6–7, 9–12.

24. N. Lockey, 'Saatchi's Push for Ads on BBC', *Television Weekly*, 16 November 1984; B. Grantham and J. Robinson, 'Licence Fee Pressure Piles up', *Television Weekly*, 21 December 1984.

25. Cockerell, *Live from Number 10*, p. 292; T. Bell, 'My Media Week', *Media Week*, 26 July 1985; N. Tebbit, *Upwardly Mobile* (Futura, 1989), pp. 252–3, 260.

26. T. Brooks, 'ISBA Presses Hard for Adverts on the BBC', *Media Week*, 5 July 1985; Incorporated Society of British Advertisers, *Financing Broadcasting – the Case for Advertising on the BBC* (ISBA, n.d.), inside cover, pp. 3, 14; 'Lobbying Boob', *Television Weekly*, 25 January 1985.

27. 'Doubts about the BBC £10 Car Radio Fee', *Broadcast*, 9 November 1984; N. Lockey, 'Saatchi's Push for Ads on BBC', *Television Weekly*, 16 November 1984; 'Tory Committee Seeks Cuts as Corporation Urges £65 Fee', *Broadcast*, 14 December 1984; T. Douglas, 'Should Auntie Go Commercial?', *The Times*, 17 December 1984; N. Stavely, 'Adverts on the BBC: Sundry Empires Strike Back',

Admap, June 1985, p. 296; P. Fiddick, 'New Pitch for BBC Ads', *Guardian*, 7 November 1986.

Chapter 3: The Press and the BBC in the 1980s

1. R. Snoddy, 'BBC Cheques and Balances', *Media Week*, 26 July 1985. See also R. Brooks and Sue Summers, 'Making the Money Go Round', *Sunday Times*, 2 December 1984.
2. Leapman, *Last Days* and Milne, *DG: The Memoirs of a British Broadcaster* (Coronet, 1989), cover the role of the press and the BBC and this section draws on them. I am not aware of any other attempt to map out the relationship between the press and the BBC in this period. The attacks on the BBC mirrored other concerted attacks by the national press on targets of government policy, notably the NUM, Labour local authorities and the peace movement; see, Hollingsworth, *Press and Political Dissent*; Curran and Seaton, *Power without Responsibility*.
3. Curran and Seaton, *Power without Responsibility*, p. 91; Hollingsworth, *Press and Political Dissent*, p. 33; M. Brown, 'The Family Firm in a Shifting Market', *Independent*, 15 February 1989; Kavanagh, *Thatcherism*, p. 95.
4. Hollingsworth, *Press and Political Dissent*, p. 33; R. Ingrams, Column, *Observer*, 14 May 1989; H. Young, *One of Us* (Macmillan, 1989). p. 557, n. 15; I. Dawnes, 'Thatcher, Resignation List Awards Businessmen and Tory Grandees', *Financial Times*, 21 December 1990; R. Harris, *Good and Faithful Servant: the Unauthorized Biography of Bernard Ingham* (Faber and Faber, 1991), pp. 88, 181; B. Ingham, *Kill the Messenger* (Fontana, 1991), p. 306; Paxman, *Friends*, p. 70. On the way Mrs Thatcher cultivated the national press in the run up to the 1979 election, see W. Shawcross, *Murdoch* (Pan, 1993), pp. 210–12.
5. A. Milne, *DG*, (Coronet, 1989) pp. 158, 160ff.
6. See S. Young, Letter, *Daily Telegraph*, 22 February, 1985; ibid., Leader, 28 March 1985; S. Day Lewis, 'Preserving a Public Service', ibid., 6 May 1985; M. Leapman, *The Last Days of the Beeb*, rev. edn (Coronet, 1987), p. 262; Cockerell, *Live from Number 10*, p. 316; O. Pritchett, 'Why the BBC Wants your £65', *Sunday Telegraph*, 23 December 1984; R. Snoddy, 'BBC Faces Independent Audit' and 'The BBC Sharpens up its Act', *Financial Times*,

21 July and 22 September 1984; Editorial, *Financial Times*, 4 July 1986.

7. A more detailed and systematic study of the content, motives and effects of this coverage is needed. These comments are based on random sampling, but I hope that they reflect the general tenor of the coverage of the papers mentioned. P. Johnson, 'Begging Bowl Economics', *Spectator*, 5 January 1985; C. Goodhall, 'Licence to Spend Money', *Spectator*, 9 February 1985; 'Freer Airwaves, More Jobs', *Economist*, 13 April 1985.

8. D. Barker, 'Copyright Challenge to TV Weeklies', *Guardian*, 16 February 1984; 'Fair Trading Office Rules in Listings', *Broadcast*, 21 December 1984; M. Brown, 'A Tilt at the Listings', *Guardian*, 28 October 1985; 'Euro MPs to Look into TV Listings Duopoly', *UK Press Gazette*, 11 April 1988; M. Brown, 'BBC Buys Control of Magazine Publisher', *Independent*, 6 July 1988; R. Snoddy, 'Government to End TV Listings Duopoly', *Financial Times*, 29 September 1989; *Broadcasting Act* 1990, Section 176.

9. M. Hastings, 'Who Will Halt the Runaway Beeb?', *Standard*, 21 January 1984; S. Clarke, 'Yes the BBC is Biased', ibid., 18 November 1986; A. Rawnsley, 'Tory Link with Media Monitors is Revealed', *Guardian*, 20 November 1986.

10. Milne, *DG*, pp. 242–3; DH, 'Young Tories Back Panorama Report', *Broadcast*, 23 March 1984; Leapman, *Last Days*, pp. 261–2; 'What the Papers Said', *Broadcast*, 5 April 1985; 'Opinion', *UK Press Gazette*, 12 August 1985; H. Herbert, 'Over the Top with Percy Toplis', *Guardian*, 15 September 1986; Editorial, *Daily Mail*, 8 December 1989.

11. G. Levy, 'Big Spender with a Begging Bowl', *Daily Express*, 20 October 1984; Leapman, *Last Days*, pp. 261–2; 'What the Papers Said', *Broadcast*, 5 April 1985; 'Opinion: High Time for the BBC to Get its Act Together', *UK Press Gazette*, 12 August 1985; 'Opinion: Time for Action at the BBC', *Daily Express*, 22 October 1986.

12. See Curran and Seaton, *Power without Responsibility*; Seymour-Ure, *The British Press*. On Murdoch's involvement with film and newspapers in the US, satellites and book publishing in the 1980s, see R. Belfield, C. Hird and S. Kelly, *Murdoch: the Decline of an Empire* (Macdonald, 1991); S. Woodman, 'Murdoch Buys Fox Studios in $162m Deal', *Media Week*, 29 March 1985; A. Brummer, 'TV Plans Force Murdoch to Sell Chicago Newspaper', *Guardian*, 1 July 1986; M. Brown, 'Free Market TV Backed', *Guardian*, 5 July

1986; L. Buckingham, 'Murdoch Takes Collins', *Guardian*, 7 January 1989.

13. M. Leapman, *Barefaced Cheek: Rupert Murdoch* , rev. edn (Coronet, 1984), p. 315; quote from *The Times* editor in J. Pilger, *A Secret Country* (Vintage, 1989), p. 259; A. Marwick, *British Society since 1945*, 2nd edn (Penguin, 1990), p. 377; R. Ingrams, columns in *Observer*, 5 February and 14 May 1989.

14. H. Evans, *Good Times, Bad Times* (Coronet, 1986), pp. 17–18, 486–7; I. Black, 'Evans Renews Attack over Sale of Times', *Guardian*, 16 February 1984; Leapman, *Barefaced Cheek*, pp. 232, 279.

15. 'Licensing of Private Dishes Gets Government Go-ahead', *Broadcast*, 31 May 1985; Editorial, 'Let DBS Rip', *Media Week*, 12 April 1985; Belfield et al., *Murdoch*, pp. 155–68, 187; A. Travis, 'Murdoch Wins Approval for Today Takeover', *Guardian*, 2 July 1987; R. Brooks, 'Auction Should be Going, Going ...', *Observer*, 10 December 1989; Shawcross, *Murdoch*, p. 511.

16. Milne, interviewed in *Television Today*, 9 May 1985; P. Foot, 'Swashbucklers Buckle at Tory Press', *New Statesman*, 14 May 1985; Hetherington quoted in M. Hollingsworth, *The Press and Political Dissent* (Pluto, 1986), p. 13; Murdoch quoted in C. Horrie and S. Clarke, *Fuzzy Monsters: Fear and Loathing at the BBC* (Heinemann, 1994), pp. 37–8; R. Evans, 'Murdoch Attacks "Fossilized" TV Standards', *The Times*, 26 August 1989; European Institute for the Media, *Events and Issues Relevant to Competition in Satellite Television between British Satellite Broadcasting and News International* (EIM, 1989), p. 8.

17. Hollingsworth, *Press and Political Dissent*, pp. 13–14; Milne, *DG*, p. 158; 'Opinion: High Time for the BBC to Get its Act Together', *UK Press Gazette*, 12 August 1985; Editorial, 'The Best TV in the World?', *Sun*, 8 November 1988; European Institute for the Media, *Events and Issues*.

18. Editorial, 'Improper Channels', *Today*, 8 November 1988.

19. M. Brown, 'Neil and his Sunday Best', *Independent*, 20 July 1988.

20. S. Summers, 'Public Tells BBC We Want Better Value for Money', *Sunday Times*, 4 March 1984; Leapman, *Last Days*, p. 251.

21. R. Brooks, 'Who Should Pay for the BBC?', *Sunday Times*, 3 June 1984; R. Brooks and S. Summers, 'Making the Money Go Round', *Sunday Times*, 2 December 1984.

22. 'Memo to Maggie', *Sunday Times*, 9 September 1984; Adam Smith Institute, *Omega*.

23. S. Summers, 'Swearing in the Jury', *Sunday Times*, 26 May 1985; P. Schlesinger, *Putting Reality Together*, reissue (Methuen, 1987) p. xix; Cockerell, *Live from Number 10*, pp. 295, 342. See below, Chapter 4, for a further discussion of the *Real Lives* incident.

24. 'Comment', *Sunday Times*, 13 November 1988; 'Buzz', *Sunday Times*, 4 December 1988. For an example of coverage of ITV-related issues which, in the style and emphasis of reporting, parallels the Summer's piece in note 20 above, see S. Clarke, 'Viewers don't Care about TV Prestige Drama', *Sunday Times*, 21 January 1990.

25. Leapman, *Last Days*, p. 248. See *The Times* for the following articles: D. Hewson, 'Advertising on BBC "Could Peg Licences"', 26 September 1984, 'Quality of BBC TV Programmes Threatened by Soaring Costs', 30 November 1984 and '£60 Licence "Would Kill BBC Plans"', 4 January 1985; Anon, 'The BBC Still Not Sending out a Clear Picture', 11 November 1984.

26. Three leaders entitled, 'Whither the BBC?', in *The Times*, 14, 15, 16 January 1985.

27. Leapman, *Last Days*, pp. 268–71; Milne, *DG*, pp. 168–71.

28. D. Housham, 'BBC Reviews 12 of its Sections', *Broadcast*, 15 March 1985; Leaders, 'Licence Fee' and 'Peacock's Progress', *The Times*, 29 March and 29 May 1985; Milne, *DG*, pp. 220, 245–6.

29. For a full discussion of this, see C. Sparks, 'Popular Journalism: Theories and Practice', in P. Dahlgren and C. Sparks, eds, *Journalism and Popular Culture* (Sage, 1992), pp. 24–44.

30. R. Harris, *Good and Faithful*, p. 86; Thatcher, *Downing Street*, p. 432; Leader, 'Mr Hurd's Garden', *The Times*, 7 November 1988.

31. Milne, *DG*, pp. 170–1, 198; 'After the Licence Fee – BBC at the Crossroads', *Stage and Television Today*, 9 May 1985. Horrie and Clarke, *Fuzzy Monsters*, pp. 22–3; P. Fiddick, 'BBC Chief Hits Back at Press Criticism', *Guardian*, 28 January 1987.

Chapter 4: The Peacock Exercise

1. B. Ingham, *Kill the Messenger* (Fontana, 1991), p. 296.

2. 'Regular BBC Check Found Overspend', *Broadcast*, 23 November 1984.

3. J. Ashton, 'Advertising and the BBC', *Labour Weekly*, 11 January 1985; 'Commons to Debate Advertising on the BBC', *Broadcast*, 14 December 1984; 'BBC Bill Defeated', *UK Press Gazette*, 21

January 1985; J. Naughtie, 'BBC Advertising Defeated after Opposition MPs Clash', *Guardian*, 16 January 1985.

4. J. Naughtie, 'BBC Discomfiture Finds a Delighted Audience on the Tory Right', *Guardian*, 29 March 1985; *Hansard*, 27 March 1985.

5. 'Parliament', *Guardian*, 1 July 1986; *Hansard*, 3 July 1986, col. 1187.

6. *Hansard*, 3 July 1986; K. Brown, 'Peacock Report "Should be Put in Waste Paper Basket"', *Financial Times*, 4 July 1986; M. Forsyth, 'Fanning the Wind of Change', *Guardian*, 7 July 1986.

7. P. Fiddick, 'Hurd Heralds Bill to Reform Broadcasting', *Guardian*, 10 November 1986; 'Prices Link for TV Licence Fee', *Guardian*, 14 January 1987; Cockerell, *Live from Number 10*, p. 339; S. Goodwin, '"Unpatriotic Bias" of BBC Attacked', *Independent*, 13 October 1990.

8. P. Gavan, 'Tory Whips are Kept off Air', *Broadcast*, 8 March 1985.

9. 'Tory Committee Seeks Cuts as Corporation Urges £65 Fee', *Broadcast*, 14 December 1984; D. Hewson, '£60 Licence Would "kill BBC Plans"', *The Times*, 4 January 1985; P. Stoddart, 'Is BBC Licensed to Ask for More?', *Broadcast*, 18 January 1985; P. Gavan, 'Tory Whips are Kept off Air', *Broadcast*, 8 March 1985; A. Peacock, 'The "Politics" of Investigating Broadcasting Finance', *Royal Bank of Scotland Review* (no. 153, March 1987), p. 12.

10. J. Naughtie, 'Tories Watch for TV Bias', *Guardian*, 3 July 1986; 'Update', *Broadcast*, 8 August 1986; P. Fiddick, 'Rifkind Protests at Broadcasting "Bias"', *Guardian*, 9 September 1986; M. Brown, 'Tory Attack on BBC "Bias" in Reporting', *Independent*, 11 November 1986; G. Jones, 'BBC "at All-time Low"', *Daily Telegraph*, 22 October 1986; Cockerell, *Live from Number 10*, p. 316.

11. Ingham, *Kill the Messenger*, p. 355. Robin Day's view, which perhaps represents a similar, but certainly more detached, view than Tebbit, or Young's, was that the clashes from 1979 to 1987 were 'errors of editorial judgement for which successive Directors-General must be blamed', Day, *Grand Inquisitor*, p. 193.

12. Cockerell, *Live from Number 10*, pp. 254–7; Ingham, *Kill the Messenger*, pp. 299–302.

13. Leapman, *Last Days*, p. 233; Harris, *Good and Faithful*, p. 99; Cockerell, *Live from Number 10*, pp. 270–2; Tebbit, *Upwardly Mobile*, p. 248; Milne, *DG*, p. 127.

14. M. Cockerell, P. Henessey and D. Walker, *Sources Close to the Prime Minister* (Macmillan, 1984), p. 115; Harris, *Good and Faithful*,

pp. 100–2, 129–30; Tebbit, *Upwardly Mobile*, p. 261. See Ingham, *Kill the Messenger*.

15. 'Tories Sue Panorama', *Guardian*, 7 February 1984; M. Linton, 'Gummer Warning to BBC on "Racist Smears"', *Guardian*, 13 February 1984; 'Tories Air Panorama Grievance', *Guardian*, 14 February 1984; Milne, *DG*, pp. 242–3.

16. Cockerell, *Live from Number 10*, pp. 295ff. Leapman, *Last Days*, and Milne, *DG*, have accounts of the *Real Lives* affair.

17. D. Barker, 'BBC "was Biased in Falkland Play Ban"', *Guardian*, 30 September 1986; Cockerell, *Live from Number 10*, pp. 311–12, which states that the 'Prime Minister saw the two cases as further evidence of the need to bring the BBC under control'; P. Fiddick, 'Governors Back BBC Ban on Play', *Guardian*, 15 April 1987. See I. Curteis, Letter, *Independent*, 29 June 1986.

18. On Mrs Thatcher's involvement, see A. Rawnsley, 'Star Reporter's Name Excluded', *Guardian*, 31 October 1986; M. Cassell and R. Snoddy, 'Tories Attack BBC over Libya', *Financial Times*, 31 October 1986; Tebbit, *Upwardly Mobile*, p. 316; Young, *The Enterprise Years*, p. 187.

19. Tebbit, *Upwardly Mobile*, p. 324; A. Travis and G. Henry, 'Tebbit Renews Attack on BBC', *Guardian*, 22 February 1990; Cockerell, *Live from Number 10*, pp. 310, 314.

20. J. Naughtie, 'Tories Watch for TV "Bias"', *Guardian*, 3 July 1986; quotes from CCO report taken from BBC, *C.C.O. Media Monitoring – the BBC Response* (BBC, 5 November 1986), pp. 2, 4; D. Barker, 'BBC Invited Tebbit to Talks a Month ago', *Guardian*, 4 November 1986; C. Reiss, 'BBC: Tebbit Names Names', *Standard*, 30 October 1986; P. Fiddick, 'Tebbit Refuels Bias Row with Uncowed BBC', *Guardian*, 6 November 1986. For a critical study of the CCO report, see L. Masterman, *Television and the Bombing of Libya: an Independent Analysis* (MK Media Press, 1987).

21. Leader, 'Dubious Tactics on BBC "Bias"', *Independent*, 1 November 1986; Leader, 'Mr Tebbit's Case', *Daily Telegraph*, 31 October 1986.

22. H. Young, *One of Us*, p. 512; Cockerell, *Live from Number 10*, p. 312; Tebbit, *Upwardly Mobile*, p. 325.

23. 'BBC Accused of "Evil Attack" on Tory MP', *Guardian*, 14 October 1986; S. Perera, 'Counsel Defends MP's Skit on Nuremburg', *Guardian*, 15 October 1986; P. Fiddick and D. Barker, 'BBC in Crisis over Libel Case Deal', *Guardian*, 20 October 1986; Tebbit, *Upwardly Mobile*, p. 324; Milne, *DG*, pp. 250–2, 263; A. Travis, 'PM Refuses Inquiry into Tebbit "Leaning" on Libel

Witnesses', *Guardian*, 22 October 1986; A. Bevins, 'Top Tory Named in BBC Row', *Independent*, 24 October 1986.

24. S. Clarke, 'Yes, the BBC is Biased', *Standard*, 18 November 1986, front-page banner headline. S. Perera, 'Panorama Accused of Left Bias in New Study on TV Reporting', *Guardian*, 19 November 1986; A. Rawnsley, 'Tory Link with Media Monitors is Revealed', *Guardian*, 20 November 1986; See also, S. Milne, 'Rightwing Group Comes out of the Bunker', *Guardian*, 23 June 1987. Interesting material linking one of Murdoch's companies with Lewis appeared in 'Murdoch in Sherwood', *The Digger*, 28 January 1988.

25. Milne, *DG*, pp. 259–64; D. Leigh et al., 'Special Branch Raids BBC', *Observer*, 1 February 1987; 'The Day in Politics', *Guardian*, 28 January 1987; Cockerell, *Live from Number 10*, p. 315; Lawson, *The View*, p. 315.

26. No title, *Guardian*, 11 April 1987; A. Travis, 'Tebbit Forces BBC to Admit Error', *Guardian*, 16 April 1987; Young, *The Enterprise Years*, p. 247; Ingham, *Kill the Messenger*, pp. 354–5.

27. C. Reiss, 'Now Howe to Halt BBC Film', *Standard*, 4 May 1988; P. Fiddick, 'Media File', *Guardian*, 6 June 1988; Leader, 'Impartial – but Only in Part', *Independent*, 11 June 1988; T. Gardam, Letter, *The Times*, 6 October 1988; R. Fitzwalker, 'Quite Right but Wrong', *Guardian*, 25 September 1989; Leader, 'Redheads under the Bed', *Independent*, 21 February 1990; S. Clark, Letter, *Guardian*, 26 February 1990; A. Travis and G. Henry, 'Tebbit Renews Attack on BBC', *Guardian*, 22 February 1990.

Chapter 5: Policy-making at the Centre

1. B. Crick, 'The 1987 General Election in Historical Perspective', in Skidelsky, ed., *Thatcherism*, p. 76; Cockerell, *Live from Number 10*, pp. 258ff.

2. Harris, *Good and Faithful*, p. 73; Ingham, *Kill the Messenger*, pp. 168–70. See J. Naughtie, 'BBC Discomfiture Finds a Delighted Audience on the Tory Right', *Guardian*, 29 March 1985.

3. Thatcher, *Downing Street*, pp. 267, 637; Cockerell, *Live from Number 10*, pp. 266–7, 274, 334; Milne, *DG*, p. 88; Lawson, *The View*, p. 722.

4. Cockerell, *Live from Number 10*, pp. 253–4, 268–9; F. Mount, 'Peacock. We Do Not Wish to Know That, Kindly Leave the Stage',

Daily Telegraph, 4 July 1986; Lawson, *The View*, p. 722; R. Harris and V. Smart, 'PM Cautions Press', *Observer*, 8 May 1988.

5. Cockerell, *Live from Number 10*, pp. 333–4; D. Barker, 'Thatcher Wants Channel 4 to Make a Profit', *Guardian*, 5 October 1983; Thatcher, *Downing Street*, p. 635; Ingham, *Kill the Messenger*, p. 344; Lawson, *The View*, pp. 577–8, 722.

6. Lawson, *The View*, pp. 383,467; Kavanagh, *Thatcherism*, pp. 26, 259; Harris, *Good and Faithful*, p. 150.

7. Tebbit, *Upwardly Mobile*, p. 218; Lawson, *The View*, pp. 107, 123; Thatcher, *Downing Street*, p. 152; Harris, *Good and Faithful*, pp. 187, 146; Kavanagh, *Thatcherism*, p. 265. See M. Jones, 'How Thatcher Played her Card and Lost the Trick', *Sunday Times*, 30 July 1989, on her precarious relations with the Cabinet 17 months before her removal from office.

8. Lawson, *The View*, p. 125; Tebbit, *Upwardly Mobile*, p. 185.

9. S. Shamoon, 'Reece and Bell: the PR Petals', *Observer*, 2 August 1989; Young, *Enterprise Years*, pp. 106–7; T. Brooks, 'Taking his Dramas out of a Crisis', *Media Week*, 8 February 1985; T. Bell, 'My Media Week', *Media Week*, 26 July 1985; P. Lennon, 'Pedlar of the Political Illusion', *Guardian*, 2 November 1992.

10. 'Broadcasting Deserves Better Treatment', *Observer*, 26 June 1988; D. Hencke, 'The Think-tank Engine', *Guardian*, 10 March 1989; L. Marks, 'Waddingtons's Game Plan', *Observer*, 29 October 1989; Horrie and Clarke, *Fuzzy Monsters*, pp. 31, 170.

11. Tebbit, *Upwardly Mobile*, pp. 232–3; Thatcher, *Downing Street*, p. 421; 'Broadcasting Deserves Better Treatment', *Observer*, 26 June 1988; A. Lycett, 'Whose Finger on the Button?', *The Times*, 20 July 1988; R. Ingrams, *Observer*, 10 December 1989.

12. Young, *Enterprise Years*, pp. 17, 32, 73; Tebbit, *Upwardly Mobile*, p. 270; 'Broadcasting Deserves Better Treatment', *Observer*, 26 June 1988; A. Lycett, 'Whose Finger on the Button?', *The Times*, 20 July 1988; R. Ingrams, *Observer*, 10 December 1989. See also A. Davidson, *Under the Hammer* (Mandarin, 1992).

13. D. Barker, 'Physicist Appointed to Cable Authority', *Guardian*, 13 November 1984; *Who's Who* (1986), entry under P. Johnson; P. Johnson, 'Begging Bowl Economics', and 'Digging the Duopoly', in *Spectator*, 4 January 1985, 2 September 1989.

14. 'The Profile: Woodrow Wyatt, Read him and Wonder', *Independent*, 13 October 1990; G. Henry, 'The Voice of Reason' and J. Pilger, 'Code for Charlatans', in *Guardian*, 8 October 1990.

15. Cockerell, *Live from Number 10*, p. 257; Leapman, *Last Days*, p. 244.

16. H. Davies, 'Do We Really Need the BBC?', *The Times*, 24 April 1983.

17. A.S.C. Ehrenberg and T.P. Barwise, 'How Much Does UK Television Cost?, *International Journal of Advertising*, no. 2, 1983 pp. 17, 23.

18. Velanjovski and Bishop, *Choice by Cable*, p. 113; H. Davies, 'Do We Really Need the BBC?', *The Times*, 24 April 1983; *The Conservative Manifesto 1983* (Conservative Central Office, 1983).

19. R. Brooks, 'Who Should Pay for the BBC?', *Sunday Times*, 3 June 1984; C. Brown, 'Ministers Aim for Radio Ads on BBC', *Guardian*, 5 June 1984; R. Snoddy, 'The BBC Sharpens up its Act', *Financial Times*, 22 September 1984.

20. Milne, *DG*, pp. 164, 218; S. Shamoon, 'The Adman's Assault on "Auntie"', *Observer*, 11 November 1984.

21. Leapman, *Last Days*, pp. 260–2; Cockerell, *Live from Number 10*, p. 294; Leader, 'Keeping "Commercials" at Bay', *Observer*, 15 December 1984; P. Fiddick, 'How the Commercial Breaks Would Stretch as the Revenue Shrank', *Guardian*, 4 February 1985.

22. R. Low, 'Thatcher Tells BBC: £55 Only', *Observer*, 16 December 1984; B. Grantham and J. Robinson, 'Licence Fee Pressure Piles Up', *Television Weekly*, 21 December 1984; 'Is BBC Licensed to Ask for More?', *Broadcast*, 18 January 1985; P. Johnson, 'Begging Bowl Economics', *Spectator*, 4 January 1985. See also J. Margolis, 'Drastic TV Shake-up Will Cut Jobs and Pay', *Mail on Sunday*, 13 January 1985.

23. J. Robinson, 'Future Ads for BBC?', *Television Weekly*, 4 January 1985.

24. R. Snoddy, 'Questions for BBC Inquiry', *Media Week*, 5 April 1985; 'Peacock Committee Delayed', *Broadcast*, 5 April 1985.

25. P. Fiddick, 'Media File', *Guardian*, 15 September 1986; R. Evans, 'Licence Fee to be Preserved', *The Times*, 12 December 1988.

26. J. Carvel and D. Barker, 'Cabinet Overruled Tebbit on Ministerial Link for BBC Attack', *Guardian*, 3 November 1986; Cockerell, *Live from Number 10*, p. 312.

27. Lawson, *The View*, p. 255; Tebbit, *Upwardly Mobile*, pp. 202–3; Thatcher, *Downing Street*, pp. 307, 634; Cockerell, 1989, p. 258.

28. Leapman, *Last Days*, p. 105; Milne, *DG*, 1989, p. 104; Tebbit, *Upwardly Mobile*, p. 247; Cockerell, *Live from Number 10*, p. 274.

29. S. Lambert, *Channel Four: Television with a Difference?* (BFI, 1982); K. Gosling, 'Colour TV Licence Rise by £12 to £46', *The Times*, 2 December 1981; Milne, *DG*, p. 218; two articles in *Admap* by W. Philips, 'Wayside Pulpit: ILR with the Brakes on', August 1981, p. 378 and 'Wayside Pulpit: Mr Thompson's flag', April 1981, pp. 144–8; Local Radio Workshop, *Capital: Local Radio and Private Profit* (Comedia, 1983), p. 111.

30. Leapman, *Last Days*, p. 201; Baker, *Turbulent Years*, pp. 85–8; Thatcher, *Downing Street Years*, p. 636; L. Marks, 'How Peacock Became a Cuckoo', *Observer*, 6 July 1986; R. Brooks, 'Whitelaw Hits out at TV Changes', *Observer*, 11 December 1988.

31. Lawson, *The View*, pp. 73–4; Kavanagh, *Thatcherism*, 1990, p. 256.

32. P. Fiddick, 'Brittan Announces Two Satellite Channels for ITV', *Guardian*, 17 September 1983; R. Snoddy, 'News Analysis', *Media Week*, 15 March 1985.

33. R. Brooks, 'Who Should Pay for the BBC?', *Sunday Times*, 3 June 1984; A. Dickson, 'Commercial Radio's Tide may be Ebbing', *Observer*, 3 June 1984.

34. R. Snoddy, 'BBC Faces Independent Audit', *Financial Times*, 21 July 1984; D. Wilby, 'Don't be Alarmed: these Reviews will Demonstrate how Efficient We Are', *Ariel*, 1 August 1984; Leapman, *Last Days*, p. 256; Milne, *DG*, p. 163.

35. L. Brittan, *Airwaves*, Winter 1984/5 (IBA), p. 5.

36. SF, 'Shaw Takes over Hurd Hot Seat', *Broadcast*, 14 August 1984; J. Robinson, 'Future Ads for BBC?', *Television Weekly*, 4 January 1985; R. Brooks and S. Summers, 'Making the Money Go Round', *Sunday Times*, 2 December 1984.

37. J. Margolis, 'Drastic TV Shake-up Will Cut Jobs and Pay', *Mail on Sunday*, 13 January 1985; A. Raphael, 'Study backs BBC Fee Rise', *Observer*, 3 February 1985; H. Thompson, 'Licence Debate is Catch 22 for BBC's Image', *Broadcast*, 25 January 1985; Milne, *DG*, p. 168.

38. Milne, *DG*, pp. 218, 172; R. Snoddy, 'BBC Cheques and Balances', *Media Week*, 26 July 1985; R. Snoddy, 'Questions for BBC Inquiry', *Media Week*, 5 April 1985.

39. *Hansard*, 27 March 1985, cols 480, 485, 487.

40. G. Henry, 'Quentin Thomas', *Broadcast*, 18 November 1988; 'After the Licence Fee – BBC at the Crossroads', *Television Today*, 9 May 1985; P. Fiddick, 'Media File', *Guardian*, 3 June 1985; L. Marks, 'How Peacock Became a Cuckoo', *Observer*, 6 July

1986; D. Barker, 'Whitehall "Tried to Blacken" Peacock Report', *Guardian*, 30 July 1986.

41. B. West, Director AIRC, Letter, *Broadcast*, 29 August 1986.

42. *Hansard*, 3 July 1986, col. 1179.

43. P. Simmonds, 'Government Plans for New TV Watchdog', *UK Press Gazette*, 22 or 29 June 1987; M. Brown, 'New Complaints Body to Keep Check on Television', *Independent*, 8 October 1987; 'Director for Watchdog Body', *The Times*, 7 November 1988.

44. Thatcher, *Downing Street*, p. 46; J. Lloyd, 'Serving Thatcher's Children', *Financial Times*, 20 July 1988; D. Walker, 'Diary', *The Times*, 8 November 1988; Mrs Thatcher's relations with the civil service are discussed in P. Henessey, *Whitehall*, rev. edn (Fontana, 1990), especially Chapter 15.

Chapter 6: The Peacock Exercise

1. R. Snoddy, 'A Light which may be Ignored', *Financial Times*, 4 July 1986; P. Fiddick, 'How the Commercial Breaks would Stretch as the Revenue Shrank', *Guardian*, 4 February 1985; see the interesting lecture by B. Thorne, *The BBC's Finances and Cost Control* (BBC Lunchtime Lecture, Eighth Series, no.3, 1970).

2. J. Davies, 'UK and European TV Policy-Making in an Information-Poor Environment' (Paper presented at the Programme on Information and Communication Technologies Conference, Newport, Wales, 1992), pp. 6–8; Home Office, *Review of a Working Group of Officials of the Home Office Treasury and Independent Broadcasting Authority. May 1985* (Broadcasting Department, Home Office, February 1986). I am grateful to Jonathan Davies for supplying me with information and references on the subject of the levy. The problem goes back further than the 1980s. See C. Heller, *Broadcasting and Accountability* (BFI, 1978), p. 51, where the following comment is made about the 'poverty of information provided about broadcasting by the broadcasting organisations'. 'It is remarkable, to say the least, that the two authorities responsible for supervision of expenditure of over £300 million on public service broadcasting should present their accounts in thirteen pages in the case of the BBC (including notes) and ten pages in the case of the IBA (including notes but excluding the details of individual ITV companies, which have to be obtained from company reports). This provides an inadequate basis for informed discussion of existing

services, let alone broader consideration of national options in broadcasting.'

3. R. Snoddy, '"£73.9m Surplus" for BBC', *Financial Times*, 8 November 1983; BBC, *Annual Report* 1985 (BBC, 1984), p. 144; S. Blanchard, *The Audio and Audio-visual Media Industries in London* (GLC Economic Policy Group – Strategy Document no. 7, June 1983), p. 49.
4. See Chapter 1, note 8, above; Thorne, *The BBC's Finances*, p. 6; P. Fiddick, 'A Licence to Survive', *Guardian*, 4 February 1985; A. Ehrenberg and T.P. Barwise, *How Much Does UK Television Cost?* (London Business School, 1982); Peat Marwick Mitchell, *Value for Money Review* (London, BBC, 31 January 1985). See the informative article by M. Cave, 'Financing British Broadcasting', *Lloyds Bank Review*, no. 157 (July 1985), pp. 25, 35.
5. 'Tory Committee Seeks Cuts as Corporation Urges £65 Fee', *Broadcast*, 14 December 1984; SC, 'Shaw Calls for a Broadcast Inquiry', *Broadcast*, 23 November 1984; B. Grantham and J. Robinson, 'Licence Fee Pressure Piles up', *Television Weekly*, 21 December 1984; D. Housham, 'Brinton's Hazard Warning', *Television Weekly*, 18 January 1985; 'BBC Inquiry: Mini Annan is not on', *Broadcast*, 1 February 1985.
6. 'BBC Inquiry: Mini Annan is not on', *Broadcast*, 1 February 1985. See the work of Jonathan Davies, PICT paper March 1992; S. Brittan, 'The Fight for Freedom in Broadcasting', *Political Quarterly*, vol. 58, no. 1 (Jan.–March 1987), p. 4; Lawson, *The View*, p. 721; Thatcher, *Downing Street*, p. 636.
7. L. Marks, 'How Peacock Became a Cuckoo', *Observer*, 6 July 1986; Cockerell, *Live from Number 10*, p. 294.
8. D. Smith, 'Free Market Economist's Critical Support of BBC', *The Times*, 28 March 1985: biographical details for this note and those up to and including note 14 are also based on Home Office, *Peacock Report: Viewers and Listeners to be in Driving Seat* (Home Office, Press Release, 3 July 1986).
9. G. Hodgson, 'Now is the Time for all Right-thinking Men ...', *Sunday Times Magazine*, 4 March 1984; Kavanagh, *Thatcherism*, p. 54; Brittan, 'The Fight for Freedom', pp. 6, 20, where he quotes from his book, *Capitalism and the Permissive Society* (Macmillan, 1978), p. 298; Milne, *DG*, p. 172.
10. P. Monteith, 'Peacock Choice Comes under Fire', *Broadcast*, 24 May 1985; Leapman, *Last Days*, p. 127ff; Brittan, 'The Fight for Freedom', pp. 6–7.

11. P. Monteith, 'Peacock Choice Comes under Fire', *Broadcast*, 24 May 1985; Arts Council of Great Britain, *Faces and Names* (ACGB, August 1985).

12. P. Monteith, 'Peacock Choice Comes under Fire', *Broadcast*, 24 May 1985; M. Whorle, 'Peacock Shows its True Blue Colours', *Media Week*, 24 May 1985; 'Ads on the Beeb Spell Doom for Broadcasting', *Labour Research* (February 1986), p. 11.

13. P. Monteith, 'Peacock Choice Comes under Fire', *Broadcast*, 24 May 1985; 'Ads on the Beeb Spell Doom for Broadcasting', *Labour Research* (February 1986), p. 11.

14. M. Whorle, 'Peacock Shows its True Blue Colours', *Media Week*, 24 May 1985; S. Summers, 'Swearing in the Jury', *Sunday Times*, 26 May 1985; Brittan, 'The Fight for Freedom', p. 6.

15. Brittan, 'The Fight for Freedom', p. 7; M. Whorle, 'Peacock Shows its True Blue Colours', *Media Week*, 24 May 1985; P. Fiddick, 'Media File', *Guardian*, 3 June 1985. See also S. Summers, 'Swearing in the Jury', *Sunday Times*, 26 May 1985 and Anon, 'Taking a Break from a Brown Study', *Broadcast*, 7 June 1985. Peacock denied he was hired to force the BBC to take advertisements: see E. Gorman, 'Peacock, "I'm no Hired Gun"', *Broadcast*, 5 April 1985.

16. Brittan, 'The Fight for Freedom', p. 6; Home Office, *Report of the Committee on Financing the BBC* (Cmnd. 9824, HMSO, July 1986), para. 2 [hereafter, *Peacock*] for details of the Committee's activities. Home Office, *Peacock Committee* (Home Office, Press Release, 29 May 1985); 'Update', *Broadcast*', 19 July 1985. The organisations involved were the Association of Independent Radio Contractors, Broadcasting Department of the Home Office, Cable Television Association, Conservative Party, Incorporated Society of British Advertisers, IBA, Independent Television Contractors, Labour Party, Liberal Party, National Consumer Council, National Economic Research Associates, Newspaper Society, Social Democratic Party: source Home Office Information Sheet. Those excluded included the broadcasting unions, NUJ, ABS/ETA, and media pressure groups, the Campaign for Press and Broadcasting Freedom, Voice of the Listener, and the Community Radio Association.

17. A. Davidson, 'Beating the Peacock Team into Submission', *Marketing*, 30 January 1986; R. Snoddy, 'Peacock's Tale of Woe', *Media Week*, 31 January 1986; L. Marks, 'How Peacock Became a Cuckoo', *Observer*, 6 July 1986; Brittan, 'The Fight for

Freedom', p. 6; R. Snoddy, 'Inquiry Rejects Advertising on BBC Television', *Financial Times*, 16 May 1986; A. Raphael, 'Peacock: Plans for Pay-as-you-see TV', *Observer*, 18 May 1986.

18. Hetherington, in Kavanagh and Seldon, eds, *The Thatcher Effect*, p. 298; Editorial, *Broadcast*, 12 September 1986; P. Fiddick, 'Peacock Gave Minority Views a Rough Ride, says Hetherington', *Guardian*, 8 September 1986.

19. Milne, *DG*, pp. 221-2; P. Fiddick, 'Peacock Gave Minority Views a Rough Ride, says Hetherington', *Guardian*, 8 September 1986; P. Fiddick, 'Static Problem', *Guardian*, 15 September 1986; Home Office, *Peacock: Viewers and Listeners to be in Driving Seat* (Press Release), 3 July 1986.

20. Peacock, 'The "Politics"', p. 4; H. Lee, 'Split over Sale of Radio 1 and 2', *Daily Telegraph*, 4 July 1986; D. Barker and J. Naughtie, 'Peacock Urges Auction of all 15 ITV Franchises', *Guardian*, 27 June 1986.

21. Insufficent time has passed for a complete assessment of the significance of the Peacock Committee to be made. But there can be little doubt that its activities, assumptions and recommendations would repay detailed critical historical analysis in years to come. Here I only deal with the key issues dealt with in the report.

22. *Peacock*, paras 1, 272, and list of research papers commissioned in Appendix D.

23. R. Collins et al., *The Economics of Television: the UK Case* (Sage, 1988) welcomes the focus on economics in *Peacock*, but does not fully accept the policies advocated by the report. Nicholas Garnham has described how under capitialism 'Culture as part of material production itself' is 'directly subordinate to or at least in a closely determined articulation with the laws of development of capital': see 'Contribution to a Political Economy of Mass Communication' in his *Capitalism and Communication: Global Culture and the Economics of Information* (Sage, 1990), p. 32. The *Peacock* report develops an argument in favour of the benefits that would be brought to the UK by making UK broadcasting 'directly subordinate to or at least' placed 'in a closely determined articulation with the laws of development of capital'.

24. ACTT, *Preliminary Submission to the Committee on Financing the BBC* (ACTT, August 1985).

25. The calculation of the number of institutional submissions is based on my analysis of a list in Appendix B of the report. See S. Barnett

and D. Docherty, *The Peacock Debate in the UK* (Broadcasting Research Unit Working Paper, n.d., but probably 1986), p. 1.

26. Organisations against advertisements on the BBC, but not in the BRU summary included, ACTT, BETA, British Film and Television Producers Association, Society for Education in Film and Television, Campaign for Press and Broadcasting Freedom.

27. Labour Party, *Labour Party Submission to the Peacock Inquiry* (Labour Party, n.d.), pp. 1–2; Liberal Party, *Liberal Party Policy Briefing: Financing the BBC* (Liberal Party, September 1985), para. 1; 'The Union's Response to the Peacock Committee', *BETA News* (September/October 1985), pp. 27–28; NUJ, *Evidence from the National Union of Journalists to the Peacock Committee on Financing the British Broadcasting Corporation* (NUJ, n.d.), paras 2.28, 6.1; Equity, *Memorandum Submitted by the Councils of British Equity to the Committee on Financing the BBC* (Equity, 27 August 1985), p. 6.

28. AIRC, *Initial Evidence to the Home Office Committee on Financing the BBC* (AIRC, August 1985), paras 4(i)–4(iii).

29. R. Snoddy, 'Peacock's Tale of Woe', *Marketing Week*, 31 January 1986.

30. *Peacock*, para. 598.

31. For a different perspective on the problems with the contemporary media and of ways to address them, see Curran and Seaton, *Power without Responsibility*; J. Curran, 'The Different Approaches to Media Reform', in J. Curran et al., eds, *Bending Reality: the State of the Media* (Pluto 1986). One of the more bizarre aspects of *Peacock* is the absence of this kind of debate from its pages.

32. *Peacock*, paras 16–27, and, more explicitly, 459–50; M. Harris, *London Newspapers in the Age of Walpole* (Associated University Press, 1987), p. 8; Curran and Seaton, *Power Without Responsibility*, pp. 7–127. For a sustained criticism of the assumptions underlying Peacock's conventional account of press freedom, see J. Keane, *The Media and Democracy* (Polity, 1991).

33. *Peacock*, paras 28–35.

34. The work of Scannell, Cardiff, Briggs, Curran and Seaton provides a much more satisfactory approach to this problem *because* they analyse public service broadcasting historically.

35. *Peacock*, Chapter 4, especially para. 183. On the operation of the market in the media in the United States, see B.H. Bagdikian, *The Media Monopoly*, 2nd edn (Beacon Press, 1987). For a sharp criticism of the Committee's use of the UK publishing market as

a model for broadcasting, see Collins et al., *Economics of Television*, p. 126.

36. *Peacock*, paras 197, 580. See the work of Briggs and Scannell and Cardiff for some basic perspectives on the original set of ideas about the purposes of broadcasting, work overlooked or ill absorbed by the Committee. For a criticism of a method similar to Peacock's, in its idealism, ahistoricism and the way its conclusions are embedded in its premises, see the critique of Louis Althusser in E.P. Thompson, *The Poverty of Theory* (Merlin, 1978).

37. *Peacock*, paras 592, 593, 598.

38. *Peacock*, paras 603–10, Table 12.1: The Three Stages.

39. Department of National Heritage, *The Future of the BBC: a Consultation Document* (Cm 2098, HMSO, November 1992), para. 6.9; P. Fiddick, 'Peacock Gave Minority Views a Rough Ride, says Hetherington', *Guardian*, 8 September 1986.

40. Davidson, *Under the Hammer*, pp. 279, 281; P. Fiddick, 'Peacock Gave Minority Views a Rough Ride, says Hetherington', *Guardian*, 8 September 1986.

41. Peacock, pp. 136–46 for the quotes taken from the Stage 1 recommendations.

42. *Peacock*, paras 683, 685, 688.

43. *Peacock*, paras 693, 694, 696–8.

44. *Peacock*, paras 700–708.

45. Brittan, 'The Fight for Freedom', p. 4; Peacock, 'The "Politics"', pp. 4–6.

Chapter 7: The Policy Framework after Peacock

1. 'Debate Shows Members are Divided over Some Proposals', *The Times*, 4 July 1986; H. Lee, 'Split over Sale of Radios 1 and 2', *Daily Telegraph*, 4 July 1986.

2. These all appeared on 4 July 1986: 'Peacock's Fuzzy Vision', *Today*; 'A Peacock and a Sitting Duck', *Guardian*; 'The Future of Broadcasting', *Financial Times*.

3. Leader, *The Times*; 'Opinion: Let Viewers Pay their Money and Take their Choice', *Daily Express*, both on 4 July 1986.

4. These all appeared on 4 July 1986: 'Peacock Grounded', *Daily Telegraph*, and 'Another Bit of Committeeitis', *Daily Mail*, both 4 July 1986. See also D. Barker, 'Cabinet Split on Free-market TV',

Guardian, 28 June 1986; and P. Donovan, 'Peacock's Ruffled Feathers', *Today*, 4 July 1986.

5. R. Snoddy, 'The Peacock Report', *Financial Times*, 4 July 1986; Editorial, 'Questions of Independence', *Broadcast*, 11 July 1986; P. Fiddick, 'BBC Image Defended', *Guardian*, 27 November 1986; B. Cox, 'Peacock and Ostriches', *New Statesman*, 29 August 1986; Peacock, 'The "Politics"', pp. 13, 15. See also D. Barker, 'Broadcasters Cool on Vision of the Future', *Guardian*, 4 July 1986.

6. D. Barker and J. Naughtie, 'Peacock Urges Auction of All 15 ITV Franchises', *Guardian*, 27 June 1986; D. Barker and J. Carvel, 'Hurd Supports Proposal for Free Market in Broadcasting', *Guardian*, 4 July 1986; Milne, *DG*, p. 232; L. Marks, 'How Peacock Became a Cuckoo', *Observer*, 6 July 1986; A. Peacock, 'Peacock Attacks ITV Franchise Proposal', *Financial Times*, 6 February 1989; Thatcher, *Downing Street*, pp. 635–6.

7. D. Hurd, *Home Secretary's Speech to the Royal Television Society Convention Dinner, 8 November 1986* (Press text, Home Office, 1986); Lawson, *The View*, pp. 128, 720–3; Brittan, 'The fight for freedom', p. 3.

8. See J. Davies's, 'UK and European TV Policy-making'; Lawson, *The View*, pp. 720–3.

9. Lawson, *The View*, p. 599; Young, *Enterprise Years*, pp. 38, 39, 251–2; Tebbit, *Upwardly Mobile*, p. 268; *Who's Who* (1993); Thatcher, *Downing Street*, p. 875.

10. H. Davies, 'Do We Really Need the BBC?', *The Times*, 24 April 1983; A. Lycett, 'Whose Finger on the Button?', *The Times*, 20 July 1988.

11. Milne, *DG*, pp. 149–53; Baker, *Turbulent Years*, p. 87; B. West, Letter, *Broadcast*, 14 August 1984; R. Snoddy, 'Commercial Radio Station to Sue Pirates', *Financial Times*, 9 November 1984; NH, 'Jackie Injunction Sought by Mercury', *Broadcast*, 16 November 1984.

12. C. Hughes, 'Hurd converted to Free-market Broadcasting', *Independent*, 8 November 1988; Thatcher, *Downing Street*, pp. 636–7; A. Lycett, 'Whose Finger on the Button?', *The Times*, 20 July 1988; Davidson, *Under the Hammer*, pp. 13–15; M. Leapman, 'Satellite Only Plan for TV', *Independent*, 11 June 1988; M. Brown, 'Satellite Proposal Perplexes TV Chiefs', *Independent*, 13 June 1988; Young, *Enterprise Years*, pp. 352–3.

13. A. Raphael, 'Study Backs BBC Fee Rise', *Observer*, 3 February 1985.

14. Milne, *DG*, p. 232; S. de Bruxelles, 'Radio Scheme Axed by Cabinet', *Observer*, 29 June 1986; D. Barker, 'Hurd Postpones

Action on Broadcasting Report', *Guardian*, 2 July 1986. See also R. Snoddy, 'A Light which May be Ignored', *Financial Times*, 4 July 1986.

15. All quotes from *Hansard*, 3 July 1986, cols 1176–89.

16. 'Government Will Act on Peacock', *Broadcast*, 11 July 1986; D. Hurd, *Home Secretary's Speech to the Royal Television Society Convention Dinner, 8 November 1986* (Press text, Home Office, 1986).

17. D. Barker, 'Ministers to Peer into the Future of Television', *Guardian*, 6 August 1986; N. Higham and M. Wohrle, 'Rift in Whitehall over Peacock's Long-term Policy', *Broadcast*, 8 August 1986.

18. A. Travis, 'Hurd Freezes Licence Fee and BBC Changes', and 'Spectre of Tebbit's Pressure against BBC Hovers over Debate on Peacock', both in *Guardian*, 21 November 1986. On DTI and the independents, see A. Lycett, 'Whose Finger on the Button?', *The Times*, 20 July 1988 and N. Higham and M. Wohrle, 'Rift in Whitehall over Peacock's Long-term Policy', *Broadcast*, 8 August 1986.

19. 'Prices Link for the TV Licence Fee', *Guardian*, 15 January 1987; Home Office, *Radio Choices and Opportunities* (HMSO, 1987).

20. K. Harper, 'Monopolies Inquiry into TV Working', *Guardian*, 29 March 1988; T. O'Malley, Letter, *Guardian*, 1 April 1988; 'Trying a New Tack to Break TV Unions', *Labour Research* (May 1988); *Hansard*, 16 May 1988, col. 685ff.

21. 'Peacock-pay-TV Plan Gets Cold Shoulder', *Broadcast*, 17 July 1987; Home Office, *Broadcasting in the 90s: Competition, Choice and Quality* (HMSO, CM. 517, November 1988), paras 3.8, 3.9.

22. Home Affairs Select Committee, *Third Report: the Future of Broadcasting*, vol. 1 (HMSO, June 1988), paras 93–5.

23. Home Affairs Select Committee, *Third Report*, vol. 1, pp. xlix–lii; M. Brown, 'Hurd Wants Licence Replaced by Subscription', *Independent*, 23 June 1988.

24. R. Evans, 'Rivals May Get Time on BBC TV', *The Times*, 21 October 1988; C. Hughes, ' "Pay as You View" Plan for BBC', *Independent*, 28 October 1988; R. Evans, 'A Screen Turned Upside Down', *The Times*, 11 November 1988; R. Brooks, 'Too Many Cooks', *Observer*, 13 November 1988.

25. Home Office, *Broadcasting in the 90s*, Chapter 3, paras 91–3, 150.

26. A. Milne, 'Down the US Road', *Independent*, 16 November 1988.

27. *Hansard*, 8 February 1989, cols 1010, 1037–8, 1062.

28. Mellor piloted the bill through Parliament. He accepted the broad thrust of the reforms but, in harmony with his own predisposition and Home Office thinking, modified some of the sharper aspects

of the Bill. The most significant modification he accepted was one promoted by the IBA and the ITVA which changed the auctioning process and allowed greater discretion to the awarding body to give franchises to companies with lower bids but who promised higher quality. This was the proposal advocated strongly in a high-profile publicity campaign by an organisation which was funded, in part, by a commercial TV company, the Campaign for Quality Television. When the franchises were readvertised in 1991 only four companies lost their franchises. Lawson, who had resigned as Chancellor in 1989, considered the auctioning process had been effectively watered down during the passage of the Bill to an Act, and as a result the outcome was a 'farce'. He blamed the traditionalism of the Home Office, who accepted amendments 'to the Bill insisted on by Parliament during its passage to the statute book, which Home Office Ministers (responsible for the Bill's passage) showed little disposition to resist'; Lawson, *The View*, p. 723. Thatcher endorses this view when discussing her preference for a system which, in the end, would have made franchise awards dependent on the highest bid: 'But the Home Office team argued that we had to make concessions – first in June 1989 in response to consultation on the White Paper and then at report stage of the broadcasting bill in the spring of 1990, when they said there would be great difficulties otherwise. These unfortunately muddied the transparency which I had hoped to achieve and produced a compromise which turned out to be less than satisfactory when the ITC bestowed the franchises the following year "in the old-fashioned way".' *Downing Street*, pp. 637–8.

29. G. Henry, 'TV Licence Fee to be Set Below RPI', *Guardian*, 2 October 1990.

30. For more detail, see T. O'Malley and J. Treharne, *Selling the Beeb: the BBC and the Charter Review Process* (Campaign for Press and Broadcasting Freedom, 1993). For a view of the BBC in the 1990s which by and large fits into Peacock's vision, see D. Green, *A Better BBC: Public Service Broadcasting in the '90s* (Centre for Policy Studies, March 1991).

Chapter 8: The BBC under Thatcher

1. See A. Briggs, *The BBC: the First Fifty Years* (OUP, 1985) and C. Heller, *Broadcasting and Accountability*; J. Paxman, *Friends*, p. 342, n.56.

2. BBC, *Annual Report and Handbook 1983* (BBC, 1982), p. xii; Young, *Enterprise Years*, pp. 113, 131; 'Profile', *Observer*, 31 July 1983; Horrie and Clarke, *Fuzzy Monsters*, p. 16; Cockerell, *Live from Number 10*, pp. 293–4.

3. Leader, 'The BBC's Empty Chair', *Guardian*, 12 September 1986; entry on Hussey in *Who's Who* (1987); J. Carvel and D. Barker, 'Cabinet Overruled Tebbit on Ministerial Link for BBC Attack', *Guardian*, 3 November 1986.

4. R. Brooks, 'Enter from Stage Right, Man with Hot Potato', *Observer*, 5 October 1986; B. Wenham, 'Hello Welcome and Speak up', *The Times*, 9 May 1990.

5. For an analysis of the unrepresentative social and educational background of Governors of the BBC and IBA at this time, see N. Willmot, 'Who's Running Broadcasting?', *Broadcast*, 13 February 1987; S. Faulks, 'Struggle for Power in BBC', *Sunday Telegraph*, 18 May 1986; Milne, *DG*, p. 280.

6. D. Leigh, 'MI6 Career of BBC Governor Revealed', *Observer*, 26 June 1988; Cockerell, *Live from Number 10*, p. 297; A. Milne, 'Heavy Hands on the Tiller', *Guardian*, 3 February 1992.

7. Kavanagh, *Thatcherism*, p. 84; Milne, *DG*, p. 108; W. Rees-Mogg, 'Time for the BBC Gentleman to Hand over to the Players', *Independent*, 7 October 1986; Paxman, *Friends*, p. 120; Young, *Enterprise Years*, p. 194.

8. The main source for this discussion of the BBC and satellite, where not otherwise given, is IBA, *Direct Broadcasting by Satellite* (Information sheet, IBA, n.d. but 1986; hereafter *IBA/DBS/86*).

9. Leapman, *Last Days*, p. 200; P. Fiddick, 'Deadlock on the Recipe for the Dish of the Day', *Guardian*, 1 December 1983; BBC, *Annual Report 1983*, p. 1; Milne, *DG*, p. 145.

10. P. Fiddick, 'Deadlock on the Recipe for the Dish of the Day', *Guardian*, 1 December 1983; R. Brooks, 'BBC May Quit Satellite Race' and 'Satellite Television Won't Pay – BBC', *Sunday Times*, 17, 31 July 1983.

11. P. Williams, 'Milne Amicable but Ruthless for BBC', *Broadcast*, 30 March 1984.

12. D. Barker, 'Satellite TV Plan Leads to Franchise Demand', *Guardian*, 20 January 1984; D. Barker, 'ITV Companies Make BBC Wait for Satellite Decision' and 'ITV Companies Ready to Accept Satellite Plans', *Guardian*, 7 February 1984 and 28 March 1984.

13. *IBA/DBS/86*; SF, 'Challenge to BBC's Share of DBS', *Broadcast*, 20 July 1984; SF, 'Indies: BBC Can't Call DBS Tune', *Broadcast*, 10 August 1984.

14. *IBA/DBS/86*; B. Grantham, 'DBS Project Cost Hitch', *Television Weekly*, 21 December 1984; T. Brooks, 'Taking his Dramas out of a Crisis', *Media Week*, 8 February 1985; PM, 'DBS Threatened by Licence Row', *Broadcast*, 15 March 1985; Milne, *DG*, pp. 155–6.

15. *IBA/DBS/86*; R. Negrine, 'Introduction', in R. Negrine, ed., *Satellite Broadcasting: the Politics and Implications of the New Media* (Routledge, 1988), p. 8; A. Burkitt, 'Where Does DBS Go from Here?', *Broadcast*, 28 June 1985; R. Snoddy, 'News Analysis', *Media Week*, 28 June 1985.

16. Day, *Grand Inquisitor*, pp. 194–5.

17. D. Barker, 'Lack of Money Curbs BBC Daytime TV', *Guardian*, 4 October 1983; P. Williams, 'Milne Amiable but Ruthless for the BBC', *Broadcast*, 30 March 1984; RF, 'Warning on BBC Licence Fee', *Broadcast*, 6 July 1984; 'Question-and-answer Guide to the BBC's Finances', *Ariel*, 4 July 1984; D. Wilby, '"Don't be Alarmed; these Reviews will Demonstrate how Efficient We Are"', *Ariel*, 1 August 1984.

18. NH, 'Milne Spurns Plan for BBC Adverts', *Broadcast*, 12 October 1984; 'Doubts about BBC £10 Car Radio Fee', *Broadcast*, 9 November 1984; S. Shamoon, 'The Adman's Assault on "Auntie"', *Observer*, 11 November 1984; 'Well They Would ...', *Ariel*, 14 November 1984; A.S.C. Ehrenberg, *The Funding of BBC Television* (no publisher, December 1984), title page, pp. 1, 20 and Ehrenberg, 'Putting a Price on Quality', *Observer*, 15 December 1984.

19. 'Milne Tours Phone-ins', *Broadcast*, 14 December 1984; C. Dunkley, three articles called, 'The BBC – the Best Bargain in Britain', in *Radio Times*, 19–25 January, 26 January–1 February, 2–8 February 1985; edited version of Radio 4 debate in 'Advertising and how the BBC is to be Financed', *Stage and Television Today*, 31 January 1985; P. Fiddick, 'Battle Plan that Opens a New Panorama', *Guardian*, 4 February 1985.

20. H. Thompson, 'Licence Debate is Catch 22 for BBC's Image', *Broadcast*, 25 January 1985; P. Stoddart, 'Milne Warns of Danger in Change', *Broadcast*, 25 January 1985; 'Milne Puts Cost of TV in Focus', *Broadcast*, 1 March 1985; Leapman, *Last Days*, p. 269; Milne, *DG*, p. 171.

21. '£58 Licence "Disappoints" BBC', *Broadcast*, 29 March 1985; P. Donovan, 'BBC Chief Admits: "We'll Fight for Ads if We Must"', *Daily Mail*, 1 April 1985; Milne, *DG*, pp. 183, 219.

22. Milne, *DG*, pp. 173–85; D. Barker, 'BBC Governors Look for Change Close to Top', *Guardian*, 5 June 1985.

23. D. Housham, 'The Buck Stops Here', *Broadcast*, 12 July 1985; P. Fiddick, 'BBC Aims to Axe 4,000 Jobs in £30m Switch', *Guardian*, 18 July 1985; 'Checkland Sets up "Axe" Committee', *Broadcast*, 2 August 1985; 'Update', *Broadcast*, 5 July 1985; P. Fiddick, 'Can the BBC Convince Peacock?', *Guardian*, 1 July 1985.

24. BBC, *Financing the BBC: the BBC's Initial Submission to the Peacock Committee* (BBC, 27 August 1985, typescript), paras 1.7.6.1–2, 7.4, 17.1–3, 5.1.

25. A. Travis, 'Managing Board Overruled on Film', *Guardian*, 1 August 1985; N. Higham and D. Frampton, 'Resignation Pressures Grow in "Censor" Crisis', *Broadcast*, 9 August 1985; Editorial, 'Back-to-front Logic', *Media Week*, 2 August 1985; A. Milne, 'Heavy Hands on the Tiller', *Guardian*, 3 February 1992.

26. Milne, *DG*, pp. 226–32; R. Snoddy, 'Peacock's Tale of Woe', *Media Week*, 31 January 1986; M. Wohrle, 'Research Row Erupts over BBC Funding Surveys', *Media Week*, 31 January 1986; *Peacock*, para. 577; Peacock, 'The "Politics"', p. 12.

27. S. Faulks, 'Struggle for Power in BBC', *Sunday Telegraph*, 18 May 1986.

28. W. Rees-Mogg, 'Time for the BBC Gentlemen to Hand over to the Players', *Independent*, 7 October 1986; S. Hearst, 'Swiping the Bouncer Bowled at the BBC', *Independent*, 24 October 1986.

29. H. Stephenson in *Guardian*, 31 January 1987; Tebbit, *Upwardly Mobile*, p. 325; Milne, *DG*, p. 248.

30. A. Spackman, 'Tory MP to Drop Second Libel Case', *Independent*, 27 October 1986; D. Barker, 'BBC Inquiry Set to Disprove "Bias" Claims on US Bombing', *Guardian*, 30 October 1986; BBC, *Statement from the Director General* (BBC News Release, 30 October 1986); Tebbit, *Upwardly Mobile*, p. 326.

31. P. Fiddick, 'The Inner Conflicts behind Milne's Downfall' and 'Governors Try to Curb Power of BBC', *Guardian*, 30, 31 January 1987.

32. P. Fiddick, 'Checkland Choice a Rebuff for Hussey' and 'ITV Man to be Second in Command at the BBC', *Guardian*, 22 February, 21 March 1987.

33. Thatcher, *Downing Street*, p. 637; P. Fiddick, 'Tricky Decisions to be Left to BBC Staff' and 'Departures Clear Checkland's Decks', *Guardian*, 20 March, 16 June 1987.

34. A. Foster, 'Tuning into Thatcherism', *Management Today* (February 1988), pp. 39, 44; R. Bolton, 'Out of the Frying-pan', *FTT & BETA News* (November 1991), p. 6.

35. D. Hencke and P. Fiddick, 'BBC Chief Attacked for Cover-up', *Guardian*, 7 March 1987; Tebbit, *Upwardly Mobile*, p. 326; J. Lloyd, 'Serving Thatcher's Children', *Financial Times*, 20 July 1988; A. Foster, 'Tuning into Thatcherism', *Management Today* (February 1988), p. 42. On Birt's background and centralising policy for BBC journalism, see Horrie and Clarke, *Fuzzy Monsters*, pp. 83–8, 92–4 and Chapter 8.

36. A. Rawnsley, 'MOD Threat Halts Documentary', *Guardian*, 12 May 1987; Cockerell, *Live from Number 10*, pp. 330–1; P. Fiddick, '"Low-level" BBC Brush with Tebbit', *Guardian*, 3 June 1987.

37. P. Fiddick, 'BBC to Build up Specialism in Current Affairs', *Guardian*, 6 July 1987; S. Griffin, 'Birt is Killing Current Affairs, Protest Staff', *Broadcast*, 24 July 1987; D. Swingewood, 'BBC Drops Panorama, "Spycatcher" Story', *UK Press Gazette*, 3 August 1987; A. Foster, 'Tuning into Thatcherism', *Management Today* (February 1988), p. 42. Further allegations about Birt's influence on the pulling or delay of programmes which might have offended the government appear in Horrie and Clarke, *Fuzzy Monsters*, pp. 166, 190–1, 210.

38. P. Fiddick, 'More Room at the Top in BBC Shake-up' and 'Departures Clear Checkland's Decks', *Guardian*, 18, 16 June 1987; R. Harris, 'Now Labour Attacks BBC over Bias', *Observer*, 25 October 1987; Young, *Enterprise Years*, pp. 151, 266; A. Foster, 'Tuning into Thatcherism', *Management Today* (February 1988), p. 41; R. Bolton, 'Gambling away the Future', *FTT & BETA News* (March 1992), p. 10.

39. P. Fiddick, 'Freelance Era at BBC', *Guardian*, 1 April 1987; 'Broadcasters Face New Hazards', *Journalist* (April/May 1987).

40. N. Higham, 'BBC Ready to Let its Radio Transmitters', *Broadcast*, 24 July 1987; A. Foster, 'Tuning into Thatcherism', *Management Today* (February 1988), pp. 41, 43; M. Brown, 'BBC Uncovers Plan for Major Changes', *Independent*, 22 October 1987.

41. B. Woffinden, 'Has BBC Journalism Lost its Spirit of Inquiry?', *Listener*, 10 March 1988; R. Brooks, 'Rees-Mogg on Cue as Chief

TV Watchdog', *Observer*, 15 May 1988; 'News', *Broadcast*, 3 June 1988; M. Brown, 'Tough New Code on TV Violence is Expected', *Independent*, 4 October 1988; Cockerell, *Live from Number 10*, p. 345.

42. R. Snoddy and R. Evans, 'Hurd Unveils Biggest TV Shake-up in 30 Years', *Financial Times*, 8 November 1988; Cockerell, *Live from Number 10*, p. 347; A. Sutherland, 'BBC's Great Escape – but for How Long', *Sunday Times*, 13 November 1988.

43. M. Checkland, 'Seeing Auntie into her Seventies', *Observer*, 17 December 1989; G. Henry, 'BBC Constrained Says Checkland', *Guardian*, 2 March 1990; P. Stoddart, 'Still Fighting the Flab with a Calculating Eye', *Sunday Times*, 4 February 1990.

44. R. Snoddy, 'LWT may Float off Advertising Team', *Financial Times*, 28 December 1988; R. Snoddy, 'BBC Willing to Run Subscription Service', *Financial Times*, 26 January 1989; S. Cook, 'Pay to Watch Plan by BBC', *Guardian*, 7 February 1989; J. Thynne, 'Press Barons are Banned from ITV Takeovers', *Daily Telegraph*, 20 May 1989.

45. G. Henry, 'Producers Protest Wins TV Share Scrutiny', *Guardian*, 17 July 1989; A. Finney, 'Independent Producers Getting a Look-in', *Sunday Correspondent*, 1 October 1989; G. Henry, 'TV Programme Quota, "Will Not Reduce Costs"', *Guardian*, 31 August 1990; 'BBC Breaks New Ground with Sponsorship Deal', *Independent*, 7 February 1990.

46. Monopolies and Mergers Commission, *Labour Practices in TV and Film Making: a Report under Section 79 of the Fair Trading Act 1973* (CM.66, HMSO, April 1989), p. 89, Appendix 3.3, para. 1; R. Creasy and M. Palmer, '1,500 BBC Jobs to Go', *Today*, 26 April 1988; M. Brown, 'The Man at the Cutting Edge of the BBC', *Independent*, 8 November 1989.

47. E. Johnstone, untitled typescript, distributed at 'Fighting the Cuts Conference' organised by BETA, 1 April 1990.

48. BETA, *Policy Digest: Principal Policy Statements Passed at BETA Annual Conferences 1985–88* (BETA, n.d.), p. 11; 'Newsfile', *Independent*, 13 July 1988; G. Henry, 'Lightning Strike Hits "Bizarre" BBC', *Guardian*, 3 July 1989; R. Bolton, ' "Staff Have Lost Confidence in Senior Management" Says Bolton', *BETA News* (November/December 1989), p. 4; BETA, *The BBC Division Newsletter* (BETA's BBC Division, February 1991).

49. O'Malley and Treharne, *Selling the Beeb*, p. 10.

Chapter 9: The Erosion of Autonomy

1. H. Wicks, *Keeping My Head* (Socialist Platform Books, 1992), p. 62; P. Golding and G. Murdock, 'Culture, Communications and Political Economy', in J. Curran and M. Gurevitch, eds, *Mass Media and Society* (Edward Arnold, 1991), p. 25.
2. Golding and Murdock, 'Culture, Communications', p. 24.
3. A. Milne, 'Tight Ship's Strained Seams', *Guardian*, 13 January 1992. See also Collins, *Broadcasting and Audio-Visual Policy*, p. 162.
4. See, for example, N. Garnham, *Capitalism and Communications* (Sage, 1990).
5. R. Miliband, *The State in Capitalist Society* (Quartet, 1973), pp. 210–11.
6. Miliband, *The State*, p. 51.
7. An excellent example of this work is J. Eldridge, ed., *Getting the Message: News Truth and Power* (Routledge, 1993). The two readers are: M. Gurevitch et al., *Culture, Society and the Media* (Methuen, 1982) and J. Curran and M. Gurevitch, eds, *Mass Media and Society* (Edward Arnold, 1991).
8. Miliband, *The State*, pp. 50, 238, 209, and Miliband, 'State Power and Class', *New Left Review* (no. 138, 1983), p. 65.
9. H. Davies, 'Class', in J. Seaton and B. Pimlott, eds, *The Media in British Politics* (Avebury, 1987), p. 26; R. Williams, 'The Growth and Role of the Mass Media', in C. Gardener, ed., *Media, Politics & Culture: a Socialist View* (Macmillan, 1979), pp. 15–16; J. Curran, 'Communications, Power and Social Order', in Gurevitch et al., *Culture*, p. 227.
10. N. Garnham, 'Contribution to a Political Economy of Mass Communication', in N. Garnham, *Capitalism*, p. 42; M. Gallagher, 'Negotiation of Control in Media Organizations and Occupations', in Gurevitch et al., *Culture*, p. 157.
11. N. Garnham, 'Public Service versus the Market', in Garnham, *Capitalism*, p. 121.

Bibliography

AIRC, *Initial Evidence to the Home Office Committee on Financing The BBC* (AIRC, August 1985)

ACTT, *Preliminary Submission to the Committee on Financing the BBC* (ACTT, August 1985)

Adam Smith Institute, *Omega Report: Communications* (ASI, May 1984)

Admap, Editorial, December 1984

Anon, 'Profile', *Observer*, 31 July 1983

Anon, 'Tories Sue Panorama', *Guardian*, 7 February 1984

Anon, 'Tories Air Panorama Grievance', *Guardian*, 14 February 1984

Anon, 'Question-and-answer Guide to the BBC's Finances', *Ariel*, 4 July 1984

Anon, 'Memo To Maggie', *Sunday Times*, 9 September 1984

Anon, 'Doubts about BBC £10 Car Radio Fee', *Broadcast*, 9 November 1984

Anon, 'Well They Would ...', *Ariel*, 14 November 1984

Anon, 'Regular BBC Check Found Overspend', *Broadcast*, 23 November 1984

Anon, 'The BBC Still Not Sending out a Clear Picture', *The Times*, 11 November 1984

Anon, 'Tory Committee Seeks Cuts as Corporation Urges £65 Fee', *Broadcast*, 14 December 1984

Anon, 'Commons to Debate Advertising on the BBC', *Broadcast*, 14 December 1984

Anon, 'Milne Tours Phone-ins', *Broadcast*, 14 December 1984

Anon, Leader, 'Keeping "Commercials" at Bay', *Observer*, 16 December 1984

Anon, 'Fair Trading Office Rules in Listings' , *Broadcast*, 21 December 1984

Anon, Leader, 'Whither the BBC?' in *The Times*, 14 January 1985.

Anon, Leader, 'Whither the BBC?' in *The Times* 15 January 1985.

Anon, Leader, 'Whither the BBC?' in *The Times*, 16 January 1985.

Anon, 'Is BBC Licensed to Ask for More?', *Broadcast*, 18 January 1985

Anon, 'BBC Bill Defeated', *UK Press Gazette*, 21 January 1985

Anon, 'Lobbying Boob', *Television Weekly*, 25 January 1985.

Anon, 'Advertising and how the BBC is to be Financed', *Stage and Television Today*, 31 January 1985

Anon, 'BBC inquiry: Mini Annan is not on', *Broadcast*, 1 February 1985

Anon, 'Milne Puts Cost of TV in Focus', *Broadcast*, 1 March 1985

Anon, Leader, *Daily Telegraph*, 28 March 1985

Anon, '£58 Licence "Disappoints" BBC', *Broadcast*, 29 March 1985

Anon, Leader, 'Licence Fee', *The Times*, 29 March 1985

Anon, 'Peacock Committee Delayed', *Broadcast*, 5 April 1985

Anon, 'What the Papers Said', *Broadcast*, 5 April 1985

Anon, 'Editorial: Let DBS Rip', *Media Week*, 12 April 1985

Anon, 'Freer Airwaves, More Jobs', *Economist*, 13 April 1985

Anon, 'After the Licence Fee – BBC at the Crossroads', *Stage and Television Today*, 9 May 1985

Anon, Leader, 'Peacock's Progress', *The Times*, 29 May 1985

Anon, 'Licensing of Private Dishes Gets Government Go-ahead', *Broadcast*, 31 May 1985

Anon, 'Taking a Break from a Brown Study', *Broadcast*, 7 June 1985

Anon, 'Update', *Broadcast*, 5 July 1985

Anon, 'Update', *Broadcast*, 19 July 1985

Anon, 'Update', *Broadcast*, 26 July 1985

Anon, 'Checkland Sets up "Axe" Committee', *Broadcast*, 2 August 1985

Anon, Editorial, 'Back-to-front Logic', *Media Week*, 2 August 1985

Anon, 'Opinion: High Time for the BBC to Get its Act Together', *UK Press Gazette*, 12 August 1985

Anon, 'Ads on the Beeb Spell Doom for Broadcasting', *Labour Research* (February 1986)

Anon, 'Parliament', *Guardian*, 1 July 1986

Anon, Editorial, 'The Future of Broadcasting', *Financial Times*, 4 July 1986.

Anon, 'Peacock's Fuzzy Vision', *Today*, 4 July 1986

Anon, 'A Peacock and a Sitting Duck', *Guardian*, 4 July 1986

Anon, Leader, *The Times*, 4 July 1986

Anon, 'Opinion: Let Viewers Pay their Money and Take their Choice', *Daily Express*, 4 July 1986

Anon, 'Peacock Grounded', *Daily Telegraph*, 4 July 1986

Anon, 'Another Bit of Committeeitis', *Daily Mail*, 4 July 1986

Anon, 'Debate Shows Members are Divided over some Proposals', *The Times*, 4 July 1986

Anon, Editorial, 'Questions of Independence', *Broadcast*, 11 July 1986

Anon, 'Government Will Act on Peacock', *Broadcast*, 11 July 1986

Anon, 'Update', *Broadcast*, 8 August 1986

Anon, Editorial, *Broadcast*, 12 September 1986

Anon, Leader, 'The BBC's Empty Chair', *Guardian*, 12 September 1986

Anon, 'BBC Accused of "Evil Attack" on Tory MP', *Guardian*, 14 October 1986

Anon, 'Opinion: Time for Action at the BBC', *Daily Express*, 22 October 1986

Anon, Leader, 'Mr Tebbit's Case', *Daily Telegraph*, 31 October 1986

Anon, Leader, 'Dubious Tactics on BBC "bias"', *Independent*, 1 November 1986

Anon, 'Prices Link for TV Licence Fee', *Guardian*, 15 January 1987

Anon, 'The Day in Politics', *Guardian*, 28 January 1987

Anon, no title, *Guardian*, 11 April 1987

Anon, 'Broadcasters Face New Hazards', *The Journalist* (April/May 1987)

Anon, 'Peacock-pay-TV Plan Gets Cold Shoulder', *Broadcast*, 17 July 1987

Anon, 'Murdoch in Sherwood', *The Digger*, 28 January 1988

Anon, 'Euro MPs to Look into TV Listings Duopoly', *UK Press Gazette*, 11 April 1988

Anon, 'Trying a New Tack to Break TV Unions', *Labour Research* (May 1988)

Anon, 'News', *Broadcast*, 3 June 1988

Anon, Leader, 'Impartial – But Only in Part', *Independent*, 11 June 1988

Anon, 'Broadcasting Deserves Better Treatment', *Observer*, 26 June 1988

Anon, 'Newsfile', *Independent*, 13 July 1988

Anon, 'Director for Watchdog Body', *The Times*, 7 November 1988

Anon, Leader, 'Mr Hurd's Garden', *The Times*, 8 November 1988

Anon, Editorial, 'The Best TV in the World?', *Sun*, 8 November 1988

Anon, Editorial, 'Improper Channels', *Today*, 8 November 1988

Anon, 'Comment', *Sunday Times*, 13 November 1988

Anon, 'Buzz', *Sunday Times*, 4 December 1988

Anon, Editorial, *Daily Mail*, 8 December 1989

Anon, 'BBC Breaks New Ground with Sponsorship Deal', *Independent*, 7 February 1990

Anon, Leader, 'Redheads under the Bed', *Independent*, 21 February 1990

Anon, 'The Profile: Woodrow Wyatt, Read Him and Wonder', *Independent*, 13 October 1990

Arts Council of Great Britain, *Faces and Names* (ACGB, August 1985)

J. Ashton, 'Advertising and the BBC', *Labour Weekly*, 11 January 1985

BBC, *Financing the BBC: the BBC's Initial Submission to the Peacock Committee* (BBC, 27 August 1985, typescript)

BBC, *Annual Reports*, 1983, 1985, 1986 (BBC, various dates)

BBC, *Statement from the Director General* (BBC News Release, 30 October 1986)

BBC, *C.C.O. Media Monitoring – the BBC Response* (BBC, 5 November 1986, typescript)

B.H. Bagdikian, *The Media Monopoly*, 2nd edn (Beacon Press, 1987)

K. Baker, *The Turbulent Years: My Life in Politics* (Faber and Faber, 1993)

D. Barker, 'Lack of Money Curbs BBC Daytime TV', *Guardian*, 4 October 1983

D. Barker, 'Thatcher Wants Channel 4 to Make a Profit', *Guardian*, 5 October 1983

D. Barker, 'Satellite TV Plan Leads to Franchise Demand', *Guardian*, 20 January 1984

D. Barker, 'ITV Companies Make BBC Wait for Satellite Decision', *Guardian*, 7 February 1984

D. Barker, 'Copyright Challenge to TV Weeklies', *Guardian*, 16 February 1984

D. Barker, 'ITV Companies Ready to Accept Satellite Plans', *Guardian*, 28 March 1984

D. Barker, 'Physicist Appointed to Cable Authority', *Guardian*, 13 November 1984

D. Barker, 'BBC "Must Look to Costs"', *Guardian*, 30 April 1985

D. Barker, 'BBC Governors Look for Change Close to Top', *Guardian*, 5 June 1985

D. Barker and J. Naughtie, 'Peacock Urges Auction of All 15 ITV Franchises', *Guardian*, 27 June 1986

D. Barker, 'Cabinet Split on Free-market TV', *Guardian*, 28 June 1986

D. Barker, 'Hurd Postpones Action on Broadcasting Report', *Guardian*, 2 July 1986

D. Barker and J. Carvel, 'Hurd Supports Proposal for Free Market in Broadcasting', *Guardian*, 4 July 1986

D. Barker, 'Broadcasters Cool on Vision of the Future', *Guardian*, 4 July 1986

D. Barker, 'Whitehall "Tried to Blacken" Peacock Report', *Guardian*, 30 July 1986

D. Barker, 'Ministers to Peer into the Future of Television', *Guardian*, 6 August 1986

D. Barker, 'BBC "Was Biased in Falkland Play Ban"', *Guardian*, 30 September 1986

D. Barker, 'BBC Inquiry Set to Disprove "Bias" Claims on US Bombing', *Guardian*, 30 October 1986

D. Barker, 'BBC Invited Tebbit to Talks a Month ago', *Guardian*, 4 November 1986

S. Barnard, *On Radio: Music Radio in Britain* (Open University Press, 1989)

S. Barnett and D. Docherty, *The Peacock Debate in the UK* (Broadcasting Research Unit Working Paper, n.d.)

R. Belfield, C. Hird and S. Kelly, *Murdoch: the Decline of an Empire*, (Macdonald, 1991)

T. Bell, 'My Media Week', *Media Week*, 26 July 1985

T. Benn, *Out of the Wilderness: Diaries 1964–67* (Hutchinson 1987).

BETA, 'The Union's Response to the Peacock Committee', *BETA News* (September/October 1985)

BETA, *Policy Digest: Principal Policy Statements Passed at BETA Annual Conferences 1985–88* (BETA, n.d.)

BETA, *The BBC Division Newsletter* (BETA's BBC Division, February 1991)

A. Bevins, 'Top Tory Named in BBC Row', *Independent*, 24 October 1986

I. Black, 'Evans Renews Attack over Sale of Times', *Guardian*, 16 February 1984

S. Blanchard, *The Audio and Audio-visual Media Industries in London* (GLC Economic Policy Group – Strategy Document no. 7, June 1983)

R. Bolton, 'Gambling Away the Future', *FTT and BETA News* (March 1992)

R. Bolton, ' "Staff Have Lost Confidence in Senior Management" says Bolton', *BETA News* (November/December 1989)

R. Bolton, 'Out of the Frying-pan', *FTT and BETA News* (November 1991)

A. Briggs, *The BBC: the First Fifty Years* (OUP, 1985)

A. Briggs, 'Obituary: Lord Swann', *Guardian*, 24 September 1990

L. Brittan, *Airwaves* (IBA, Winter 1984/5)

S. Brittan, 'The Fight for Freedom in Broadcasting', *Political Quarterly*, vol. 58, no. 1 (January–March 1987)

Broadcasting Act 1990

Broadcasting Research Unit, *Summary of Evidence to the Peacock Committee* (BRU, n.d.)

R. Brooks, 'BBC May Quit Satellite Race', *Sunday Times*, 17 July 1983

R. Brooks, 'Satellite Television Won't Pay – BBC', *Sunday Times*, 31 July 1983

R. Brooks, 'Who Should Pay for the BBC?', *Sunday Times*, 3 June 1984

R. Brooks and Sue Summers, 'Making the Money Go Round', *The Times*, 2 Dec 1984

R. Brooks, 'Enter from Stage Right, Man with Hot Potato', *Observer*, 5 October 1986

R. Brooks, 'Rees-Mogg on Cue as Chief TV Watchdog', *Observer*, 15 May 1988

R. Brooks, 'Too Many Cooks', *Observer*, 13 November 1988

R. Brooks, 'Whitelaw Hits out at TV Changes', *Observer*, 11 December 1988

R. Brooks, 'Auction Should be Going, Going ...', *Observer*, 10 December 1989

T. Brooks, 'Taking his Dramas out of a Crisis', *Media Week*, 8 February 1985

T. Brooks, 'ISBA Presses Hard for Adverts on the BBC', *Media Week*, 5 July 1985

C. Brown, 'Ministers Aim for Radio Ads on BBC', *Guardian*, 5 June 1984

K. Brown, 'Peacock Report "Should be Put in Waste Paper Basket"', *Financial Times*, 4 July 1986

M. Brown, 'A Tilt at the Listings', *Guardian*, 28 October 1985

M. Brown, 'Free Market TV Backed', *Guardian*, 5 July 1986

M. Brown, 'Tory Attack on BBC "Bias" in Reporting', *Independent*, 11 November 1986

M. Brown, 'New Complaints Body to Keep Check on Television', *Independent*, 8 October 1987

M. Brown, 'BBC Uncovers Plan for Major Changes', *Independent*, 22 October 1987

M. Brown, 'Satellite Proposal Perplexes TV Chiefs', *Independent*, 13 June 1988

M. Brown, 'Hurd Wants Licence Replaced by Subscription', *Independent*, 23 June 1988

M. Brown, 'BBC Buys Control of Magazine Publisher', *Independent*, 6 July 1988

M. Brown, 'Neil and his Sunday Best', *Independent*, 20 July 1988

M. Brown, 'Tough New Code on TV Violence is Expected', *Independent*, 4 October 1988

M. Brown, 'The Family Firm in a Shifting Market', *Independent*, 15 February 1989

M. Brown, 'The Man at the Cutting Edge of the BBC', *Independent*, 8 November 1989

A. Brummer, 'TV Plans Force Murdoch to Sell Chicago Newspaper', *Guardian*, 1 July 1986

L. Buckingham, 'Murdoch Takes Collins', *Guardian*, 7 January 1989

A. Burkitt, 'Where Does DBS Go from Here?', *Broadcast*, 28 June 1985

S.C., 'Shaw Calls for a Broadcast Inquiry', *Broadcast*, 23 November 1984

S.C., 'Public Poll Prefers Ads to Licence Increase', *Broadcast*, 30 November 1984

J. Carvel and D. Barker, 'Cabinet Overruled Tebbit on Ministerial Link for BBC Attack', *Guardian*, 3 November 1986

M. Cassell and R. Snoddy, 'Tories Attack BBC over Libya', *Financial Times*, 31 October 1986

S. Castle, 'Manifesto Bid by Radical Right', *Independent on Sunday*, 8 July 1990

M. Cave, 'Financing British Broadcasting', *Lloyds Bank Review*, no. 157 (July 1985)

M. Checkland, 'Seeing Auntie into her Seventies', *Observer*, 17 December 1989

S. Clark, Letter, *Guardian*, 26 February 1990

S. Clarke, 'Yes, the BBC is Biased', *Standard*, 18 November 1986

S. Clarke, 'Viewers Don't Care about TV Prestige Drama', *Sunday Times*, 21 January 1990

M. Cockerell, P. Henessey and D. Walker, *Sources Close to the Prime Minister* (Macmillan, 1984)

M. Cockerell, *Live from Number 10: the Inside Story of Prime Ministers and Television*, 2nd edn (Faber and Faber, 1989)

R. Collins, N. Garnham, G. Locksley, *The Economics of Television: the UK Case* (Sage, 1988)

R. Collins, *Broadcasting and Audio-visual Policy in the European Single Market* (John Libbey, 1994)

Conservative Party, *The Conservative Manifesto 1983* (Conservative Central Office, 1983)

S. Cook, 'Pay to Watch Plan by BBC', *Guardian*, 7 February 1989

B. Cox, 'Peacock and Ostriches', *New Statesman*, 29 August 1986

R. Creasy and M. Palmer, '1,500 BBC Jobs to Go', *Today*, 26 April 1988

R. Crossman, *The Diaries of a Cabinet Minister. Volume Three. Secretary of State for Social Services 1968–70* (Book Club Associates, by arrangement with Hamish Hamilton and Jonathan Cape, 1977)

J. Curran et al., eds, *Bending Reality: the State of the Media* (Pluto, 1986)

J. Curran and J. Seaton, *Power without Responsibility*, 4th edn (Routledge, 1991)

J. Curran and M. Gurevitch, eds, *Mass Media and Society* (Edward Arnold, 1991)

I. Curteis, Letter, *Independent*, 29 June 1986

P. Dahlgren and C. Sparks, eds, *Journalism and Popular Culture* (Sage, 1992)

D'Arcy MacManus Masius, *Funding the BBC from Advertising* (DMM, September 1984)

A. Davidson, 'Beating the Peacock Team into Submission', *Marketing*, 30 January 1986

A. Davidson, *Under the Hammer* (Mandarin, 1992)

J. Davies, *UK and European TV Policy-Making in an Information-Poor Environment* (Paper presented at the Programme on Information and Communications Technologies Conference, Newport, Wales, March 1992)

H. Davies, 'Do We Really Need the BBC?', *The Times*, 24 April 1983

Robin Day, *Grand Inquisitor* (Pan, 1990)

S. Day Lewis, 'Preserving a Public Service', *Daily Telegraph*, 6 May 1985

I. Dawnes, 'Thatcher, Resignation List Awards Businessmen and Tory Grandees', *Financial Times*, 21 December 1990

S. de Bruxelles, 'Radio Scheme Axed by Cabinet', *Observer*, 29 June 1986

Department of National Heritage, *The Future of the BBC: a Consultation Document* (CM. 2098, HMSO, November 1992)

R. Desai, 'Second-Hand Dealers in Ideas: Think Tanks and Thatcherite Hegemony', *New Left Review* (no. 203, 1994), pp. 27–64

A. Dickson, 'Commercial Radio's Tide may be Ebbing', *Observer*, 3 June 1984

P. Donovan, 'BBC Chief Admits: "We'll Fight for Ads if We Must"', *Daily Mail*, 1 April 1985

P. Donovan, 'Peacock's Ruffled Feathers', *Today*, 4 July 1986

T. Douglas, 'Should Auntie Go Commercial?', *The Times*, 17 December 1984

C. Dunkley, three articles all called 'The BBC – the Best Bargain in Britain', in *Radio Times*, 19–25 January, 26 January–1 February, 2–8 February 1985

D. Edgar et al., *The New Right and the Church* (Jubilee Group, 1985)

A. Ehrenberg and T.P. Barwise, *How Much does UK Television Cost* (London Business School, 1982)

A.S.C. Ehrenberg and T.P. Barwise, 'How Much Does UK Television Cost?', *International Journal of Advertising*, no. 2, 1983

A.S.C. Ehrenberg, *The Funding of BBC Television* (no publisher, December 1984)

A.S.C. Ehrenberg, 'Putting a Price on Quality', *Observer*, 15 December 1984

J. Eldridge, ed., *Getting the Message: News, Truth and Power* (Routledge, 1993)

Equity, *Memorandum Submitted by the Councils of British Equity to the Committee on Financing the BBC* (Equity, 27 August 1985)

European Institute for the Media, *Events and Issues Relevant to Competition in Satellite Television between British Satellite Broadcasting and News International* (EIM, 1989)

H. Evans, *Good Times, Bad Times* (Coronet, 1986)

R. Evans, 'Rivals May Get Time on BBC TV', *The Times*, 21 October 1988

R. Evans, 'A Screen Turned upside down', *The Times*, 11 November 1988

R. Evans, 'Licence Fee to be Preserved', *The Times*, 12 December 1988

R. Evans, 'Murdoch Attacks "Fossilized" TV Standards', *The Times*, 26 August 1989

R.F., 'Warning on BBC Licence Fee', *Broadcast*, 6 July 1984

S.F., 'Challenge to BBC's Share of DBS', *Broadcast*, 20 July 1984

S.F., 'Indies: BBC Can't Call DBS Tune', *Broadcast*, 10 August 1984

S.F., 'Shaw Takes over Hurd Hot Seat', *Broadcast*, 14 August 1984

S. Faulks, 'Struggle for Power in BBC', *Sunday Telegraph*, 18 May 1986

P. Fiddick, 'Brittan Announces Two Satellite Channels for ITV', *Guardian*, 17 September 1983

P. Fiddick, 'Deadlock on the Recipe for the Dish of the Day', *Guardian*, 1 December 1983

P. Fiddick, 'How the Commercial Breaks would Stretch as the Revenue Shrank', *Guardian*, 4 February 1985

P. Fiddick, 'Battle Plan that Opens a New Panorama', *Guardian*, 4 February 1985

P. Fiddick, 'A Licence to Survive', *Guardian*, 4 February 1985

P. Fiddick, 'Media File', *Guardian*, 3 June 1985

P. Fiddick, 'Can the BBC Convince Peacock?', *Guardian*, 1 July 1985

P. Fiddick, 'BBC Aims to Axe 4,000 Jobs in £30m Switch', *Guardian*, 18 July 1985

P. Fiddick, 'Peacock Gave Minority Views a Rough Ride, says Hetherington', *Guardian*, 8 September 1986

P. Fiddick, 'Rifkind Protests at Broadcasting "Bias"', *Guardian*, 9 September 1986

P. Fiddick, 'Media File', *Guardian*, 15 September 1986

P. Fiddick, 'Static Problem', *Guardian*, 15 September 1986

P. Fiddick and D. Barker, 'BBC in Crisis over Libel Case Deal', *Guardian*, 20 October 1986

P. Fiddick, 'Tebbit Refuels Bias Row with Uncowed BBC', *Guardian*, 6 November 1986

P. Fiddick, 'New Pitch for BBC Ads', *Guardian*, 7 November 1986

P. Fiddick, 'Hurd Heralds Bill to Reform Broadcasting', *Guardian*, 10 November 1986

P. Fiddick, 'BBC Image Defended', *Guardian*, 27 November 1986

P. Fiddick, 'BBC Chief Hits Back at Press Criticism', *Guardian*, 28 January 1987

P. Fiddick, 'The Inner Conflicts behind Milne's Downfall', *Guardian*, 30 January 1987

P. Fiddick, 'Governors Try to Curb Power of BBC', *Guardian*, 31 January 1987

P. Fiddick, 'Checkland Choice a Rebuff for Hussey' *Guardian*, 22 February 1987

P. Fiddick, 'Tricky Decisions to be Left to BBC Staff', *Guardian*, 20 March 1987

P. Fiddick, 'ITV Man to be Second in Command at the BBC', *Guardian*, 21 March 1987

P. Fiddick, 'Freelance Era at BBC', *Guardian*, 1 April 1987

P. Fiddick, 'Governors Back BBC Ban on Play', *Guardian*, 15 April 1987

P. Fiddick, '"Low-level" BBC Brush with Tebbit', *Guardian*, 3 June 1987

P. Fiddick, 'Departures clear Checkland's Decks', *Guardian*, 16 June 1987

P. Fiddick, 'More Room at the Top in BBC Shake-up', *Guardian*, 18 June 1987

P. Fiddick, 'BBC to Build up Specialism in Current Affairs', *Guardian*, 6 July 1987

P. Fiddick, 'Media File', *Guardian*, 6 June 1988

P. Fiddick, 'Pleas to Safeguard ITV Profits', *Guardian*, 28 November 1988

A. Finney, 'Independent Producers Getting a Look-in', *Sunday Correspondent*, 1 October 1989

R. Fitzwalter, 'Quite Right but Wrong', *Guardian*, 25 September 1989

P. Foot, 'Swashbucklers Buckle at Tory Press', *New Statesman*, 14 May 1985

T. Forester, ed., *Computers in the Human Context* (Basil Blackwell, 1989)

M. Forsyth, 'Fanning the Wind of Change', *Guardian*, 7 July 1986

A. Foster, 'Tuning into Thatcherism', *Management Today* (February 1988)

N. Fraser, 'IBA Looks Forward to Life after Death', *Observer*, 10 December 1989

T. Gardam, Letter, *The Times*, 6 October 1988

C. Gardener, ed., *Media, Politics & Culture: a Socialist View* (Macmillan, 1979)

N. Garnham, *Capitalism and Communication: Global Culture and the Economics of Information* (Sage, 1990)

P. Gavan, 'Tory Whips are Kept off Air', *Broadcast*, 8 March 1985

C. Goodhall, 'Licence to Spend Money', *Spectator*, 9 February 1985

S. Goodwin, '"Unpatriotic Bias" of BBC Attacked', *Independent*, 13 October 1990

E. Gorman, 'Peacock, "I'm no Hired Gun"', *Broadcast*, 5 April 1985

K. Gosling, 'Colour TV Licence Rise by £12 to £46', *The Times*, 2 December 1981

D. Graham, 'De-regulation – the Only Path to Freedom', *Stage & Television Today*, 2 May 1985

D. Graham, 'Broadcasting Market Forces', *New Statesman*, 24 May 1985

B. Grantham, 'DBS Project Cost Hitch', *Television Weekly*, 21 December 1984

B. Grantham and J. Robinson, 'Licence Fee Pressure Piles up', *Television Weekly*, 21 December 1984

D. Green, *A Better BBC: Public Service Broadcasting in the '90s* (Centre for Policy Studies, March 1991)

S. Griffin, 'Birt is Killing Current Affairs, Protest Staff', *Broadcast*, 24 July 1987

M. Gurevitch et al., *Culture, Society and the Media* (Methuen, 1982)

D.H., 'Young Tories Back Panorama Report', *Broadcast*, 23 March 1984

N.H., 'Milne Spurns Plan for BBC Adverts', *Broadcast*, 12 October 1984

N.H., 'Would Ad Finance Plan Aid the BBC?', *Broadcast*, 5 October 1984

N.H., 'Jackie Injunction Sought by Mercury', *Broadcast*, 16 November 1984

Hansard, 22, 27 March 1985; 3 July 1986; 16 May 1988; 8 February 1989

I. Hargreaves, *Sharper Vision: the BBC and the Communications Revolution* (Demos, 1993)

K. Harper, 'Monopolies Inquiry into TV Working', *Guardian*, 29 March 1988

M. Harris, *London Newspapers in the Age of Walpole* (Associated University Press, 1987)

R. Harris, 'Now Labour Attacks BBC over Bias', *Observer*, 25 October 1987

R. Harris and V. Smart, 'PM Cautions Press', *Observer*, 8 May 1988

R. Harris, *Good and Faithful Servant: the Unauthorized Biography of Bernard Ingham* (Faber and Faber, 1991)

M. Hastings, 'Who Will Halt the Runaway Beeb?', *Standard*, 21 January 1984

S. Hearst, 'Swiping the Bouncer Bowled at the BBC', *Independent*, 24 October 1986

C. Heller, *Broadcasting and Accountability* (BFI, 1978)

D. Hencke and P. Fiddick, 'BBC Chief Attacked for Cover-up', *Guardian*, 7 March 1987

D. Hencke, 'The Think-tank Engine', *Guardian*, 10 March 1989

P. Henessey, *Whitehall*, rev. edn (Fontana, 1990)

G. Henry, 'Quentin Thomas', *Broadcast*, 18 November 1988

G. Henry, 'Producers Protest Wins TV Share Scrutiny', *Guardian*, 17 July 1989

G. Henry, 'Lightning Strike hits "Bizarre" BBC', *Guardian*, 3 July 1989

G. Henry, 'BBC Constrained Says Checkland', *Guardian*, 2 March 1990

G. Henry, 'TV Programme Quota, "Will Not Reduce Costs"', *Guardian*, 31 August 1990

G. Henry, 'TV Licence Fee to be Set Below RPI', *Guardian*, 2 October 1990

G. Henry, 'The Voice of Reason', *Guardian*, 8 October 1990

H. Herbert, 'Over the Top with Percy Toplis', *Guardian*, 15 September 1986

D. Hewson, 'Advertising on BBC "Could Peg Licences"', *The Times*, 26 September 1984

D. Hewson, 'Quality of BBC TV Programmes Threatened by Soaring Costs', *The Times*, 30 November 1984

D. Hewson, '£60 Licence would "Kill BBC Plans"', *The Times*, 4 January 1985

N. Higham and D. Frampton, 'Resignation Pressures grow in "Censor" crisis', *Broadcast*, 9 August 1985

N. Higham and M. Wohrle, 'Rift in Whitehall over Peacock's Long-term Policy', *Broadcast*, 8 August 1986

N. Higham, 'BBC Ready to Let its Radio Transmitters', *Broadcast*, 24 July 1987

G. Hodgson, 'Now is the Time for all Right-thinking Men …', *Sunday Times Magazine*, 4 March 1984

M. Hollingsworth, *Press and Political Dissent* (Pluto, 1986)

T. Hollins, *Beyond Broadcasting: into the Cable Age* (BFI, 1984)

Home Affairs Select Committee, *Third Report: the Future of Broadcasting*, vol. 1 (HMSO, June 1988)

Home Office, *Review of the ITV and ILR Levy Structure 1984–5, May 1985* (Broadcasting Department, Home Office, February 1986)

Home Office, *Peacock Committee* (Home Office, Press Release, 29 May 1985)

Home Office, *Report of the Committee on Financing the BBC* (CMND. 9824, HMSO, July 1986)

Home Office, *Peacock Report: Viewers and Listeners to be in Driving Seat* (Home Office, Press Release, 3 July 1986)

Home Office, *Radio Choices and Opportunities* (HMSO, 1987)

Home Office, *Broadcasting in the 90s: Competition, Choice and Quality* (HMSO, CM. 517, November 1988)

C. Horrie and S. Clarke, *Fuzzy Monsters: Fear and Loathing at the BBC* (Heinemann, 1994)

D. Housham, 'Brinton's Hazard Warning', *Television Weekly*, 18 January 1985

D. Housham, 'BBC Reviews 12 of its Sections', *Broadcast*, 15 March 1985

D. Housham, 'The Buck Stops Here', *Broadcast*, 12 July 1985

C. Hughes, '"Pay as you View" Plan for BBC', *Independent*, 28 October 1988

C. Hughes, 'Hurd Converted to Free-market Broadcasting', *Independent*, 8 November 1988

D. Hurd, *Home Secretary's Speech to the Royal Television Society Convention Dinner, 8 November 1986* (Press text, Home Office, 1986)

Independent Broadcasting Authority, *Direct Broadcasting by Satellite* (Information sheet, IBA, n.d. but 1986)

Incorporated Society of British Advertisers, *Financing Broadcasting – the Case for Advertising on the BBC* (ISBA, London, n.d.)

B. Ingham, *Kill the Messenger* (Fontana, 1991)

R. Ingrams, Column in *Observer*, 5 February, 14 May 1988, 10 December 1989

P. Johnson, 'Begging Bowl Economics', *Spectator*, 5 January 1985

P. Johnson, 'Digging the Duopoly' in *Spectator*, 2 September 1989

E. Johnstone, untitled typescript, distributed at 'Fighting the Cuts Conference' organised by BETA, 1 April 1990

G. Jones, 'BBC "at All-time Low"', *Daily Telegraph*, 22 October 1986

M. Jones, 'How Thatcher Played her Card and Lost the Trick', *Sunday Times*, 30 July 1989

D. Kavanagh and A. Seldon, eds, *The Thatcher Effect: a Decade of Change* (Oxford University Press, 1989)

D. Kavanagh, *Thatcherism and British Politics: the End of Consensus*, 2nd edn (Oxford University Press, 1990)

J. Keane, *The Media and Democracy* (Polity, 1991)

S. Koss, *The Rise and Fall of the Political Press in Britain* (Fontana, 1990)

Labour Party, *Labour Party Submission to the Peacock Inquiry* (Labour Party, n.d.)

S. Lambert, *Channel Four: Television with a Difference?* (BFI, 1982)

N. Lawson, *The View from No 11: Memoirs of a Tory Radical* (Bantam Press, 1992)

M. Leapman, *Barefaced Cheek: Rupert Murdoch* (Coronet, 1984)

M. Leapman, *The Last Days of the BEEB* (Coronet, 1987)

M. Leapman, 'Satellite Only Plan for TV', *Independent*, 11 June 1988

H. Lee, 'Split over Sale of Radio 1 and 2', *Daily Telegraph*, 4 July 1986

D. Leigh et al., 'Special Branch Raids BBC', *Observer*, 1 February 1987

D. Leigh, 'MI6 Career of BBC Governor Revealed', *Observer*, 26 June 1988

P. Lennon, 'Pedlar of the Political Illusion', *Guardian*, 2 November 1992

G. Levy, 'Big Spender with the Begging Bowl', *Daily Express*, 20 October 1984

Liberal Party, *Liberal Party Policy Briefing: Financing the BBC* (Liberal Party, September 1985)

M. Linton, 'Gummer Warning to BBC on "Racist Smears"', *Guardian*, 13 February 1984

J. Lloyd, 'Serving Thatcher's Children', *Financial Times*, 20 July 1988

Local Radio Workshop, *Capital: Local Radio and Private Profit* (Comedia, 1983)

N. Lockey, 'Saatchi's Push for Ads on BBC', *Television Weekly*, 16 November 1984

R. Low, 'Thatcher Tells BBC: £55 Only', *Observer*, 16 December 1984

A. Lycett, 'Whose Finger on the Button?', *The Times*, 20 July 1988

P.M., 'DBS Threatened by Licence Row', *Broadcast*, 15 March 1985

D. MacKenzie and J. Wajcman, eds, *The Social Shaping of Technology*, (Open University Press, 1988)

J. Margolis, 'Drastic TV Shake-up Will Cut Jobs and Pay', *Mail on Sunday*, 13 January 1985

L. Marks, 'How Peacock Became a Cuckoo', *Observer*, 6 July 1986

L. Marks, 'Waddington's Game Plan', *Observer*, 29 October 1989

A. Marwick, *British Society since 1945*, 2nd edn (Penguin, 1990)

L. Masterman, *Television and the Bombing of Libya: an Independent Analysis* (MK Media Press, 1987)

Media Week, Editorial, 'No Time to Submit', 5 July 1985

R. Miliband, *The State in Capitalist Society* (Quartet, 1973)

R. Miliband, 'State Power and Class', *New Left Review* (no. 138, 1983)

J. Miller and A. Sutherland, 'How a "Dead Duck" Started a TV Big Bang', *Sunday Times*, 13 November 1988

A. Milne, 'Down the US Road', *Independent*, 16 November 1988

A. Milne, *D.G: The Memoirs of a British Broadcaster* (Coronet, 1989)

A. Milne, 'Tight Ship's Strained Seams?', *Guardian*, 13 January 1992

A. Milne, 'Heavy Hand on the Tiller', *Guardian*, 3 February 1992

S. Milne, 'Rightwing Group Comes out of the Bunker', *Guardian*, 23 June 1987

Monopolies and Mergers Commission, *Labour Practices in TV and Film Making: a Report under Section 79 of the Fair Trading Act 1973* (CM. 66, HMSO, April 1989)

P. Monteith, 'Peacock's Choice Comes under Fire', *Broadcast*, 24 May 1985

D. Morrison, *Invisible Citizens: British Public Opinion and the Future of Broadcasting* (John Libbey, 1986)

F. Mount, 'Peacock. We Do Not Wish to Know That, Kindly Leave the Stage', *Daily Telegraph*, 4 July 1986

J. Naughtie, 'BBC Advertising Defeated after Opposition MPs Clash', *Guardian*, 16 January 1985

J. Naughtie, 'BBC Discomfiture Finds a Delighted Audience on the Tory Right', *Guardian*, 29 March 1985

J. Naughtie, 'Tories Watch for TV Bias', *Guardian*, 3 July 1986

R. Negrine, ed., *Satellite Broadcasting: the Politics and Implications of the New Media* (Routledge, 1988)

NUJ, *Evidence from the National Union of Journalists to the Peacock Committee on Financing the British Broadcasting Corporation* (NUJ, n.d.)

R. Oakely, 'Privatized Policy-making for the Tory Right', *The Times*, 17 February 1989

T. O'Malley, Letter, *Guardian*, 1 April 1988

T. O'Malley and J. Treharne, *Selling the Beeb: the BBC and the Charter Review Process* (Campaign for Press and Broadcasting Freedom, 1993)

J. Paxman, *Friends in High Places. Who Runs Britain?* (Penguin, 1991)

A. Peacock, 'The "Politics" of Investigating Broadcasting Finance', *Royal Bank of Scotland Review* (no. 153, March 1987), pp. 3–16.

A. Peacock, 'Peacock Attacks ITV Franchise Proposal', *Financial Times*, 6 February 1989

Peat Marwick Mitchell, *Value for Money Review* (BBC, 31 January 1985)

S. Perera, 'Counsel Defends MP's Skit on Nuremburg', *Guardian*, 15 October 1986

S. Perera, 'Panorama Accused of Left Bias in New Study on TV Reporting', *Guardian*, 19 November 1986

W. Phillips, 'Wayside Pulpit: Mr Thompson's Flag', *Admap*, April 1981

W. Phillips, 'Wayside Pulpit: ILR with the Brakes on', *Admap*, August 1981

J. Pilger, *A Secret Country* (Vintage, 1989)

J. Pilger, 'Code for Charlatans', *Guardian*, 8 October 1990

O. Pritchett, 'Why the BBC Wants your £65', *Sunday Telegraph*, 23 December 1984

A. Raphael, 'Study Backs BBC Fee Rise', *Observer*, 3 February 1985

A. Raphael, 'Peacock: Plans for Pay-as-you-see TV', *Observer*, 18 May 1986

A. Rawnsley, 'Star Reporter's Name Excluded', *Guardian*, 31 October 1986

A. Rawnsley, 'Tory Link with Media Monitors is Revealed', *Guardian*, 20 November 1986

A. Rawnsley, 'MOD Threat Halts Documentary', *Guardian*, 12 May 1987

W. Rees-Mogg, 'Time for the BBC Gentleman to Hand over to the Players', *Independent*, 7 October 1986

C. Reiss, 'BBC: Tebbit Names Names', *Standard*, 30 October 1986

C. Reiss, 'Now Howe to Halt BBC Film', *Standard*, 4 May 1988

J. Robinson, 'Future Ads for BBC?', *Television Weekly*, 4 January 1985

M. Rutherford, 'The BBC's Pride and Prejudice', *Financial Times*, January 1985

Saatchi and Saatchi, *Funding the BBC – the Case for Allowing Advertising* (London, Saatchi and Saatchi, October 1984)

P. Scannell and D. Cardiff, *A Social History of British Broadcasting Volume 1, 1922–1939* (Blackwell, 1991)

P. Scannell, P. Schlesinger, C. Sparks, eds, *Culture and Power* (Sage, 1992)

P. Schlesinger, *Putting Reality Together* (Methuen, 1987)

J. Seaton and B. Pimlott, *The Media in British Politics* (Avebury, 1987)

C. Seymour-Ure, *The British Press and Broadcasting since 1945* (Blackwell, 1991), p. 216

S. Shamoon, 'The Adman's Assault on "Auntie"', *Observer*, 11 November 1984

S. Shamoon, 'Reece and Bell: the PR Petals', *Observer*, 2 August 1989

C. Shaw, ed., *Rethinking Governance and Accountability* (BFI, 1993)

W. Shawcross, *Murdoch* (Pan, 1993)

A. Sherman, 'Why the BBC Needs its own Monitors', *Guardian*, 8 December 1986

P. Simmonds, 'Government Plans for New TV Watchdog', *UK Press Gazette*, 22 or 29 June 1987

R. Skidelsky, ed., *Thatcherism* (Basil Blackwell, 1990)

D. Smith, 'Free Market Economist's Critical Support of BBC', *The Times*, 28 March 1985

R. Snoddy, '"£73.9m Surplus" for BBC', *Financial Times*, November 1983

R. Snoddy, 'BBC Faces Independent Audit', *Financial Times*, 21 July 1984

R. Snoddy, 'The BBC Sharpens up its Act', *Financial Times*, 22 September 1984

R. Snoddy, 'Commercial Radio Station to Sue Pirates', *Financial Times*, 9 November 1984

R. Snoddy, 'News Analysis', *Media Week*, 15 March 1985

R. Snoddy, 'Questions for BBC Inquiry', *Media Week*, 5 April 1985

R. Snoddy, 'News Analysis', *Media Week*, 28 June 1985

R. Snoddy, 'BBC Cheques and Balances', *Media Week*, 26 July 1985

R. Snoddy, 'Peacock's Tale of Woe', *Media Week*, 31 January 1986

R. Snoddy, 'Inquiry Rejects Advertising on BBC Television', *Financial Times*, 16 May 1986

R. Snoddy, 'A Light which may be Ignored', *Financial Times*, 4 July 1986

R. Snoddy, 'The Peacock Report', *Financial Times*, 4 July 1986

R. Snoddy and R. Evans, 'Hurd Unveils Biggest TV Shake up in 30 Years', *Financial Times*, 8 November 1988

R. Snoddy, 'LWT may Float off Advertising Team', *Financial Times*, 28 December 1988

R. Snoddy, 'BBC Willing to Run Subscription Service', *Financial Times*, 26 January 1989

R. Snoddy, 'Government to End TV Listings Duopoly', *Financial Times*, 29 September 1989

A. Spackman, 'Tory MP to Drop Second Libel Case', *Independent*, 27 October 1986

N. Stavely, 'Advertising on the BBC: Sundry Empires Strike Back', *Admap*, June 1985.

H. Stephenson in *Guardian*, 31 January 1987

W. Stevenson and N. Smedley, eds, *Responses to the White Paper* (BFI, 1989)

P. Stoddart, 'Is BBC Licensed to Ask for More?', *Broadcast*, 18 January 1985

P. Stoddart, 'Milne Warns of Danger in Change', *Broadcast*, 25 January 1985

P. Stoddart, 'Still Fighting the Flab with a Calculating Eye', *Sunday Times*, 4 February 1990

P. Stothard, 'Who Thinks for Mrs Thatcher', *The Times*, 31 January 1983.

S. Summers, 'Public Tells BBC We Want Better Value for Money', *Sunday Times*, 4 March 1984

S. Summers, 'Swearing in the Jury', *Sunday Times*, 26 May 1985

A. Sutherland, 'BBC's Great Escape – but for how Long', *Sunday Times*, 13 November 1988

D. Swingewood, 'BBC Drops Panorama, "Spycatcher" Story', *UK Press Gazette*, 3 August 1987

N. Tebbit, *Upwardly Mobile* (Futura, 1989)

Television Weekly, 4 January 1985

M. Thatcher, *The Downing Street Years* (Harper Collins, 1993)

E.P. Thompson, *The Poverty of Theory* (Merlin, 1978)

H. Thompson, 'Licence Debate is Catch 22 for BBC's Image', *Broadcast*, 25 January 1985

B. Thorne, *The BBC's Finances and Cost Control* (BBC Lunchtime Lecture, Eighth Series, no. 3, 1970)

J. Thynne, 'Press Barons are Banned from ITV Takeovers', *Daily Telegraph*, 20 May 1989

A. Travis, 'Managing Board Overruled on Film', *Guardian*, 1 August 1985

A. Travis, 'PM Refuses Inquiry into Tebbit "Leaning" on Libel Witnesses', *Guardian*, 22 October 1986

A. Travis, 'Hurd Freezes Licence Fee and BBC Changes', *Guardian*, 21 November 1986

A. Travis, 'Spectre of Tebbit's Pressure against BBC Hovers over Debate on Peacock', *Guardian*, 21 November 1984

A. Travis, 'Tebbit Forces BBC to Admit Error', *Guardian*, 16 April 1987

A. Travis, 'Murdoch Wins Approval for Today Takeover', *Guardian*, 2 July 1987

A. Travis and G. Henry, 'Tebbit Renews Attack on BBC', *Guardian*, 22 February 1990

J. Tunstall, *The Media in Britain* (Constable, 1983)

J. Tunstall, 'Coming up for Air', *Times Higher Education Supplement*, 22 January 1988

J. Tunstall and M. Palmer, *Media Moguls* (Routledge, 1992)

C. Veljanovski and W. Bishop, *Choice by Cable* (Institute of Economic Affairs, February 1983)

C. Veljanovski, ed., *Freedom in Broadcasting* (Institute of Economic Affairs, 1989)

C. Veljanovski, 'Time for a Redefined Image', *Sunday Times*, 14 May 1989.

D. Walker, 'Diary', *The Times*, 8 November 1988.

B. Wenham, 'Hello Welcome and Speak up', *The Times*, 9 May 1990

B. West, Letter, *Broadcast*, 14 August 1984

B. West, Letter, *Broadcast*, 29 August 1986

M. Whorle, 'Peacock Shows its True Blue Colours', *Media Week*, 24 May 1985

M. Wohrle, 'Research Row Erupts over BBC Funding Surveys', *Media Week*, 31 January 1986

Who's Who (1986, 1987, 1993)

H. Wicks, *Keeping My Head* (Socialist Platform Books, 1992)

D. Wilby, ' "Don't be Alarmed; these Reviews will Demonstrate how Efficient we Are"', *Ariel*, 1 August 1984

P. Williams, 'Milne Amicable but Ruthless for BBC', *Broadcast*, 30 March 1984

R. Williams, *Television: Technology and Cultural Form* (Fontana, 1974)

N. Willmot, 'Who's Running Broadcasting?', *Broadcast*, 13 February 1987 ·

H.H. Wilson, *Pressure Group* (London, 1961)

B. Woffinden, 'Has BBC Journalism Lost its Spirit of Inquiry?', *Listener*, 10 March 1988

S. Woodman, 'Murdoch Buys Fox Studios in $162m Deal', *Media Week*, 29 March 1985

H. Young, *One of Us* (Macmillan, 1989)

Lord Young, *The Enterprise Years: a Businessman in the Cabinet* (Headline, 1991)

S. Young, Letter, *Daily Telegraph*, 22 February 1985

Index